悦读丛书

浙江省社科普及全额资助项目

浙江省社科规划一般课题

——14KPCB01YB——

我们的价值观

美丽浙江人的故事

楼青 厉芳 谭淑滢 编著

浙江工商大学出版社
ZHEJIANG GONGSHANG UNIVERSITY PRESS

图书在版编目(CIP)数据

我们的价值观 : 美丽浙江人的故事 / 楼青, 厉芳, 谭淑滢编著. — 杭州 : 浙江工商大学出版社, 2016.5

ISBN 978-7-5178-1487-0

Ⅰ. ①我… Ⅱ. ①楼… ②厉… ③谭… Ⅲ. ①人物—生平事迹—浙江省—现代 Ⅳ. ①K820.855

中国版本图书馆 CIP 数据核字(2015)第 297957 号

我们的价值观——美丽浙江人的故事

楼 青 厉 芳 谭淑滢 编著

责任编辑 王 英 任晓燕

责任校对 陈艳君

封面设计 林朦朦

责任印制 包建辉

出版发行 浙江工商大学出版社

(杭州市教工路 198 号 邮政编码 310012)

(E-mail:zjgsupress@163.com)

(网址:http://www.zjgsupress.com)

电话:0571－88904980,88831806(传真)

排　　版 杭州朝曦图文设计有限公司

印　　刷 浙江云广印业股份有限公司

开　　本 710mm×1000mm 1/16

印　　张 13.25

字　　数 254 千

版 印 次 2016 年 5 月第 1 版 2016 年 5 月第 1 次印刷

书　　号 ISBN 978-7-5178-1487-0

定　　价 38.80 元

浙江工商大学出版社营销部邮购电话 0571-88904970

前　言

浙江省第十三次党代会提出，要积极倡导以“务实、守信、崇学、向善”为内涵的当代浙江人的共同价值观。作为社会主义核心价值体系的重要组成部分，共同价值观不仅为浙江精神、民族精神和时代精神提供源源不断的精神动力，更能在新形势下为帮助确立正确的社会主义荣辱观、推进社会主义核心价值体系建设、塑造文明高尚的社会风尚发挥重大的作用。

真、善、美的种子，在钱塘江两岸处处生根。默默无闻的小人物，汇聚成闪耀道德光芒的“最美”群像：最美妈妈吴菊萍惊世一举，最美司机吴斌忍痛一刹，最美爸爸黄小荣勇敢一跃，最美女儿方亚儿一生坚守……这些像蒲公英一样播散的“最美现象”，已经成为时下浙江最美丽的风景。本书紧扣当代浙江人“务实、守信、崇学、向善”的共同价值观，从近年来浙江省涌现出的“最美”群像中精选出 67 个故事，并按照务实、守信、崇学、向善四个主题，将每个主题分为内涵、力量、名言和故事四个层次，来讴歌百姓建设“美丽浙江”的精神风貌，展现具有时代感的“最美浙江人”的形象，进而体现浙江地域特点和人文特色，引领崇德向善的社会风尚。

“最美现象”已为浙江注入了强大的正能量，也为实现“中国梦”增添了来自于百姓、根源于生活的无穷的道德力量。随着改革开放进一步深入，为了向全世界传递浙江人共同的价值观和浙江精神，我们编撰了这本图文并茂、中英文对照的小册子。通过一个个典型人物的具体事例，我们期望这本小册子可以向中外读者诠释当代浙江人的共同价值观的内涵，激发读者对真、善、美的感悟。书中每个人物故事均配有英文和人物素描，以便于外国朋友阅读。

2015 年 3 月 28 日

CONTENTS | 目录

第二章 守信 Trustworthiness

第三章 崇学 Studiousness

第一章
务实 Pragmatism

一　务实内涵
Connotation of Pragmatism

"务实",即脚踏实地、科学理性和实事求是。在我国的传统文化中,王符提出:"大人不华,君子务实。"汉代哲学家王充主张"实事疾妄",体现的就是务实精神。"务实"作为传统美德,仍在我们当代生活中发挥着重要的作用。

Pragmatism means being earnest and down-to-earth, being scientific and rational and seeking the truth. In the traditional culture of our country, Wang Fu put forward "excellent people will not appear better than they are, while prestigious people devote themselves to pragmatism". Wang Chong, a philosopher in the Han Dynasty, taught that we should "seek the truth and criticize falsehood", which as well as embodied the spirit of pragmatism. As a traditional virtue, pragmatism still plays an important role in our contemporary society.

二　务实力量
Force towards Pragmatism

"务实"作为一种核心价值观,告诉我们要排斥虚妄,拒绝空想,鄙视华而不实，指引我们追求充实而有活力的人生。

Pragmatism acts as one of the core values, instructing us to criticize fabrication, reject day-dreaming, and despise the superficially clever and guiding us to pursue a pragmatic and dynamic life.

三　务实名言
Quotations on Pragmatism

熟能生巧。　　Practice makes perfect.

不劳则无获。　　No pains, no gains.

早起的鸟儿有虫吃。　　It's the early bird that catches the worm.

千里之行，始于足下。

A thousand-li journey is started by taking the first step.

实践是检验真理的唯一标准。

Experience is the sole criterion for testing truth.

四　务实故事
Stories on Pragmatism

故事一　王法金——新时代的马天民 Ma Tianmin in the New Age

【人物介绍】Character Introduction

王法金，民警，1961年生，浙江湖州人。他曾获得“全国劳动模范”“全国五一劳动奖章”“全国我最喜爱的十大人民警察”“全国公安系统一级英模”和“全国特级优秀民警”等多个荣誉称号。

Wang Fajin, policeman, born in 1961, is

from Huzhou, Zhejiang Province. Wang Fajin has had a series of honorary titles: "National Model Worker" "National May 1st Labor Medal" "National Top Ten of My Favorite Policemen" "Class-A Hero and Model of National Public Security System" and "National Super-Excellent".

【人物事迹】Character Story

警察常常因为"勇敢"而受人尊敬,但王法金,湖州市吴兴区公安分局月河派出所副所长,却因为"点子"赢得群众的爱戴。每一个"点子"虽然平凡、琐碎,但都来自他对人民警察职责的深刻理解,更需要勇气和创新精神。王法金的"点子"从哪里来? 王法金说:"点子来源于社区百姓的需要。"

2000年4月担任社区民警后,王法金全身心投入到社区工作中。他自己掏钱印制警民联系卡和给住户的公开信,还挨家挨户送上门;在小区里挂出26块警民联系牌,贴上自己的照片,写上自己的联系电话。十多年来,他总是随身携带一个小本子,随时记下居民家和小区里的琐事、杂事,并想方设法帮助解决。无论谁家的水管坏了、钥匙丢了,他们都会想到王法金,"有困难,找老王"成了社区群众挂在嘴边的一句话。

王法金以"黄手帕工程"密切警民关系为切入点,积极为无业人员解决"饭碗头",编写《王法金警务工作法》,创办"朝霞工程"挽救失足青少年,成为为群众排忧解难的贴心人,保一方平安的用心人,与时俱进、改革基层警务的有心人,求真务实、模范践行"三个代表"重要思想的带头人,被群众亲切地称为"新时代的马天民"。2008年上映的电影《民警王法金》,根据王法金的真实事迹改编,旨在歌颂这位在平凡岗位中却做出不平凡业绩的、赢得了百姓认可和赞誉的社区民警。

The police are always respected for their "bravery", while Wang Fajin, the deputy director of Yuehe Police Station, Bureau of Wuxing District of Huzhou City, is respected and loved by the civilians for his "ideas". Every idea comes from his deep insight into the duties of the police. Ordinary and trivial as it as, it comes with more courage and creation. Where do the ideas come from? Wang Fajin says, "They are from the need of the civilians."

In April, 2000, Wang Fajin became a community policeman. Since then, he has devoted himself wholeheartedly to the community work. He spent his own money printing police-civilian contact cards and letters to the civilians, made a door-to-door delivery. He put up 26 police-civilian contact posters in the community, having his photos and telephone posted. He always takes a notebook and writes down any problem he has met anytime and tries to solve it. The civilians in the community will ask Wang for help if the toilet plunge is broken or the key is lost. They bear it in mind, "when you are in trouble, go to ask Lao Wang for help."

In order to launch "the Yellow Handkerchief Project" to maintain close ties between police and civilians, Wang devoted himself wholeheartedly to the community work, making great contributions to resolve the problems of unemployment. What's more, he edited "Wang Fajin's Work Method" and innovated "Project" to rescue juvenile delinquents, which makes him become a helpful policeman who's always willing to solve problems and secure the safety for the civilians. Wang keeps pace with the times to reform fundamentals, with the virtues of loyalty, sincerity and pragmatism. He's the leader of the "Three Represents", kindly called "Ma Tianmin in the New Age" by civilians.

The film *A Peek into the Life of a Chinese Policeman*, released in 2008, is based on the true story of Wang, which tells how a Chinese community policeman devotes himself wholeheartedly to his work and makes extraordinary achievements, eventually winning recognition and praise from the civilians.

【人物启迪】Character Enlightenment

警民情是密不可分的鱼水情。作为一名基层民警,王法金善用、巧用沟通技巧,用自己的聪明智慧和辛勤劳动,创造了平安社区,构建了和谐的警民情。

The police and the people are as inseparable as fish and water. As a community policeman, Wang Fajin succeeds in creating a safe community and constructing a harmonious relationship between the police and the people with his proficient communication skills, intelligence and pragmatic innovation.

故事二　郑小平——独臂鸿雁 Messager with One Arm

【人物介绍】Character Introduction

郑小平，邮递员，1967年生，浙江台州人。他曾获得“2012年度浙江骄傲人物”和“第三届浙江省道德模范”等荣誉称号。

Zheng Xiaoping, postman, born in 1967, is from Taizhou, Zhejiang Province. Zheng Xiaoping has got the honorary titles: "The Pride of Zhejiang Province in 2012" and "The 3rd Session of Moral Model in Zhejiang Province".

【人物事迹】Character Story

郑小平于1989年10月参加工作，虽然他的右手先天残疾，但对工作认真负责：无论刮风下雨，还是严寒酷暑，他都坚守岗位，25年如一日，投递准确率达到100%，被称为“独臂鸿雁”。郑小平克服身体障碍，练就一只灵巧的左手，分发报刊工作做得和其他邮递员一样熟练；他还苦练单手骑车本领，载着30多千克报刊，自行车骑得又平又稳。他助残济困，服务群众，想方设法为群众做好事，解难事，特别是残疾人遇到困难时，他总是结合自身经历鼓励对方，并尽己所能，倾力相助。

78岁的村民吴华祝订阅了《参考消息》17年，只有一天没收到。到了第二天才知道，是因为小平的妻子出车祸，他去医院了。村民蒋明君说自己订阅报纸20年从没间断，“去年那么大的雪，小平都把报纸给送过来，特别感动”。

郑小平在投递途中认识了50多岁的残疾人丁兴法。他在几年前因工伤导致下肢瘫痪，后又不慎被开水烫伤，长年卧床，家境十分困难。陷入困境的丁兴法不想活了，村里人说丁兴法是“晦气人”，都避而远之。可郑小平听说后，赶到丁兴法床前，鼓励他说：“我也是残疾人，现在不也过得很好，你一定要对生活有信心。”临走时，并不富裕的郑小平留下了300元。自此，郑小平在邮路上多了一个“停留站”。每次投递经过时，他都会去看看，逢年过节时还会专程探望。

村民郑学通高度残疾，靠双手支撑两条凳子行走，挑水、买东西都非常艰难。郑小平12年来一直悉心照顾他，为他理发，帮助他干家务，直到老人去世。村民项小香、黄菊兰夫妇膝下无儿女，靠在外地工作的亲戚寄生活费。两位老人因腿脚不方便，每次都要委托他代领汇款。自2011年开始，郑小平还自费给当地戚城小学的十多名贫困生订了一份报纸和一种刊物。这些年，像这样的事郑小平做了很多。

如今，尽管人们的沟通联系方式发生了翻天覆地的变化，但是郑小平还在用最淳朴的方式，真心地为村民们传递着外界的信息，从未倦怠。他憨厚地说："我非常热爱这份工作，小时候看到邮递员送报纸到家里，我就非常羡慕，这是我的梦想。这条邮路上的村民就像我的亲人一样，我要在邮路上一直走下去。"

Zheng Xiaoping began to have a job in October, 1989. Despite the fact that he is disabled in his right arm, he's responsible for his own job, no matter what the weather looks like. Working as a postman and being loyal to his own occupation, he's cordially reputed as "Messager with One Arm", spending 25 years at work like one single day. He's also renowned for his high efficiency (up to 100%) of posting. Overcoming the inconvenience the disability brings about, he practices his left arm, with which he manages the job as proficiently as other postmen. He also trains himself as a rider with the sole arm, riding with more than 30 kg papers on the bike stably. Zheng is always willing to help the disabled and impoverished, serve the civilians and work out problems for others. Especially when some problems occur to people who are disabled, he's always the one who would like to share his experience, encourage them and do his best to help.

Wu Hua, one of the villagers, has been the reader of *Reference News* for 17 years. Every day he can read *Reference News* delivered by Zheng but the day when Zheng's wife went to hospital because of a car accident. Jiang Mingjun, one of the villagers who had subscribed newspaper for 20 years, said, "Last year, it snowed heavily, but Zheng Xiaoping posted newspaper timely. It's really moving."

Zheng made an acquaintance with Ding Xingfa, who was over 50 years old and unfortunately disabled. A few years ago, Ding Xingfa was paralyzed due to an industrial accident. What's worse, he was accidentally scalded by boiling water. As a result, he led a miserable life lying on the bed all years long. He was so desperate that he even wanted to commit suicide. Ding Xingfa's villagers avoided meeting him, considering him a guy with bad luck. After hearing about Ding Xingfa's experience, Zheng went to Ding Xingfa's bed, encouraged him and said, "I am disabled, too. But I also lead a happy life now. In the same way, you should have confidence in life." Not rich himself, Zheng gave Ding Xingfa 300 RMB before leaving. Since then, Zheng has another "post" on his way to delivery. He not only drops in on Ding Xingfa on his way to delivery, but also pays special visits to him during the holidays.

The villager, Zheng Xuetong suffered from high severe disability, walking with his two hands supported by two stools. It was difficult for him to fetch a pail of water and go shopping. Zheng Xiaoping had been taking care of him for 12 years, barbering him and doing chores, until the old man passed away. The couple, Xiang Xiaoxiang and Huang Julan, are childless and depend on the money sent by their far-off relatives to make a living. They are too old to draw the money from the post office, so they entrust Zheng Xiaoping to do it on their behalf. Zheng also subscribed to newspaper and magazines for the poor students of the primary school in Qi Cheng, at his own expense since 2011. Zheng has done numerous good deeds like this over these years.

Nowadays, although the way of communication has undergone enormous changes, Zheng still bridges the villagers with the outside world by delivering mails to them, which he is never tired of. He says simply but honestly, "I love my job. When I was a little kid, I admired the postman who delivered newspapers to my house. Therefore, being a postman has been my dream. The villagers are my family, and I will pursue my job forever."

【人物启迪】Character Enlightenment

25 年如一日,投递行程超过 32 万千米,相当于绕地球赤道 8 圈,郑小平却不曾延误一个包裹,误投一封信件,或丢失一份报纸。他始终如一把每件小事做到尽善尽美,不出一点差错。做好一件小事,就是完成一件大事。

Spending 25 years at work like one single day, Zheng Xiaoping covers more than 320000km by bike which equals revolving the equator of the earth for 8 times. What impresses us is that he has never delayed a parcel, delivered a wrong letter, or lost a newspaper. Do small things consistently, perfectly and correctly, and you will realize they are big things.

故事三 孙炎明——警界保尔“Pavel Korchagin” in Public Security Organization

【人物介绍】Character Introduction

孙炎明，警察，1962年生，浙江东阳人。孙炎明先后荣获“金华市优秀人民警察”“浙江省百名优秀基层民警”“2010年度感动中国十大人物”等荣誉称号。

Sun Yanming, policeman, born in 1962, is from Dongyang, Zhejiang Province. He has been awarded a series of honorary titles, such as “The Excellent Policeman in Jinhua City” “The Top One Hundred Excellent Grassroots Policemen in Zhejiang Province” and “The Top Ten People who Moved China in 2010”.

【人物事迹】Character Story

孙炎明从警28年来，对党和公安事业无限忠诚，爱岗敬业、恪尽职守，把公安工作当作自己的天职，有“警界保尔”之称。作为管教民警，孙炎明始终认为，自己的工作对象是一个特殊群体，他们曾经危害社会，如何让他们认罪服法、改造自我、重新回归社会是自己的责任。为了使在押人员勇于改过自新，他坚持以人为本，平等对待每一名在押人员，教育挽救了一大批失足人员。

孙炎明分管的监室在全所始终保持两项最好：在押人员秩序最好，教育转化的效果最好。在在押人员的眼中，孙炎明是他们的“贴心人”。自调入看守所工作以来，每年的春节，老孙都跟在押人员一同度过。平时，在押人员在生活中遇到问题都愿意向他反映，而他也像一位慈父，认真仔细地了解情况，不厌其烦地做好疏导教育工作。

一个东阳小伙子偷了辆摩托车，被刑事拘留后，他想不开，嚷嚷着要自杀。孙炎明把他叫出监室，扭过头让他看看后脑的疤痕，对他说："你知道我这后脑的疤痕是咋回事吗？是打架打出来的吗？当然不是！是不小心跌出来的吗？也不是。这是开刀动手术留下的。脑袋上开刀动手术，够吓人了吧！我再告诉你更可怕的，我得的是脑癌，我现在跟你谈话，说不定明天就死了，可我今天仍要好好过。你还这么年轻，知错就改，仍有美好的未来呢！"听了孙炎明的经历，看着他的伤疤，这个小伙子愣住了，羞愧地说不出话来。打那以后，他自觉遵守监规，再也不寻死觅活了。

孙炎明每年都会接到已在外地劳改的服刑人员的来信，都是感谢他挽救的内容。孙炎明说："我不要他们记住我，我只要他们记住我的话，好好做人就行。"

2004 年被确诊为脑癌以后，孙炎明面对绝症的威胁，始终保持积极乐观的人生态度，以超越常人的顽强毅力，克服病痛带来的折磨，坚守岗位，把工作当成了自己的生命。"说实在的，我们一家现在能够这样坦然面对，都是老孙的乐观心态在影响着我们。"孙炎明的妻子张春香说，看到丈夫笑对病魔，几十年来积下的辛酸劳苦，都化为欣慰与自豪。女儿谈到爸爸时，说："人最大的幸福是有人爱、有事做、有理想，我爸爸做到了！他总说他很幸福，因为警察这份神圣而崇高的职业，就是要把奉献作为自己的一种责任、承诺和义务，让生命在奉献中得到升华。爸爸现在做的就是快乐工作、快乐生活，奉献自我，不留遗憾。"

Dedicated and responsible as he is, Sun Yanming devoted himself wholeheartedly to the Communist Party and the Public Security. Being prominently reputed as "Pavel Korchagin" in public security, he takes his job as his bounden duty. As a policeman, Sun always believes that these prisoners he faces with are a different group of people who have done some damage to the society. It's his duty to help them plead guilty, transform them to new men and send them back to society again. In order to help the prisoners correct their errors and make a fresh start, he claims the principle of being man-oriented and insists that every prisoner should be treated fairly and receive education, rescuing a bunch of people who took a wrong step in their lives.

The prison cells charged by Sun maintain the two "bests" all the time:

the best in regulatory order and the best in educating the prisoners. The prisoners regard Sun as their close friend. Since he has been working in the detention center, he spends every Spring Festival with the prisoners. If they encounter any problem in their lives, they would turn to him for help. And Sun always carefully listens to them and talks to them patiently, just like a father.

Once a young man from Dongyang in Zhejiang Province, stole a motorcycle and was detained later. He felt ashamed and yelled to commit suicide. Sun called him out of his cell, showed him the scar in the back of his head and said, "Do you know how I got this scar? Is it caused by a fight? Obviously not. Was it caused by an accidental tumbling? Surely not! It is the result of an operation. You are scared, aren't you? Let me tell you something more terrible. I have got a brain cancer. Though I'm talking to you right now, I may die tomorrow, but I still cherish today. You are still young and you can still have a bright future!" After hearing of Sun's experience and seeing his scar, this young man was shocked and regretted what he had done. Since then, he consciously abided by the prison regulations and never yelled to commit suicide again.

Every year Sun will receive many letters from his former prisoners in other jails, the contents of which show their gratitude to his help. Sun says, "I do not expect them to remember me; I just want them to remember my words and become good citizens."

Unfortunately, in 2004, his illness was diagnosed as the brain cancer. Facing the threat of his fatal illness, he always keeps optimistic and positive attitudes towards his life, overcoming torments his illness brings about with his unusual persistence. Not only does he keep working while being ill but he regards his job as his own life. "To tell the truth, it is Sun's positive attitude that encourages us to face life bravely." said Zhang Chunxiang, Sun's wife. She also added that she was proud and relieved because her husband faced cancer optimistically. Speaking of him, his daughter said, "The greatest happiness lies in loving and being loved, engaging in one's career, and pursuing one's dreams. My dad possesses all of them. He always says he is very happy, because police work is a sacred and noble profession, and he regards devotion to his career as his responsibility, commitment, spirit, and duty. His life is meaningful because of his job. What my dad is pursuing is to work and live happily, devote himself and leave no regrets behind him."

【人物启迪】Character Enlightenment

孙炎明没有惊天动地的英雄壮举,没有振聋发聩的豪言壮语,有的只是朴实的工作作风和不图名利的奉献。对理想的执着追求,对事业与岗位的执着坚守,让他这个平凡的基层监管警察不再平凡。

There are no mock heroic undertakings or undue brave words. In Sun's working life, he shows his down-to-earth style of work and dedication without seeking any fame or gain. The pursuit of dream and the persistence in his career and his duty make a big difference of him as a policeman who comes from the grassroots.

故事四　钟杏菊——自家医生 Our Family Doctor

【人物介绍】Character Introduction

钟杏菊,医生,1954 年生,浙江嵊泗人。钟杏菊同志 2008 年被评为全国卫生系统先进工作者,2010 年被评为"感动浙江卫生"十大人物,2011 年被评为"全国三八红旗手""浙江省敬业奉献模范"和"浙江省优秀共产党员"。

Zhong Xingju, doctor, born in 1954, is from Shengsi, Zhejiang Province. Zhong Xingju has been awarded the titles, including "The Excellent Worker in the National Hygiene System of zhejiang province" in 2008, "The Top Ten People who Moved Hygiene System of Zhejiang Province" in 2010, and obtained reputations in 2011 including "The National March 8th Red-Banner Holder" "Dedication and Commitment Role-Model in Zhejiang Province" and "Excellent Member of Communist Party of Zhejiang Province".

【人物事迹】Character Story

在烟波浩渺、碧浪连天的东海，有一个1.2平方千米的小岛——壁下岛，这个小岛隶属浙江省舟山市嵊泗县。这个小岛上没有蔬菜，到嵊泗县城要乘3个多小时的船，每天只有一班，阵风8级以上就要停船，一年里有1/3的时间无法通航。就是在这样艰苦的条件下，一位女医生为了岛上百姓的健康坚守了36个年头。扎根海岛36年，钟杏菊数十载如一日，始终把"立志从医为乡亲、哪有困难就有我"作为自己的职业道德准则，满腔热情地为病人服务、为患者排忧解难，忠诚地履行一个基层医务工作者的神圣职责，赢得了群众的广泛赞誉，被海岛渔民称为"自家医生"。岛上其他社会服务机构都撤离后，唯有她坚守至今。

"我是渔家的女儿，更是一名共产党员，为渔民看病是我的本分。"钟杏菊说。从小在大盘岛上长大的钟杏菊，对小岛有着别样的感情，更知道一名医生对渔民的重要性。11岁那年，当她和父亲眼睁睁地看着母亲因缺医少药而感染肺结核，最终不治身亡时，她就下定决心：一定要学医。

从医36年来，无论白天黑夜、刮风下雨，钟杏菊出诊总是随叫随到，从未让海岛渔民失望过。一天深夜，渔民崔忠良在海上作业时被起网机绳索绞断腿骨大出血，船老大边往回开，边用对讲机紧急呼救。钟杏菊立刻赶到码头，等伤员一到立即施行伤口消毒、输液，并将伤员送往舟山骨伤科医院治疗。渔船驶向舟山的路上，钟杏菊守护着伤员，一夜没合眼，次日凌晨终于将伤员顺利送达。因为治疗及时，崔忠良不但保住了性命，也保全了下海生产能力，这让他对钟杏菊感激不已："把生命托付给她，我们放心！"一次，大盘岛上一位60多岁的老阿婆突然晕倒在地，呼吸不畅。一个电话打到壁下，钟杏菊在告知患者家属注意事项的同时，乘坐丈夫驾驶的自家的机动渔船火速赶到大盘岛，及时对昏迷中的阿婆实施抢救，老人终于转危为安。

在钟杏菊工作过的地方，只要提起她的名字，乡亲们都会由衷地说："杏菊是我们渔民自家的医生，她坚守小岛，肩挎药箱，风里来浪里去，为我们送医送药、除病消灾，真比亲人还要亲！"

Bixia Island is located in the East China Sea, a vast expanse of misty, rolling blue waters. The small island of 1.2 km^2 is under the jurisdiction of Shengsi, Zhoushan, Zhejiang Province. There are no vegetables. It takes more than 3 hours to commute between Bixia Island and Shengsi. Only one boat is available every day when there is no strong gale. It is not open to navigation during 1/3 of a year. Under such difficult conditions, a female doctor has been working for the people on the island for 36 years. Setting down on the island for 36 years, Zhong Xingju insists on her own career moral principles, believing that she is the one who can provide aids for those who are sick on the island. Zhong enthusiastically offers her services for the patients, relieves them of worries and helps solve their problems. She faithfully performs her sacred duty as a medical worker who comes from the grassroots. With her great contributions to her job, she gains the prominent reputations from people as a "family doctor". Despite of the fact that other social serving organizations were retrieved from the island, she still insists on staying there.

"I am the daughter of a fisherman and also a communist. It is my duty to cure the diseases of fishermen." Zhong says. She has grown up on Dapan island, and has a special feeling for this area ever since. Therefore, she is fully aware of the importance of a doctor for the fishermen. At the age of 11, when she and her father witnessed her mother died of tuberculosis for the lack of medical treatments, she made up her mind: "I will be a doctor in the future."

Having been a doctor for 36 years, Zhong always gets to the patient in time no matter what the weather looks like, never letting down the local fishermen. For instance, one night, a fisherman, Cui Zhongliang, got hurt by a fishing rope and his leg was broken. While the captain drove the boat back, he used intercom to call for Zhong. Zhong rushed to the pier. After she disinfected the wounded area and transfused the patient, she accompanied the patient to Zhoushan Orthopedic Hospital immediately. On the way, Zhong took good care of the patient and did not fall asleep at all for the whole night. The next morning the wounded man was finally sent to the hospital. Thanks to timely treatment, Cui Zhongliang was safe, and luckily enough, he could continue to work on a fishing boat after recovery. Therefore, he is very grateful to Zhong for her timely help. "We trust her even with our life!" he says. In another case, a granny over sixty suddenly fell down on the ground unconsciously on the Dapan island. The granny's relatives called Zhong for help. After Zhong instructed the relatives some first aid measures on the phone, she boarded her husband's motor boat and rushed to Dapan Island. Thanks to her timely treatment, the granny finally came back to life.

When speaking of Zhong, all the folks will sincerely comment, "Zhong is really a noble doctor. She stays on the island to cure our diseases and sends us the medicine despite bad weather and working conditions. We all regard her as our family doctor!"

【人物启迪】Character Enlightenment

当今社会,医疗事故多发,医患矛盾日益尖锐。的确,作为医务工作者不仅要有精湛的技术,还要有一颗救死扶伤的心。钟杏菊三十余年如一日守护海岛居民,用自己的实际行动谱写着医者仁心。

Nowadays, there occur malpractices and conflicts between doctors and patients sometimes. Indeed, as medical personnel, they are supposed to possess superb medical skills and dedication for healing the wounded and rescuing the dying. Zhong Xingju has been staying on the island for more than 30 years, practicing her own story of being a doctor.

故事五 俞佳友——为民记者 A Journalist of the People and for the People

【人物介绍】Character Introduction

俞佳友,记者,1974 年生。他曾获得"浙江省优秀农村工作指导员""省杰出青年""省第二届道德模范"和"浙江省优秀新闻工作者"等荣誉称号。

Yu Jiayou, journalist, was born in 1974. He has been awarded a series of honorary titles: "The Excellent Instructor for Rural Areas in Zhejiang Province" "The Outstanding Youth in Zhejiang

Province" "The 2nd Session of Moral Model in Zhejiang Province" and "the Excellent Journalist in Zhejiang Province".

【人物事迹】Character Story

俞佳友从事新闻工作10多年来,采写了大量感人至深的报道,展示了新时期一位党报记者炽热的职业精神、社会责任和爱民情怀。他深入一线,参加过"98抗洪""2008年杭城抗击风雪"和汶川地震的采访报道。每逢重大事件,他的第一选择就是"到现场去",发回最鲜活的新闻。他的许多新闻作品在社会上反响较好,有的作品获得了浙江省新闻奖。

2009年,俞佳友受浙江日报报业集团委派,到经济欠发达的青田县万阜乡任农村工作指导员。万阜乡到青田县城是近3小时车程的盘山公路。2000户人家分散在海拔500多米高的群山间,又穷困又封闭。下乡第一天,俞佳友就开始徒步探访农户。农村长大、当过兵的他没有被艰苦条件吓住,反而被淳朴的乡民感动。俞佳友说:"农民确实要出去,但不应是现在。他们没有知识没有技能,只能沦为廉价劳动力。金窝银窝不如自己的草窝啊。"在这种思路之下,俞佳友非常看重两件事,第一是寻找农业产业化的发展路径,第二是巩固基础教育,拓宽孩子们的视野。而这两大问题的成功解决,靠的是他对自己记者身份的巧妙运用。

挂职锻炼期间,他利用自己做农业新闻的优势,帮助当地农民种植高山蔬菜,并借助报社和网络平台,打开蔬菜销路,使村民脱贫致富。为打响高山蔬菜的知名度,他为高山蔬菜申请注册商标,联系干菜加工商,在意大利开出第一家万阜干菜销售店,将干菜产品销往欧洲。

俞佳友还热心公益事业,引导社会力量帮助解决难题,通过报道拉开媒体爱心助学的序幕。"开往青田万阜的爱心列车"为314名学生筹集到款物价值70多万元,填补了蒲州村40多万元的自来水工程资金缺口,使村民喝上了干净水。万阜乡男孩夏明明不幸患上骨癌,无钱医治,他连续跟踪报道,帮助筹款11万余元。两年多来,他积极发动社会力量,共为困难群众捐献了150余万元的财物,被群众形象地称为"为民记者"。

在万阜的两年,他始终没有放下手中的笔,策划报道了230余件新闻,为万阜乡赢来了社会各界的关注和帮助。作为记者,他总是不畏艰险冲在一线,忠实地履行着一个记者的职责,写出了大量的精彩、动人的报道。

Yu Jiayou has been working as a journalist for more than 10 years. He has written a lot of touching reports which shows a communist journalist's professionalism, social responsibility, and concern for people. Yu went to the frontier of news events, participated in the "1998 Fight against Flood" "2008 Hangzhou Fight against Snow Disaster" and Wenchuan earthquake. When it comes to big events, he chooses to "go to the spot" to send back the most vivid pieces of news. His works have good reflections on the whole society. Some even have won the Press Award of Zhejiang Province.

In 2009, assigned by Zhejiang Daily Press Group, Yu went to Wanfu village, an underdeveloped area in Qingtian county, working as a village guide. It takes nearly 3 hours' drive on the winding roads to arrive at Wanfu from Qingtian. About 2000 families have scattered among the mountains over 500 m. Therefore, the villagers are impoverished and isolated from the outside world. On the first day of his arrival, Yu began to visit the villagers. Growing up in the rural area and once being a soldier, Yu was not intimidated by the harsh conditions, instead, he was deeply moved by the simplicity of the villagers. Although, he only has worked there for one year, Yu believes that, "Our villagers really need to go out to work, but it is not the suitable time now. They have neither enough knowledge nor skills, as a result, they are reduced to a cheap labor force. East or west, home is best." Considering the present situation, Yu lays great emphasis on two urgencies: the first one is to realize agricultural industrialization, and the second is to educate children in these rural areas and broaden their horizons. Yu eventually tackled these problems by wisely using his knowledge as an agriculture journalist.

He took advantage of being an agriculture journalist, offering the local peasants help to grow Gaoshan vegetables. He accessed the newspaper and network platform, innovating a new vegetable selling strategy, which contributed to the wealth of the local people. In order to make more people aware of the vegetables, he applied for a brand for it, contacting the dried vegetable processor to start a first Wanfu dried vegetable shop in Italy, pioneering a market for the dried vegetable in Europe.

Yu also engages in public welfare projects enthusiastically and guides social strength to help solve social problems. After his report of the media helping students in need, the charity program "The Caring Train Driving to Wanfu Village, Qingtian County" has raised funds and materials for 314 students over 700 000 RMB. He also helps to raise more than 400 000 RMB to build infrastructures of providing clean water for the local residents in Puzhou village. Yu's continuous tracking reports also help to raise more than 110 000 RMB for a boy, Xia Mingming, in Wanfu village who suffers from cancer in the bones, but didn't have enough money for treatment. For more than two years, Yu activates social strength to donate a total of more than 1.5 million RMB for people in need, eventually regarded as a journalist of the people and for the people.

Within the two years of staying in Wanfu, he insists on writing and sending 230 reports to different newspapers. His incessant reports gained assistances from the society. Working as a journalist, he's always at the frontline, responsible for his job and writing a large number of excellent and touching reports.

【人物启迪】Character Enlightenment

无论身在哪里,无论做什么,俞佳友认真、勤恳地对待生活和工作的态度一直没变。他写了很多报道,他的文字始终没有离开当地群众的生活。他在为群众谋福利中,实现了一名新闻工作者应有的社会价值。

Yu Jiayou is very conscientious and diligent, whatever he does and wherever he is. Such attitudes towards life and work have never changed. He has written many reports about the lives of people living in rural areas. Harboring such belief to work for the interests of people, he realizes his social value as a journalist.

故事六　吴强忠——最美人民公仆 The Most Beautiful Public Servant

【人物介绍】Character Introduction

吴强忠,庆元县松源镇政府维稳中心主任,1955 年生。他先后获得“全国人民满意司法员”“全国十大法制新闻人物”“全国百名感动中国人物”等 82 项荣誉。

Wu Qiangzhong, born in 1955, is the director of the Center of Maintaining Social Stability in Songyuan, Qingyuan county. By far, he is prominently reputed as “The Most Satisfying Judge”, one of “The Top Ten National Outstanding People in the Justice System”, and one of “The Top One Hundred People who Moved China”, about 82 honorary titles in total.

【人物事迹】Character Story

吴强忠，早在 25 年前就已经是在生死线走过一回的人了。1990 年，年富力强的吴强忠被查出患了尿毒症，必须进行肾移植手术才能延续生命。然而，进行肾移植手术至少需要 8 万余元的费用，这对于他这样一个当时每月只有 90 余元工资，且未享受公费医疗待遇的乡镇聘用干部来说，无疑是个天文数字。正在吴强忠和他的家人陷入绝望之际，当地政府及群众向他伸出了援助之手，帮助他解决了手术费用，使他成功进行了肾移植手术，因此他对党和人民无比感激。1993 年，吴强忠开始担任松源镇司法所所长。上班第一天，他就暗下决心：一定要竭尽全力做好工作，为推进基层依法治理、维护农村社会稳定做出贡献，以出色的工作成绩报答党和政府及群众的救命之恩。

吴强忠始终牢记为人民服务的宗旨,以高度的责任感和强烈的事业心扎根基层,在平凡的岗位上做出了不平凡的业绩。为了快速、及时制止并有效化解矛盾纠纷,吴强忠将司法所全体干部的办公电话及手机号码印制成“便民卡”,向各村(社区)广为散发,公开承诺不分白天黑夜,遇有纠纷情况,调解人员城内 15 分钟、郊区 60 分钟内到达现场，并且由自己带头前往。这一举措被当地干部群众誉为“司法 110”。多年来，不管多么复杂的矛盾纠纷，只要到吴强忠的手里，总能被化解，让怒目相对的双方握手言和。

一起遗留 6 年之久、金额达 200 多万元的土地征地款分配纠纷案，县政府组成工作队进驻四个多月没有结果，吴强忠接手此案后短时间成功化解纠纷；一起 33 名原告诉至法院 18 个月也没结果的食用菌错菌索赔纠纷案，到了吴强忠手里 15 天被化解；两起棘手的山林纠纷案，半天化解……吴强忠调处化解的各类疑难矛盾纠纷举不胜举。历年来，他先后调处化解纠纷 1760 余件，接待信访、代访、陪访 5090 余件，提供法律法规的咨询服务 62880 人次。

特别是在 1990 年进行肾移植手术后，他担任该镇维稳中心主任、综治工作中心主任、信访办主任、司法所所长等十多个职务，还兼驻一个 1300 余人口的大村，所任职承担的工作在考核中的成绩都名列前茅。他的敬业精神和奉献精神催人奋进，他是构建社会和谐的道德标杆。

Wu Qiangzhong had a brush with death 18 years ago. In 1990 he was attacked suddenly by uremia in the prime of his life. To keep alive, he must take a kidney transplant operation. However, the cost for taking such an operation would exceed 80 000 RMB, which was far beyond Wu's affordability as he got a monthly wage of 90 RMB at that time, and being a contracted cadre in towns, was not entitled to enjoy the free medical care. The whole family fell into deep despair and they even prepared themselves to answer the call from God of death. At that very time the local government and people gave a helping hand to Wu and made it possible for him to have a kidney transplant operation. The operation has turned out to be a successful one and Wu Qiangzhong has felt extremely grateful to the party and the people ever since. In 1993 Wu Qiangzhong began to act as the director of Songyuan Judicial Bureau. From the first day of his assumption of duty, he made up his mind to repay the whole society by devoting himself to promoting the popularization of ruling by law in towns and villages and maintaining social stability in the rural areas.

Not only does Wu Qiangzhong keep the principle in mind that he should serve the people, but he's taking actions to work hard for the fundamental public with a great sense of responsibility. Though working at an ordinary position he devotes himself wholeheartedly and accomplishes extraordinary achievements. In order to mediate the issues quickly and effectively, Wu has a convenience card printed and delivered among the people. On the card are written the office numbers and mobile numbers of all the cadres of the judicial office. It says in cases of issues, the mediators and he himself will arrive at the scene within 15 minutes in suburb areas and 60 minutes in rural areas. The centre is prominently reputed as the "110" in judicial system. Over the years, no matter how complicated the issues are, Wu will solve them skillfully. Issues resolved, and people become friendly to each other again.

There once was a land expropriation compensation case which lasted for over 6 years and involved nearly 2 000 000 RMB. The county government made up a special team to work on this, yet turned out to be fruitless after 4 months' struggle. Finally Wu Qiangzhong took over this thorny issue and got it settled successfully in a short time. He also solved a compensation dispute caused by edible mushroom in which 33 citizens got involved and took to court for 18 months. What is more, he made it a miracle to resolve another disputes in the mountain forest with only half a day. Such instances are too numerous to mention. Over the years Wu has solved and mediated more than 1760 disputes one after another, handled complaint letters and visits from civilians over 5090 times, and provided counseling for more than 62 880 civilians in the aspect of laws and regulations.

After the kidney transplant operation in 1990, he has been the director of the safety centre, comprehensive working centre, complaints office, administration of justice, etc., and at the same time he is responsible for a village with a population of 1300 people. He is ranked at the top according to his working outcomes. His loyalty and commitments encourage the public, which consists of the social harmony.

【人物启迪】Character Enlightenment

有人整天为“小家”忙碌，而有人却时时刻刻为“大家”操劳。吴强忠从家长里短、鸡毛蒜皮的小事着手，用质朴的忠心、爱心、热心、耐心关爱着“大家”，维护着社会的稳定与正义。

Some people are busy for their own family, while some people are busy for the whole big family. Wu Qiangzhong is busy for the trifles and issues of the big family and devotes himself wholeheartedly to serve people, maintaining the social safety and justice with his loyalty, love, enthusiasm and patience.

故事七 张思洋——大学生的好保姆 A Good Keeper of College Students

【人物介绍】Character Introduction

张思洋,杭州经济技术开发区公安分局白杨派出所副所长兼下沙高教园区民警,1976 年生。他先后荣获"全国优秀人民警察""浙江省优秀人民警察"等荣誉称号。

Zhang Siyang, born in 1976, is the deputy chief in Baiyang police office, Bureau of Hangzhou Economic and Technology Exploring Area, and a policeman in Xiasha Higher Education District. He has been awarded titles including national and Zhejiang's "Prominent Public Policeman".

【人物事迹】Character Story

"欢迎您的孩子来到杭州下沙高教园区学习!"伴随着这样一封录取通知书,下沙各高校数万新生的家长还收到一封特殊的信件。这封信印刷精美,制作细致,一面是洋洋洒洒千余字的涉及十个方面的安全注意事项,一面是下沙新城的地图,还有一个民警的头像。"我是下沙高教园区派出所民警张思洋,你们叫我张警官或张 Sir 就可以了。"张思洋还公布了自己的手机号码和邮箱,欢迎学生和家长随时联系。9 月初开学后,张思洋警官每晚都在给高校新生讲课,最忙时一天连讲 3 场, 14 所高校都差不多轮一遍。高校治安问题错综复杂,骗子、小偷和其他各类犯罪嫌疑人的犯罪手法五花八门。通过一堂课,张思洋生动全面地介绍校园安全知识和预防手段,并运用故事、图片、视频和自己富有节奏感的讲课方式，让在场的学生受益。

工作9年来，张思洋为学生上安全课1100多次。一年365天，他几乎每天都在工作。他把手机号码告诉每位师生，始终履行24小时随叫随到的承诺，被称为大学生的“好保姆”。他利用业余时间建立网上警务室、“张思洋在线”微博、大学生QQ群，为高校师生提供服务，及时化解高校各种矛盾，先后从死亡线上拉回180多个学生，成功调解高校大学生意外死亡事件约50起。

在张思洋看来，只有师生平安，才能保证高校真正的平安。园区大学虽然都配备辅导员，但这些辅导员普遍年纪轻，很多都是刚刚走上工作岗位的大学生，生活阅历少，工作经验不丰富，他们能不能及时发现、跟踪和解决学生出现的各种问题，张思洋不放心。为此，张思洋抽出业余时间，在园区各高校轮流举办辅导员课堂，讲述自己多年来的经历和故事。不少辅导员在本校听了还不够，又跑到其他学校听。他向大家保证——24小时接受咨询，24小时做辅导员们的辅导员。

他还在高校推行校园警务室，创新学生社区管理模式，为打造省内最安全高教园区做出了贡献。一双小眼睛使得张思洋成了下沙高校学子最熟悉的人，这双小眼睛也凝聚着一名大学城人民警察的大视野、大胸怀和大境界。

Along with the Admission Notice, all the parents whose children will attend the colleges in Xiasha Higher Education District in Hangzhou receive a special letter. This open letter is beautifully printed and artistically bound. On one side of it, there are the lists of safety precautions on campus, and a map of Xiasha New City and a head portrait of a police officer on the other side. Below the portrait, it writes, "I am Zhang Siyang, the police officer in charge of areas around Xiasha Higher Education District. Please feel free to contact me via email or mobile phone whenever there is an emergency or problem." It is a knotty issue to keep the campus a safe place, since there are different types of crimes such as theft and swindling. The best way to improve safety is to equip students and staff with correct precautions. Hence, Zhang Siyang would get very busy in each September, as it is the time for colleges to reopen and huge number of students pour into the campus. He will make lectures to the freshmen in different colleges every night during that period. He ever made 3 lectures in one day. Could you imagine that? By adopting stories, photos and videos,

Zhang Siyang gives his lectures in a lively and comprehensive way, which makes a deep impression on the attendants.

About 1100 classes about safety have been given to students by Zhang Siyang during 9 years. He almost works everyday without any break. He is called a good keeper by the college students, owing to his promise that he is ready for any emergency by calling him. Having access to the extra time to set up online police office, he also applies to other network platforms such as Weibo and QQ to provide instant assistances and resolve problems on campus. Not only has he succeeded in rescuing 180 students, but he has solved about 50 accidents as well.

Zhang Siyang pays close attention to the safety of both the college students and teaching staff. There are student advisors in all the colleges at Xiasha Higher Education District. But these advisors are all quite young. To many of them, it is their first job to work as student advisors. With insufficient life and work experience, could they find out and tackle all the problems which faces the college students? That is a question from Zhang Siyang. Thus Zhang Siyang often makes lectures to the student advisors in these colleges in his spare time, to share his own experiences with them. These lectures are very popular with the student advisors. Zhang even promises to them that he would be available and could offer advice and suggestions round the clock.

Furthermore, he has launched an appeal to set up police offices in the universities and innovated the governing mode of students' communities. Zhang has made his great contributions to the safety of Higher Education District. Almost every college students in the Higher Education District knows Zhang Siyang who has a distinctive feature of small but sharp eyes. He is a policeman with a broad vision and mind.

【人物启迪】Character Enlightenment

"亲爱的同学,同窗挚友即将离别,大家适当饮酒。有同学醉睡在马路边,十分危险。一句老话:不能乐极生悲。"张思洋就这样像关爱自己的孩子一样关爱着学生。只要人人都献出一点爱,世界将变成美好的人间。

"Dear students, it is time to say goodbye to your classmates. You shouldn't drink excessively. Some students have been found lying on the road, drunken like a dog. It's very dangerous. Remember the old saying: Extreme joy begets sorrow." Zhang Siyang takes the college students as his own children. As long as everyone offers a bit of love, the world will become more beautiful.

故事八　蒋定军——十字路口的艺术家 The Artist at the Crossroad

【人物介绍】Character Introduction

蒋定军,交警,1979 年出生,浙江杭州人。他曾获得“全国优秀人民警察”“全国优秀青年卫士”等多项荣誉称号。

Jiang Dingjun, born in 1979, is a traffic policeman from Hangzhou, Zhejiang Province. He has been awarded the titles including "National Outstanding Policeman" and "National Excellent Young Soldier".

【人物事迹】Character Story

蒋定军所在的松木场路口,连接省政府和黄龙体育中心,车流量大,交通管理任务繁重。有人给蒋定军计算过,每天他一班岗要打 1000 多次手势,喊话 1300 多句,在路口穿梭往复就要走上 3 公里,5 年下来,刚好绕了赤道一圈。蒋定军在交通管理的工作中摸索总结出一套独特的处理交通违章的方法,既严格执法又热情服务。

2009 年的一个夏天,蒋定军处理一次违章,是一辆本田轿车随意变更车道。整个处理过程,共计 2 分钟。蒋定军一共敬了四次礼,并始终面带微笑。标准的普通话,洪亮的声音,一锤定音式的裁定和一系列认真规范的身体语言,使得违章司机在事后只用了四个字形容自己的被罚经历——心服口服。

一次,蒋定军看到一名中年男子没有走人行横道就穿马路,蒋定军微笑地走过去阻止,但这名男子理也没理。蒋定军抢走两步,站在他前面敬礼:“你好,同志!请你积极配合……”没等说完,这名男子一转身又往前走。一个往前闯,一个不停地在旁边敬礼,引来不少人观望。一名老同志看不下去站出来说:“这个民警虽然年轻,你知道他向你敬了多少礼?我为杭州有这样的民警感到骄傲,为你这种行为感到耻辱。”迫于群众的压力和乱闯马路的违章行为,这名男子低头认错。蒋定军说:“我纠正你的违章,是为你的安全考虑。如果出了意外,你将承担大部分的责任。”这名男子点头称是,并解释说因为心情不好才这样,下次不会再这样过马路了。“心情不好,更应该小心过马路。”经过五分钟的解释,蒋定军说:“这次不处罚你了,希望你以后不要乱穿马路。”这名男子连忙为自己刚才的态度道歉。

蒋定军所在的西湖交警大队曾收到一位叫章月清市民的来信,内容是这样的:“我是居住在松木场社区的一位市民,患有哮喘并且身体有残疾,请领导们替我感谢松木场岗亭的蒋定军同志。前几天,我在路上哮喘复发,是这位好心的同志扶我上出租车,并且交给我三百元钱。后来,我去还他钱,他坚决不要。我十分感动,非常感激他。”

从警 11 年来,他共纠正、处理各类违章(违法)行为 6 万余起,没有一起群众投诉,还受到各类表扬 150 多次,赢得了广大群众的爱戴和信赖。

Jiang Dingjun is a traffic policeman working at the crossing of Songmuchang Road, adjacent to Zhejiang Povincial Government Building and the Huanglong Sports Center, the largest sports facility in Zhejiang. There is always an incessant stream of vehicles and heavy traffic regulations at that crossing. It is calculated that every shift Jiang Dingjun makes more than 1000 traffic gestures, gives more than 1300 instructions, and walks back and forth at the crossing with covering 3 kilometers which equals revolving the equator once. He has summed up a set of unique methods to process traffic violations, and provider strict but enthusiastic services.

In the summer of 2009, Jiang Dingjun perfectly processed one violation. a man driving Honda changed his courses randomly. Jiang took 2 minutes to process the traffic violation with salutations, smiles, standard Mandarin, sonorous voice, a fair judgment, and a series of standardized gestures. The driver later acknowledged that he was completely convinced of this wrong doing.

One day, Jiang Dingjun caught a middle-aged man crossing the road without obeying the traffic rules. He walked towards that man with smile and tried to stop him, but he was ignored totally. He insisted, but the man kept ignoring him. This drew the attention of the passers-by. Among them a senior citizen could not put up with it and stepped out to support Jiang Dingjun. Finally that man acknowledged his wrong behavior and explained that he did this just because he was in a bad mood. Instead of fining that man, Jiang Dingjun educated him until he promised that he would correct himself and obey the traffic rules in the future.

Traffic Police Brigade of Xihu District received a letter from a Hangzhou citizen named Zhang Yueqing. In this letter it said that "I am writing to express my heartedly gratitude to Jiang Dingjun, one of your traffic policemen. I live in Songmuchang Community. I am a disabled man and suffers from asthma. Several days ago I was under a sudden asthma attack. It was Jiang Dingjun who kind-heartedly helped me and arranged a taxi for me to go to the hospital promptly. Besides, he handed to me 300 RMB. He refused me to pay the money back. I am so moved and I feel extremely grateful for his kind help."

During 11 years of his work, Jiang has corrected and processed over 60 000 traffic violations among which there are no complaints. Besides, he has received praise for more than 150 times, winning the love and trust from people.

【人物启迪】Character Enlightenment

每个人都有属于自己的人生舞台,十字路口就是蒋定军的舞台。交通指挥的动作是单调乏味的,但他的每一个手势不仅标准有力,而且还带着某种节奏感。他是在路口“跳舞”的交警,舞出了一片蓝天。

Everyone has his own stage on which he is an actor. The crossing is the stage of Jiang Dingjun. Directing traffic is dull and tedious. But his every gesture is standard, precise and powerful, with beautiful kind of rhythm. He is the traffic policeman who is dancing at the crossing under the blue sky.

故事九　周兆木——环保卫士 An Environmental Protection Activist

【人物介绍】Character Introduction

周兆木，退休人员，1950 年出生。1986 年转业到富阳市环保局，富阳市环保局原副局长。他曾获得“地球奖”“全国环境保护系统精神文明建设先进个人”“浙江省环保先锋人物”等多个荣誉称号。

Zhou Zhaomu, retired, was born in 1950. He transferred from the army to Fuyang Environmental Protection Bureau in 1986, and is the former deputy bureau director. He has been granted "the Earth Award" "Excellent Individual for Construction of Spiritual Civilization in the National Environmental Protection System" and "Environmental Pioneer in Zhejiang Province".

【人物事迹】Character Story

周兆木出生在农村，中学毕业后参军。1986 年他转业被调入刚刚成立的富阳市环保局，不久又被分配去筹建“排污收费管理站”。收费站筹建完成，挂起了排污收费管理站的牌子，但排污费却收不上来。周兆木几经思考，认为收不上费只是现象，从根本上说这还是对环境保护的认识问题，对排污收费只有从认识上提高了，在制度上有了保障，这项工作才能顺利开展。于是周兆木一再向上级建议，应将排污费的收缴与企业的污染治理、项目审批、政策倾斜这三者结合起来，上级采纳了这一合理建议。新的收费办法一经颁布，不但排污费收缴有章可循，企业的环保面貌也大为改观。仅 1999 年至 2001 年这三年，富阳的排污收费就达 4060 万元，后来又将其中的 80%返还企业，使富阳市完成了 100 多个治污建设项目。

1996 年开始，周兆木担任富阳市环保局副局长，分管环境管理和环境监理。当时富阳市提出“既要金山银山，更要绿水青山”的口号，让周兆木更受鼓舞。他不管严寒酷暑，不到一年就跑遍了全市的每一个角落，并对排污严重的企业采取了强制手段，限期关停。

龙羊山区是富阳市有名的偏远山区，但有一家卫生纸造纸厂在这深山中。由于这个厂排放的污水污染了当地的水源，群众意见很大。周兆木对此很焦急，一连在山上颠簸了六趟，却找不到厂长。有人笑着对周兆木说，民间的规矩是“事不过三”，你们已经来了六趟，心也算尽到了，过段时间再说吧。周兆木笑了，说：“如果有这规矩，那它也得依着环保改。”老周的执着，终于感动了这位造纸厂的厂长，厂长终于露面了。周兆木与厂长长谈，讲道理，提措施，终于说服了他，污水得到了治理。由他组织和参与的“环境保护公众有奖举报活动”实施六年来，共受理群众举报 3782 个，举报企业 4050 家(次)，查实违法企业 1299 家(次)，兑现举报奖金 250 万元。经过十多年的治理，富阳市终于贴上了“生态”的标签。

周兆木进入富阳市环保系统 19 年，现在退下来当调研员，为了环保宣传从未放下过手里的笔。这些年他先后在有关人员配合下，制作环保宣传图板 200 余块，环保宣传小册子 1000 余册，摘录、编辑宣传资料 5000 余份，并利用业余时间积极为报刊撰写调研报告和新闻报道 1000 多篇。在富阳市，如果要找环保方面的资料，马上会有人告诉你，“找周兆木呀，环保局的周兆木，他是环保方面的百科全书！”

Zhou Zhaomu was born in rural area and joined the army after his graduation from middle school. He was transferred from the army to the newly established Fuyang Environmental Protection Bureau in 1986. Later, he was in charge of building the pollution charge and management office. At the beginning, he found it hard to collect the fee from factories that emitted effluents. After thinking carefully, Zhou claimed it was a phenomenon. It could be solved smoothly if people had an awareness of environmental protection and pollution charge with the guidance of the government policies. To solve the problem, Zhou suggested that the charge collection be linked with enterprises' anti-pollution measurements, government's approval and preferential policy. The suggestion was adopted. The businesses began to pay the fee and adopt measures to cut down pollution. From 1999 to 2001, 40.6 million RMB was collected and Fuyang's environment was greatly improved. Later, about 32 million RMB was refunded to enterprises for implementing over 100 anti-pollution projects.

In 1996, Zhou was promoted to be the deputy director of the Fuyang Environmental Protection Bureau and was in charge of environment supervision and management. The slogan "We Want Economic Prosperity and Environmental Protection" inspired Zhou a lot. No matter what the weather was like, he visited every corner of the city and shut down some enterprises that were not up to the anti-pollution standards.

As everyone knows, Longyang is a remote mountain area in Fu Yang. But in the remote mountains there lies a paper mill producing toilet paper. Local people had a lot of complaints about the mill which discharged the sewage and polluted the water source. Zhou Zhaomu felt very worried, bumping over the mountainside at least six times to find the mill owner. Some people smiled to Zhou and said, "As the old saying goes: three and out. You have been here for six times. You've done what you should do. There's no use for you to come." Zhou smiled and said with a firm tone, "If there goes such saying, it should have been changed for the sake of environmental protection." The dedication of Zhou finally moved the mill owner who turned up to have a long talk with Zhou. They talked a lot. Finally, the mill owner was convinced of taking some measures and getting a sewage treatment. The activities which Zhou had organized and involved in "environmental protection prizes for report" which have been launched for more than six years. They have received a total of 3782 reports from the public, including 4050 enterprises reported and 1299 verified. The money came up to as much as 2.5 million RMB. After 10 years of hard work, Fuyang finally became an ecological-friendly city.

Zhou now is an investigator of Fuyang Environmental Protection Bureau after 19-year work in local environmental protection projects. He has devoted himself wholeheartedly to the local environmental protection projects. With the help of his colleagues, Zhou has made more than 200 post-boards for environmental protection, dispatched 1000 pamphlets on environmental protection and edited more than 5000 propaganda materials. Zhou has written about 1000 research reports and news reports for newspapers in his spare time. In Fuyang, if you need to collect some materials related to environmental protection, you would be told, "Go to ask Zhou Zhaomu for help, who is an encyclopaedia in this field."

【人物启迪】Character Enlightenment

水清了,天蓝了。夕阳下,溪水边, 孩子戏水,妈妈洗菜。我们要的不仅仅是一个山清水秀的宜居环境,更要一笔给下一代、下下一代的宝贵财富。

The water is clear and the sky is blue. At sunset and by the stream, children are padding and mothers are doing washing. We need a a livable environment with picturesque scenery but most of all, a valuable wealth for our future generations.

故事十 何剑兴——困难职工的贴心人 A Helpful Man of the Needy Workers

【人物介绍】Character Introduction

何剑兴,杭州市总工会职工维权帮扶中心主任。2003 年 1 月开通“12351”职工维权热线,2011 年他被评选为第六届“杭州市十大平民英雄”。

He Jianxing is the director of the Workers Service Center of Hangzhou Federation of Trade Unions. In January, 2003, a "12351" hotline for protecting workers' rights was opened. In 2011, He Jianxing has been named one of the "Top Ten Civilian Heroes of Hangzhou at the 6th Session".

【人物事迹】Character Story

杭州市总工会职工维权帮扶中心从 2003 年 1 月 16 日成立第一天起,就开通了“12351”职工维权热线。中心成立以来,何剑兴带领全体工作人员热心于为全市职工服务。为了让“12351”职工维权热线在第一时间得到响应,何剑兴在自己的手机上设置了呼叫转移,让这条维权热线成了名副其实的 24 小时热线。深更半夜接到求助、咨询电话已成了他的家常便饭,通话常常是一、两个小时。以亲情温暖人心从而化解将要激化的矛盾的事例不胜枚举。外来务工人员亲切地称之为“民工热线”。中心在成立之初的信访接待中,发现有2/3的来访者,是要寻找一份养家糊口的工作。对此,何剑兴在该中心成立半年后的2003年7月,独辟蹊径,开通了“星期二就业绿色通道”,即每逢周二在该中心办事大厅举办小型用工洽谈会。2007年4月,他把这一就业绿色通道延伸到社区,每逢周二就“送岗位”到社区。7年多来,何剑兴组织用工单位提供就业岗位6万余个,帮助近两万名下岗失业和外来务工人员走上了就业岗位。

从2011年4月起,杭州市总工会职工维权帮扶中心推出“职工难事现场办”直通车活动,为职工现场解难。

赵主席是杭州市春光丝织厂原工会主席,在春光丝织厂当了12年的工会主席,已经退休18年了。他还是杭州市劳动模范,老伴也被评为杭州市先进工作者。3年前,老伴不幸患病,成了植物人,一直住在医院里,每月医疗费要4000多元,两个人的退休工资基本交给了医院。“我居住的社区很了解我的情况,有一次碰到何主任就讲了我家的情况。何主任了解后说,可以享受困难救助一次性补助5000元。”赵主席说:“我很不好意思,一直以来,我是帮助别人的,可现在要别人来帮助我了。今天我是来拿救助款的。”“赵主席你不要有思想负担,”何剑兴急忙说,“像你这样的老主席、老先进,生活上遇到了困难,政府应该给予帮助的。”

知青王先生是杭州人,在黑龙江工作期间因公负伤,腿部骨折。回杭后被安排到杭州市“工纠队”维护社会治安,执勤时被犯罪嫌疑人刺伤手臂,经劳动部门鉴定为“工伤八级”,享受相应的工伤补助待遇。可王先生遇到的困难是,年满60岁的他即将办理退休手续,进入社区管理属地之后,能否继续享受工伤待遇成了他的后顾之忧。同时,由于工伤,先后有5000余元的自负自理部分的医药费无处报销,这也成了他的一个“心病”。了解到这些情况,何主任马上与王先生所在的王马社区取得联系,进行协调:“退休进入社会化管理后,其工伤待遇可继续享受;考虑到他家庭的实际情况,一直以来‘悬’在那里的5000余元医疗费,由中心通过一定程序给予补助。”

The “12351” hotline for protecting workers' rights was opened on January 16, 2003, when the Workers Service Center of Hangzhou Federation of Trade Unions was established. Since that day, He Jianxing, together with the whole staff, devoted wholeheartedly and enthusiastically to serve the local workers. In order to make the “12351” hotline work efficiently, He Jianxing set up call forwarding on his own phone. The "12351" hotline was available to the public during 24 hours. Answering those various and long calls even in the midnight is common for him. There are numerous cases to mention for resolving issues with love and warmth. It is cordially named as "the Hotline for Migrant Workers". Among the letters and calls for complaints and rights, more than 2/3 of them are from unemployed workers who are seeking for jobs to support their family. Therefore, He Jianxing launched a "Green Path for Employment on Tuesday" in July, 2003. Every Tuesday, with the local conditions there will be some mini-sized job interviews in the hall center. In April, 2007, the "Green Path for Employment on Tuesday" went into the communities. "Job Openings" was held in the community every Tuesday. For more than 7 years, He Jianxing has helped provide more than 60 000 jobs, helping nearly 20 000 laid-off and migrant workers get employed.

Since April, 2011, the Workers Service Center has launched the campaign of "Green Path for Needy Staff", aiming to solve problems for needy workers on the spot.

Mr. Zhao was the chairman of the trade union in Hangzhou Chunguang Silk Weaving Mill which went bankrupt. He had worked as the chairman for 12 years and was ever awarded the title of "the Model Workers in Hangzhou". Mr. Zhao got retired 18 years ago. However, not everything went smoothly. Three years ago, his wife, the former excellent worker of the city, suffered greatly from her illness. She has been a vegetable and confined in hospital since then, costing more than 4 000 RMB monthly on medical care which almost spent all their pension. "My communities know my trouble well. Once I happened to tell Director He about my trouble. I am informed to enjoy one-time subsidy of 5 000 RMB." Chairman Zhao said, "I feel deeply sorry for I was the person who helped others before, but now I am the person who needs help from others. Today, I am here to get the subsidy." He Jianxing comforted him in a hurry, "Don't say like that. Our government is supposed to be helpful when our old comrades and friends, just like you, are in trouble."

During the period of the "Go and work in the Mountainous and Rural Areas", Mr. Wang became a sent-down youth in Heilongjiang, where he had his legs fractured on the job. Back to Hangzhou, Mr. Wang's hometown, he was assigned to "the workers' pickets" to maintain the social order. On duty, his arms were stabbed and wounded by a criminal suspect. It was identified as an industrial injury by the Human Resources and Social Security Bureau and he could enjoy the disability compensation. What worries him the most those days is whether he can continue to enjoy the disability compensation since he is going to retire at the age of 60 and enter the management of his community. What's more, he has 5 000 RMB which can't be reimbursed. No sooner does He Jianxing know it than he makes contact with the Wangma Community where Mr. Wang is living and tries to coordinate with them, "The worker can still enjoy injury benefits in the social management after retirement. Taking his trouble into account, our center will grant him 5 000 RMB, the medical fee which can't be reimbursed."

【人物启迪】Character Enlightenment

何剑兴是园丁,在竭诚为职工群众服务、努力为他们排忧解难这块特殊的园地里辛勤耕耘,终于结出累累硕果。

He Jianxing is a "gardener", cultivating in his garden diligently. He devotes himself wholeheartedly to serving people and helping people solve their troubles. He has made numerous significant achievements.

故事十一 高彩珍——杭州的姐 A Female Taxi Driver in Hangzhou

【人物介绍】Character Introduction

高彩珍,1955 年出生,杭州外事旅游汽车公司出租车驾驶员。高彩珍先后获得"诚信驾驶员""明星驾驶员""浙江省出租车服务明星"以及杭州首届"十佳的士之星"荣誉称号。

Gao Caizhen, born in 1955, is a cab driver in the Foreign Affairs Tourism Motor Company in Hangzhou. She has been awarded some honorary titles, including "The Trustworthy Driver" "The Star Driver" "The Taxi Service Star in Zhejiang" and "The Top Ten Taxi Drivers in Hangzhou".

【人物事迹】Character Story

1984 年 11 月,高彩珍加入了杭州外事旅游汽车公司。20 多年的"的姐"经历,在她心里仅化作最质朴的两句话:"每天我都在做平凡的工作,做不平凡的事;每天我都在长知识,学习如何正确面对不同的客人,体验人间万象和生活百态。"入行 20 多年,高彩珍几乎没有一天离开过出租车,这在整个行业里都是鲜见的。她十分注重业务能力的提高,时常利用休息时间阅读安全理论书籍,学习道路交通安全法规。20 多年穿梭于杭城的大街小巷,她对杭州的道路状况早已烂熟于心;细心的她在行车途中每次遇到新的道路变化,都会用笔认真记录,久而久之她成了杭州的"活地图"。俗话说:"一方水土养一方人。"作为一名优秀的杭州出租车司机,高彩珍用自己的行动完美诠释了"天堂使者"的光辉形象。在高彩珍的心里,她的形象必须要与西湖的美景相称。

1989 年冬日的一个下午,入行不久的高彩珍在火车站拉了一位外地乘客前往市中心,在到达中华饭店后,外地乘客趁付钱之机掏出一块鹅卵石猛击她的头部,高彩珍顿时鲜血直流。面对突袭,高彩珍没有退缩,她一边牢牢地拽住歹徒的手腕,一边打开车门向旁人求救。最终,在两位好心路人的协助下,歹徒被送进了派出所。就是这样一位勇敢的"的姐",在面对弱势群体时,也总会义不容辞伸出援助之手。

从事出租车行业至今,高彩珍想乘客之所想,急乘客之所急,以几十年如一日的真诚服务赢得了乘客的信任与尊敬,也赢得了社会的认可。一次,杭州市第一医院的李医生乘她的车去会诊,结算车费的是一位打工者。由于急着送不慎从脚手架上摔下来的同乡去医院,他没有多带钱,而车费就要 200 元。高彩珍只收取了 150 元,余下的钱让他作为回程路费。还有一次,雨下得很大,一位浑身湿透的女乘客抱着小孩上了车。车到一条又窄又深的弄堂口停下,看到女乘客没有带伞,高彩珍就将自己的伞送给了她。这样的事例不胜枚举。一位外籍人士玛丽小姐经常乘高彩珍的车,对她每一次都准时到达、热情周到的服务赞不绝口。

Gao Caizhen joined Hangzhou Foreign Affairs Tourism Motor

Company in November 1984. Talking about her experience as a taxi driver over 20 years, she said, "Though the job itself is an ordinary one, I tried my best to do it well in my own way. I learnt a lot every day from this job and got to know how to deal with different customers properly." Over the years she stuck to her post and her taxi cab, which is quite rare in the field. She put great importance on improving her professional skills through reading books on personal safety and laws and regulations of traffic safety. Driving throughout the whole city of Hangzhou over 20 years, she was very familiar with this city's traffic conditions. Whenever she found there was any change on the road signs, she would write it down to remind herself. She became a walking map of Hangzhou gradually, which was a great help for tourists. Hangzhou is deemed as an earthly paradise for hundreds of years. As the old saying goes that human beings are shaped by the land around them, Gao Caizhen, being a professional taxi driver in Hangzhou, won the title of "A Paradise Messenger". She took it for granted that it was her responsibility to drive her taxi perfect for the beautiful scenery of the West Lake.

On a winter afternoon of 1989, Gao Caizhen, being a novice, picked up a nonlocal passenger at the railway station. At the arrival of Zhonghua Hotel that guy pretended to take out the money from his pocket, but actually took out a cobble stone and hit hard on her head. Immediately her head bled a lot. Facing this sudden attack, Gao Caizhen didn't cower and shrink back. Instead she grasped the hoodlum's wrist tightly and sought help from the passers-by at the same time. Eventually the hoodlum was seized and turned over to the police station with the help of two kind-heartedly passers-by. Being such a brave female taxi driver, Gao Caizhen took it duty-boundly to help the disadvantaged.

It has been more than 20 years since Gao Caizhen became a taxi driver. She takes what the passengers need and what they are worried into consideration and wins their trust and respect in return with her sincere service. Doctor Li from Hangzhou First People's Hospital once took her taxi for a patient who fell down from the scaffold accidentally. It was a migrant worker, who was the patient's fellow-villager, helped pay the fares. It happened that the fellow-villager was so hurried to help his injured friend that he didn't take enough money. Altogether the fares were supposed to be 200 RMB. When seeing it, Gao Caizhen charged only 150 RMB and asked him to take the rest of money to go back. Another example, once it rained cats and dogs. A woman who was caught in rain for a long time finally took her taxi with a little baby held in her arms. The taxi stopped at an alley, apparently deep and narrow. Seeing the female passenger didn't take an umbrella, Gao Caizhen gave her own umbrella to the passenger. There are too numerous examples to mention. A foreign passenger often takes her taxi. Every time, Gao Caizhen arrives on schedule and offers warm service which makes the foreign passenger sing high praise for her.

【人物启迪】Character Enlightenment

出租车可以说是外地人了解一个城市的窗口,许多游客对于一个城市的印象都是从出租车开始的。杭州作为著名的旅游城市,素有"人间天堂"的美称,希望能出更多的像高彩珍这样的司机。

Taxis can be said to be the windows for travelers to know the city. For many travelers, an impression on the city starts from their impression on taxis. Hangzhou is a national tourist city, renowned as "Paradise on Earth", calling for as many drivers as possible like Gao Caizhen.

故事十二　史文斌——电力服务明星 A Service Star Electrician

【人物介绍】Character Introduction

史文斌,1964 年生,杭州市电力局城北供电局抢修班班长。他曾获得杭州市和浙江省"劳动模范"、全国"电力行业用户满意服务明星"和全国"劳动模范"等多个荣誉称号。

Shi Wenbin, born in 1964, is the head of the rush-repair group of Chengbei Bureau of Power Supply, Hangzhou Electric Power Company. He has been awarded a series of titles, including "Model Worker in Hangzhou" "Model Worker in Zhejiang Province" "The Service Star of the National Electric Power System" and "The National Model Worker".

【人物事迹】Character Story

从事电力抢修工作20余年,史文斌爱岗敬业,钻研技术,练就了一手快速判断和处理故障的本领,创造了20余年"零投诉"的业绩。无论高温、台风、雷雨,只要有情况,他总是第一个赶到现场,故障不排除决不回家。他不计名利,经常在上下班途中上门为年老体弱的困难用户排除户内故障,并经常向用户传授一些简易的检查和维修方法。

有一次,大年三十的下午,到处是节日的喜庆气氛。街头不时传来"噼噼啪啪"的鞭炮声,人们正分享着节日的欢乐。儿子在阳台上挂着一串长长的爆竹,正等着爸爸回来;爱人也已经包好了饺子,备好年夜饭的酒菜。这时,阿斌的手机响了:"阿斌师傅,我是京江敬老院,我们这里有台电视突然坏了,问了修理部,查出好像是屋内电路问题,他们都说修不了。我只好求助于你,帮我们解决一下。"接完电话,阿斌迟疑了一下,但马上意识到除夕夜一台电视机对于敬老院的老人的意义所在。他二话没说,当即就去了。当他找到这位客户的住所时,眼前的情景让他心头一震:今天我来对了!原来那间宿舍里住着两位年迈的孤寡老人,两位老人看到阿斌的到来,像是一下子看到了希望。"阿斌师傅!给你添麻烦了。"老人抱歉地说。"没关系,这是我应该做的。"阿斌一边说一边检查电路。由于线路埋在墙体内,检查工作进行得比较缓慢。阿斌决定重新放置一路明线,确保老人晚上看得上电视。晚8时整,大功告成,整洁的新布线路丝毫没有破坏屋内的装修,春节晚会也准时开播。老人们满意地用微微颤动的手竖起了大拇指,敬老院李院长也感慨地说:"阿斌随叫随到,就像住在我们隔壁一样!"

史文斌勇于创新,探索并总结出表后线延伸服务的考核规范和管理方法,在全市电力系统推广。史文斌一直在思考如何把一个人的服务变成一个团队的服务,把其他党员也带动起来。最终,他以自己的名字成立了"阿斌电力服务队"。已过不惑之年的史文斌,眼下最大的希望就是儿子能接过自己的班,把阿斌服务的精神传递下去。

Having engaged in the electric rush-repair for more than 20 years, Shi Wenbin always has great passion for his own work and improves professional competence. He is expert at telling electric problems without delay and solving them in time, achieving a non-complaint record. No matter what the weather is like, such as high temperature, typhoon or thunderstorm, if there's any emergency, he's the first one on the spot with determination that he wouldn't go back home unless the problems are solved. He often helps the old and the poor resolve problems and offers some methods to check and repair for free.

On a Chinese New year's Eve, the whole city was filled with the happy atmosphere. People were enjoying their holidays and sharing their joy with their family. Here and there came the sound of firecrackers. Shi Wenbin's wife was preparing reunion dinner for the family and his son was waiting for him to come back home to set off the crackers which he put on the balcony. Bin was on his way back home, but suddenly his mobile phone rang. "Master Bin, I am calling from Jingjiang Nursing House. One of televisions here was broken down all of a sudden. Our workers of Repair Department have checked it and found that there was something wrong with the electric circuit. Unfortunately they could not fix it. That is why I call you. We do need your help and thank you very much in advance." He hardly hesitated and accepted the request, as he clearly knew what a television means to the aged people in the nursing house at this very special time. He realized that he had made a totally right decision at the very sight of two aged men in that room. Bin was their only hope. They said, "Master Bin, we feel really sorry for making this trouble for you." "It doesn't matter. That is my job!" Bin answered and began to check the circuit promptly. It went quite slowly because that the wire line was buried inside the wall. To ensure that they could watch the Spring Festival Gala on time, Bin decided to set a new open-wire line and he finished it at 8:00 p.m. Those two aged men were so happy that they gave a thumb-up to Bin. Even Mr. Li, the director of Jingjiang Nursing House, said with emotion, "Bin is on call all the time. It seems like that he lives next door to us!"

With his innovation and exploration, a new assessment and management of electric extension service has already been launched in the whole city. Shi Wenbin has been involved in thinking how to organize a service team and lead other communists. Eventually, he succeeded in setting up “A Bin Electric Service Team”. At the age of over forty, Shi Wenbin hopes that his son could become his successor and handed down the spirit of A Bin Service.

【人物启迪】Character Enlightenment

干一行爱一行。我们好像看到远远的一个背影,背着电线走街串巷,守护着城市电网,不遗余力地给千家万户带来光明。

Love whatever job you take up. We seemingly see a figure in the distance, carrying electric wire wandering about the streets, guarding the city grid and sparing no efforts to brighten thousands of households.

故事十三　高水华——残疾人企业家 A Disabled Entrepreneur

【人物介绍】Character Introduction

高水华,1964 年生,浙江省杭州海纳实业有限公司董事长。他先后获得了“全国优秀福利企业家”“省级扶残助残先进个人”“杭州市十大平民英雄”“杭州市残疾人事业爱心慈善家”“江干区十大道德模范”荣誉称号。

Gao Shuihua, born in 1964, is the Chairman of Hangzhou Haina Industrial Co., Ltd., Zhejiang Province. He has been awarded the titles including “National Outstanding Welfare Entrepreneur” “Provincial Excellent Individual for Helping the Disabled” “The Top Ten Civilian Heroes in Hangzhou” “the Loving Philanthropist Caring the Disabled People in Hangzhou” and “The Top Ten Moral Models in Jianggan District, Hangzhou”.

【人物事迹】Character Story

1988 年,高水华在一场意外事故中双腿残疾。顽强的意志和坚韧的品质使他在治疗中承受了常人难以想象的痛苦，并最终战胜磨难，重新站了起来。病床上，一直存在的创业念头迸发出强烈火花，高水华决心用智慧和双手，谱写一曲创业之歌。不甘消沉的他用仅有的7000多元开始了创业之路，创办了白石纸箱厂。成立之初的白石纸箱厂是一家默默无闻的小厂，厂房是石棉瓦简易工棚，生产设备也相当简陋。经过20年的不断发展，今天的白石纸箱厂已成长为一家拥有全电脑控制、全自动流水线设备，并通过ISO9001:2000国际质量体系认证的现代企业。它所生产的包装纸箱、特种式样纸箱、展示盒、纸托盘深受客户信赖，还被浙江省出入境检验检疫局定为出口商品定点包装产品。“追求卓越，精益求精，满足客户需求”是高水华企业的宗旨。随着企业声誉不断提高，规模迅速扩大，高水华后来又创办了杭州海纳投资有限公司和宿迁海纳担保有限公司。

事业成功的高水华从未忘记过帮助残疾人。在帮困助残这个问题上，仅仅出钱已经不能满足高水华的心愿。他想到了装修。是啊，哪个残疾困难家庭会有闲钱，花在这种他们认为“花里胡哨”的东西上啊？即使有，他们也宁愿买家电，补贴家用。但是，残疾人困难家庭的房子装修老旧，有的甚至渗漏，电线老化，影响生活质量和生活安全，他们也将就着过，这是不争的事实。如果解决了这个实际问题，他们的生活质量会好很多。于是，从2008年开始，高水华每年拿出30万元，帮助家庭困难的残疾人装修房屋。授人以鱼不如授人以渔。高水华在捐助这30万元的时候，对如何做好这件事又动起了脑筋，他请了残疾人组成的装修队装修房子，给他们创造了就业机会，拉动了残疾人就业市场。这个完美的构想既帮助了残疾人困难家庭，又解决了残疾人就业难问题，还实现了自己回报社会的梦想，是一个三赢的结果。

纸箱厂刚步入正轨，高水华就一次性拿出十几个岗位安排残疾人就业，他还办起培训班帮助残疾人尽快适应岗位。现在高水华厂里残疾人比例超过了50%，职工年人均收入增幅保持在10个百分点以上。他还热心捐助春风行动等各类公益活动，资助困难儿童和残疾人。

In 1988, Gao Shuihua became disabled in his legs because of an accident. Undergoing great suffering during the medical treatment which was unimaginable to the common people, he finally overcame hardships and stood back up with his strong will and perseverance. Lying in the hospital bed, Gao made up his mind to start his own business, which had been a dream for a long time. He didn't fall into despair and lose all hope but set up his own career. Gao Shuihua founded Baishi Cardboard Box Factory with only 7 000 RMB. During the initial stage of establishment, Baishi cardboard box factory was a small plant unknown to the public. The workshop was very shabby. In fact, it was only a bunkhouse made of asbestos tiles. The production equipment was quite crude as well. With 20 years' development, the factory has turned into a modern enterprise, adopting automatic production lines and computer-controlled equipment. Besides, the company has been authorized the ISO 9001:2000 Quality Management System Certificate. Their products such as packaging cartons, special-pattern cartons, show cases and cardboard pallets, win the trust of all their customers and were appointed as the packaging products for export commodies by Zhejiang Entry-exit Inspection and Quarantine Bureau. Gao insists on the company tenet of "Keeping, Improving and Striving for perfection". With the spreading of its reputation, the company expanded rapidly. Later, he founded Haina Investment Co., Ltd and Suqian Haina Guarantee Co., Ltd.

Gao never forgets to offer his help to the disabled after his success. Gao Shuihua is not confined to aid only with money to help the poor and the disabled. He comes up with a new idea. That's helping them in the way of house decoration. It is no denying that the poor and the disabled would never spend much money on house decoration which appears so fancy and impractical in their eyes. Even if they have some spare money, they would rather buy home appliances than decorate the houses. Their houses are generally worn out. Some of them even are leaking and the wire lines inside the house are getting old, which would definitely cause safety problems and weaken the quality of life. But these families basically do with it and leave it as it is. They would absolutely better off if someone can help them with these problems. Therefore, from 2008 Gao Shuihua takes out 300 000 RMB every year and helps the poor and the disabled to renovate their houses. Give a man a fish and you feed him for a day; teach a man to fish and you feed him for a lifetime. Apart from donating 300 000 RMB, Gao also offers the opportunity of renovating these houses to a renovation team made up of the disabled. This enhances the chances of getting employment for the disabled. By doing this, Gao not only helps the poor and the disabled directly, but also helps to solve the employment problem for the disabled and realizes his dream of repaying the society.

While his cardboard box factory is growing, Gao helps more than ten disabled men get employed and begins training programs to help them get qualified for their jobs as quickly as possible. At present, the number of the disabled in his factory exceeds 50%, with an average annual growth rate of 10% average personal income. He warm-heartedly donates money to some non-profit activities such as "Spring Wind Project", helping the children in financial trouble and the disabled.

【人物启迪】Character Enlightenment

企业小时做产品,企业大时做人品。企业家的使命是回馈社会,帮助需要帮助的人,为社会的稳定与和谐做一些力所能及的事。正所谓授人玫瑰,手有余香。

When the enterprise is small, it should focus on its products; when it grows bigger, it should focus on its brand. The mission of entrepreneurs is to reward the society, help those who need help and make contributions to the social stability and harmony. Just as the old saying goes, "The rose's in her hand, the flavor in mine."

故事十四 葛明霞——情感教学的创新者 An Innovator of Emotional Teaching Method

【人物介绍】Character Introduction

葛明霞,教师,1962 年生,宁波宁海县人。她曾多次荣获"县级优秀教师""感动甬城学子十大优秀教师""浙江骄傲"等荣誉称号。

Ge Mingxia, teacher, was born in 1962, Ninghai coutry of Ningbo City. A series of honorable titles have been granted to her, such as "The Excellent Teacher of the County" "The Top Ten Teachers who Moved Students in Yongcheng" and "The Pride of Zhejiang".

【人物事迹】Character Story

从教30多年来,葛明霞从不计较个人得失,把所有的爱都倾注在学生身上,把所有的情都洒在教育事业上。她常说,选择了教师这一职业,就意味着奉献和自我牺牲。

葛明霞是一位优秀的"魔术师"。2004年,葛明霞接任了当时在年级段中语文基础最差的初三(3)班的语文课老师,一年后的中考,全班学生语文平均成绩97.6分,名列全校第一;2005年,接任初三(10)班语文课老师,该班中考语文平均分列全校第一……不可思议的现象每年都在上演着。自2000年调入宁海县跃龙中学,葛明霞连续八年接任初三毕业班的工作,每一届接的都是年级段中语文基础最差的班级,可每年中考,她带的班级不仅语文成绩在全县名列前茅,而且各科成绩都有很大的提高,学生们在各类竞赛中获奖的也特别多。

"好孩子是夸出来的!"葛明霞说。她喜欢夸学生,尤其喜欢夸"学困生"。初三(9)班的何明泽可爱又顽皮,不喜欢读书,进初中第一次语文考试就不及格,葛老师决定等待机会。一次月考,批改试卷的老师不小心将小何的语文成绩多算了8分,葛老师决定变这个错误为机会,她在全班同学面前"狠狠"地表扬了小何,说他是一不小心就将语文考到了92分,假如真努力了,成绩肯定很快就上去了。课后,葛老师悄悄地同小何约定:"老师把这8分借给你,但期末时你要还给老师。"对着笑意盈盈的葛老师,小何认真地点点头。这之后,葛明霞开心地发现,这个原来讨厌学习的孩子变了,不仅上课认真听讲,而且还会认真地记好每一个知识点。

在教学上,她潜心钻研,成功摸索出了"以情动人、以情感人、以情育人"的"情感教学法"。她用亲情打造和谐班级,把每一个学生当成自己的孩子。从教以来,她一直坚持义务为学生辅导,不管是自己班级还是其他班级的学生,她都无偿接纳。从教30多年,葛明霞根本就记不清,自己到底牺牲了多少个休息日,为她的学生义务补过多少课,又有多少学生在她这里补过课。她总是对感觉过意不去的家长们说:"我家不缺钱,用这个钱奖励孩子吧,学生的进步就是对老师最好的回报。"

她无私付出,带出的很多徒弟都成为县市学科骨干。

Ge Mingxia has been teaching for 30 years, with all her love wholeheartedly contributed to her students and her passion to her teaching career, regardless of her own gains and losses. As she always says, her job demands commitment, contributions and self-sacrifice.

Ge Mingxia is an excellent "Magician". In 2004 she took over Class 3 Grade 9 which performs worst in Chinese at the same grade. But this class, with the average score of 97. 6 points, ranked the first in Chinese among the whole school in the High School Entrance Examination one year later. In 2005 she took over Class 10 Grade 9 and Class 10 also ranked the first in the Entrance Examination for high school. The same miracle happened each year. Since being transferred to Yuelong Middle School in 2000, Ge was in charged for Grade 9 during the continuous eight years. Every time the class she took over performed worst in Chinese for the same grade at first, but they finally turned out to be the best one. Students in the class not only performed excellently in Chinese but also made great progress in the remaining subjects. They won many prizes in various competitions.

As what Ge has ever said, a good child grows with praise. She is always praising her students, especially the students with learning difficulties. He Mingze, a student from Class 3 Grade 9, was lovely and naughty. He didn't like to study at all. He failed first in Chinese exam after he entered Yuelong middle school. Ge waited for a chance to educate him and finally got a good chance. For one of the monthly exams, a teacher who marked the exam papers gave carelessly extra 8 points to He Mingze. Ge Mingxia decided to take this mistake as a good chance and greatly praised He, saying that He could get the high score of 92 points so easily and if He could make more efforts, he definitely could get much higher score. After class Ge made a deal with He that the extra 8 points were lent to him and he must return it to Ge at the end of the term when taking the final exam. From then on, Ge found that He Mingze was making progress gradually. He not only paid all his attention to the class, but also took notes carefully at the same time.

Ge Mingxia devotes herself to the study of teaching, innovating her own "emotional teaching method". She treats her students like her own children, leading to a harmonious atmosphere in class with love. Students from both her class and others benefit a lot from her extra help in study.

Being a teacher for over 30 years, Ge could not remember how many holidays she has spared to make up missed lessons with her students voluntarily. Nor does she remember how many students come to her for taking these lessons. She always refuses to charge any money on these lessons and she talks to these students' parents, "I'm not short of money. If you want to pay me, please use the money to reward your children. I would get fully rewarded if your children make any progress."

With her selfless help, many teachers guided by her have become county-level and city-level subjects leaders.

【人物启迪】Character Enlightenment

一位理想的教师应该是距离圣人最近的人，知识渊博、学风严谨、人格高尚，对学生充满关爱，富有强烈的责任心。教师对学生的关怀无所不在，极度人性化，学生的未来即学校的未来！

An ideal teacher is supposed to be a wise man who has a profound knowledge, a rigorous academic approach, and a noble mind. With a strong sense of responsibility, an ideal teacher is supposed to love and care students deeply and reasonably. The future of students is the future of school.

故事十五　黄斌——荒岛英雄 A Hero in a Desert Island

【人物介绍】Character Introduction

黄斌，舟山环卫处的环卫工人，1981 年出生。他连续多年被评为"优秀城市美容师"，2007 年被评为"舟山市劳动模范"，2009 年被评为"浙江省十大优秀青年"，2010 年被评为"浙江省劳动模范"。

Huang Bin, born in 1981, is a sanitation worker of Zhoushan city. He has been awarded the titles for years including the"Excellent Environmental Worker", "Model Worker of Zhoushan City" in 2007, " The Top Ten Outstanding Young People of Zhejiang Province" in 2009, and "Model Worker of Zhejiang Province" in 2010.

【人物事迹】Character Story

黄斌19岁走出校门，来到舟山市团鸡山岛。团鸡山岛，面积约0.2平方千米，离舟山本岛4.5海里，是个非常不起眼的弹丸小岛，却是整个舟山岛城的垃圾填埋场。这是一座孤岛，岛上最后一个居民早在十几年前就迁走了。黄斌每天要凌晨起床，赶第一班垃圾船到达团鸡山。他的工作主要是开着推土机，不停地将垃圾车倒下的垃圾推平、压实、覆盖。最难熬的是冬夏两季。夏天坐进推土机驾驶室像坐进蒸笼一样，又必须穿上长袖长裤，否则皮肤经不住长时间的暴晒。冬天除了海风凛冽，遇上雨雪天气，黏糊糊的垃圾一脚就陷进去十几厘米，又难受又恶心。时间一长，人会不由自主地陷入空虚绝望，在他之前的一个又一个环卫工，正是因为无法忍受这样长期的孤独，最终选择离开这座岛。在无边的寂寞中，在恶劣的环境里，黄斌默默地填埋着从岛城来的每天600多吨的垃圾，无怨无悔。

Huang Bin came to work on Tuanjishan Island shortly after his graduation from high school at the age of 19. As a nondescript tiny island covering about only 0.2 square meters and 4.5 nautical miles away from Zhoushan city, Tuanjishan Island is the landfill site of the whole Zhoushan city. This barren island saw the departure of its last habitant over a decade ago. Every day Huang Bin wakes up at dawn to catch the earliest sewage vessel to Tuanjishan Island. His routine work every day is to bulldoze and ram the garbage unloaded from the garbage truck. Summer and winter are the toughest seasons for him. In summer, the bulldozer cage is as hot as a steamer, but he has to wear long-sleeved shirts and pants to prevent from sunburn; while in winter, he has to suffer freezing sea wind, and in case of rain and snow, he will get his feet bogged down into sticky and sick garbage. As time goes on, desperation caused by loneliness and illusion arises, which has forced sanitation workers to finally leave this island one after another. But Huang Bin, in spite of endless loneliness and adverse circumstances, sticks to his post and handles over 600 tons of garbage delivered every day without one word to complaint.

【人物启迪】Character Enlightenment

正因为有了他们的青春付出和坚定守护,日新月异的舟山群岛,才变得越来越干净、美丽。不问回报,只知付出,他们是当之无愧的英雄。

Thanks to the devotion and commitment by Huang Bin and his colleagues, Zhoushan Islands are becoming cleaner and more beautiful. Always contributing but expecting no returns makes them our real heroes.

故事十六 杭兰英——百姓喜爱的好支书 A Good Secretary Loved by People

【人物介绍】Character Introduction

杭兰英,浙江省上虞区祝温村党支部书记,1949年12月出生,浙江上虞人。她先后荣获“浙江省优秀党务工作者”“全国优秀党员”“浙江省劳动模范”等称号。2014年8月,浙江省委授予杭兰英“百姓喜爱的好支书”荣誉称号;2015年2月当选2014年度“全国三八红旗手标兵”候选人;2015年,她被评为“全国劳动模范”。

Hang Lanying, born in December 1949, is the Secretary of Communist Party Branch in Zhuwen village, Shangyu District of Zhejiang Province. Hang has won a series of honorary titles: “The Excellent Party Affairs Worker in Zhejiang Province” “The National Excellent Member of Communist Party” and “The Model Worker in Zhejiang Province”. In August 2014, Hang Lanying was conferred the title “A Good Secretary of Communist Party Loved by People” by Zhejiang Provincial Party Committee. In February 2015, She was nominated one of the national “March 8th Red-Banner Holders”. In 2015, Hang was honored with “National Model Worker”.

【人物事迹】Character Story

在浙江绍兴市上虞区，有一个叫祝温村的小村庄远近闻名。祝温村原本是杭州湾边上的一片滩涂地。20 多年前，村里不仅没有硬化的道路，房前屋后还满是垃圾，一下雨就污水横流，臭气熏天。如今，村容发生了翻天覆地的变化，村民的精神面貌也焕然一新。而这些改变，都是村党总支书记杭兰英带领村民一点一滴做出来的。

1986 年，村党支部改选，曾就读绍兴卫校的杭兰英是村里的“赤脚医生”。她细心负责的态度，赢得了不少村民的信任，大家一致支持她担任新的支部书记。在老支书和丈夫的动员下，杭兰英接过了这份“苦差事”。

杭兰英上任之初，村里条件很差，壮劳力大都选择外出打工。渐渐地，一部分村民挣到些钱，先富起来了，但村集体经济依然薄弱，村容村貌依旧。“要改变村里的面貌，激起村民的创业热情，就要先改善村里的基础设施。”她把目光转向推进标准农田建设，她和村干部们积极争取土地整理项目，先后投入 500 余万元，对全村 1300 亩农田进行标准化改造，建成了省级千亩高产粮食示范基地。水稻良种基地、猕猴桃基地、花卉基地……一个个农业合作社随后发展起来。许多村民在家中搞起了加工业，村民收入年年攀升。“要把工作做好，得先让老百姓真正信任我们村干部。”杭兰英立下规矩，所有项目资金直接打进公账，项目建设时再按程序做账领取，所有村委班子成员及亲戚都不得插手本村的工程建设，避免发生腐败现象。杭兰英许多亲戚都是做工程建设的，开始有人有些想法，觉得她不近人情，但杭兰英坚守住了关口。“干部清廉了，账目清楚了，村民才会放心。我做书记的，更加不能偏私！”这些年，村里大大小小的工程项目不下 50 个，总投资超过 1780 万元，但杭兰英和村干部及其亲戚从未承包、承建和插手过，账目清清楚楚。

“仓廪实而知礼节，衣食足而知荣辱。”在杭兰英的带领下，祝温村村民不仅在物质上越来越富裕，他们的精神世界也越来越充实。为改善民风，杭兰英把村民组织起来搞文艺活动，让他们在合作中加强交流。2006 年正式成立的祝温村表演队现有成员 40 余人，几年来，这支表演队已在各种比赛中多次获奖。从 2010 年开始，祝温村每年会举办一系列活动，举行“十佳和谐家庭”“十佳好婆婆”“十佳好媳妇”“十佳好少年”和“十佳爱心人士”的评选，目前全村已有 200 位村民评上了“五个十佳”，村里把当选者的照片挂在“人和文化长廊”上，村民都为能登上这个“光荣榜”感到自豪。现在，村里已经有了图书馆、文化讲堂、文化活动中心、文化长廊。任职 28 年,杭兰英把一个集体经济薄弱、班子软弱涣散、村庄管理无序的落后村,建成了享有"创业乐园、生态花园、文化公园、人和家园"美誉的新农村建设示范村,实现了从过去单纯引导农民致富的"能人治村",向全面治理的"贤人治村"模式转变。

In Shangyu District of Shaoxing City, there is a well-known village named Zhuwen Village. Zhuwen Village used to be a barren mudflat located on the edge of Hangzhou Bay without hardened roads and full of garbage everywhere. When it rained, the whole village was overwhelmed by sewage and it stank to high heaven. 20 years have seen a tremendous change in the village and villagers taking on an entirely new look. And all these changes owe to the hard-work by Hang Lanying, the secretary of Party Branch in the village, along with her villagers.

In 1986, it was time for Party Branch of the village to elect again. At that time, Hang, a student graduated from Shaoxing Medical School, was a "barefoot doctor" in the village. She was careful and responsible, so she had won the trust of many villagers. She got the whole support to be the new Secretary of Party Branch in the village. With the support of the former secretary and her husband, Hang took over this appointment which was going to challenge her a lot.

Shortly after taking office, Hang found the village in poor condition and most able-bodied adults going out to do manual work for a living. Gradually, some of them became well-off, which was still not able to make the whole village's economy prosperous. "In order to change the status of the village and stimulate the enthusiasm of the villagers, we must give top priority to the improvement of the infrastructure in the village." She plunged herself into the promotion of standard construction of farmland. Working together with her colleagues, they have actively sought the land consolidation project, invested more than 50 million RMB to transform the farmland with 1,300 acres and succeeded in building a provincial pilot base of high-yield grain farmland. Several bases have sprung up such as improved varieties of rice, kiwi fruit and flowers. Many villagers have therefore engaged in the processing industry which has made their income increase annually. "Only by gaining the trust from the villagers can we do a good job." There is a rule set by Hang: all the project funds should go directly into the public account. Once the project carries out, the funds will be received by procedure. All her colleagues and their relatives are not allowed to intervene in these projects in order to avoid corruption. At the very beginning, some of Hang's relatives who engaged in project construction couldn't understand her and thought Hang was unreasonable. But Hang refused all of them and adhered to the principle. "With honest and incorruptible officials and clear accounts, our villagers will be assured. As the secretary of the village, I can't be inequitable." Over these years, there have been more than 50 construction projects with over 1.78 million RMB of investment. Hang, her colleagues together with their relatives have never intervened in them and all the accounts have been clear.

As the Chinese saying goes, "When the granaries are full, men appreciate rites and obligation; When food and clothing are enough, men have a sense of honor and shame." Under the leadership of Hang, the villagers have begun to pay attention to their material aspects as well as their moral civilization. Hang has involved the villagers into carrying out programs of entertainment which has helped them cooperate with each other. In 2006, an entertainment team was formally set up with more than 40 villagers. Since then, the team has won some awards in various competitions. From 2010, Zhuwen village has held a series of activities, such as the election of "Top Ten Harmonious Families" "Top Ten Good Mothers-in-law" "Top Ten Good Daughters-in-law" "Top Ten Excellent Youths" and "Top Ten Loving Persons". Till now, more than 200 villagers have got the five "Top Tens". Those villagers' photos have been posted in the "Harmonious Cultural Corridors" and they are proud of being there. Now there are libraries, cultural forums, centers and corridors in the village.

28 years have witnessed the village's transformation from a backward one with weak collective economy, inefficient leadership and mismanagement to a well-known pilot village which has a good reputation of "entrepreneurship

paradise, ecological garden, cultural park and harmonious home". Hang has succeeded in achieving the transformation from the management mode that the capable man simply leads the villagers into making a fortune to the one that the wise man comprehensively and scientifically manages the village today.

【人物启迪】Character Enlightenment

情怀是一种不可思议的力量，它能感染人，甚至塑造出一个全新的精神世界。杭兰英拥有勤廉为民、公而忘私的情怀。有了这种情怀，我们才能真正立党为公、执政为民，我们才能忧民之忧、急民所急，我们才能严于律己、克己奉公，我们才能像杭兰英一样，于平凡的岗位中，迸发出不可思议的巨大力量。

Feelings are an inconceivable power which can affect people, and even create a completely new spiritual world. Hang is diligent and conscientious in serving the people, and she is so devoted to public service as to forget her private interests. With such feelings, we can build a party serving the interests of the people and stay at the helm of the state for the people, we can feel concerned about our country and people, we can become strict with ourselves and work selflessly for the public interests, and we can achieve extraordinary successes at our ordinary post like Hang Lanying.

故事十七　朱志根——浙江"水军"的功勋旗手 The Meritorious Coach of Zhejiang Swimming Team

【人物介绍】Character Introduction

朱志根，国家级教练，1957 年出生，浙江上虞人。他于 1980 年 2 月开始担任教练员，1983 年担任浙江省体工队游泳队领队，1996 年担任浙江省游泳协会副会长，1997 年担任浙江省游泳协会教练员委员会主任。他曾获 1998 年和 1999 年两届"全国十佳教练员"、2001 年"跨世纪中青年优秀教练员"和"全国体育先进工作者"等称号，是第十届全国人大代表，2004 年被评为国家级教练员，2012 年和 2013 年获"体坛风云人物"提名奖，2014 年当选为"浙江骄傲年度人物"。

Zhu Zhigen, born in 1957, is a national coach from Shangyu, Zhejiang Province. He started his career as a coach in February, 1980. Zhu served as the leader of Zhejiang swimming team in 1983, the vice president of Zhejiang Swimming Association in 1996 and the director of coaches committee in Zhejiang Swimming Association respectively in 1997. Zhu has won a series of honorary titles: "The Top Ten National Outstanding Coaches" in 1998 and 1999, "The Cross-Century Outstanding Middle-Aged and Young Coach" in 2001, "The National Excellent Sports Worker", the Deputy to the Tenth National People's Congress, "Nomination of Sports Personality" in 2012 and 2013, and "the Pride of Zhejiang Province" in 2014.

【人物事迹】Character Story

朱志根的父亲是一位经验丰富的外海运输工，朱志根懂事后就开始在渔船上帮大人做事。海水泡大的孩子水性都很好，朱志根自小便显现出游泳天赋。在他 14 岁那年，镇上举行游泳比赛，小志根居然力克众多游泳好手，从一帮大小伙子手中接连夺得 100 米、200 米仰泳第一名。这引起了浙江省队教练的关注，使得他成了一名省队队员。良好的先天条件加上系统刻苦的训练，朱志根很快在省队脱颖而出，取得了全国比赛亚军。

1980 年至今，他一直默默地从事教练工作，即使面临中国和浙江游泳事业的最低谷，他还是矢志不渝地坚守着泳坛事业，朱志根憋足一股劲：一定要为中国男泳争口气！为了这个信念，朱志根拿出了拼命三郎的劲头，他的敬业精神得到了队里工作人员的一致好评。

1996 年，朱志根提出了"以管理带动训练"，向管理要质量、要成绩。2001 年他又倡导"以科学带动管理"。其中最为突出的是"生理生化测试"，每周一由医护人员准时给运动员测试血红蛋白、血乳酸、血色素等专业项目，并及时将结果反馈给教练员，教练员再根据结果制定训练计划。另一项措施是将以前的大周期训练改成小周期训练，即每天减少 2 万米的锻炼距离，将精力转移到训练强度上，从而提高训练效率和质量。

要保证游泳队的良性发展，选苗环节一定要抓好。浙江省游泳队的生源80%以上是杭州人。针对这个特点，游泳队实行“走训制”，即由少体校推荐，每次考察1～2人，经过半年的观察和测试，队里统一商讨后决定去留。这比以往招一大批退一大批的做法节省了大量的人力和财力，同时提高了成功率。

用科学指导管理也十分必要。游泳队率先改革管理模式，变全队统一管理为分组管理。一方面充分发挥党团员以及优秀队员的骨干作用，另一方面增加了教练与队员接触的机会，让教练参与管理，提高了教练员积极性。正是靠着科学的管理，整个队伍得以全面发展，游泳队的训练风气和学习风气都日臻完善。

朱志根以先进的理念和科学的手段训练运动员，培养了吴鹏、陈桦、杨雨、汪顺、邵依雯、孙杨等一批又一批优秀运动员，每一位都是中国泳坛不同时期的代表人物，实现了中国男子游泳奥运金牌零的突破。2014年，朱志根所带队员参加了全国游泳冠军赛暨亚运会选拔赛、第十七届亚运会、全国游泳锦标赛等赛事，为浙江游泳队、中国游泳队获得优异的战绩做出了突出的贡献，继续体现着他作为浙江功勋教练员的重要作用。

Zhu Zhigen's father is an experienced maritime transport worker. When Zhu Zhigen was a little kid, he began to help adults on the fishing boats. At that time Zhu showed a great talent for swimming. There was a swimming competition held in his town when he was 14 years old. Unexpectedly, Zhu ranked the first in 100m and 200m backstroke. His fantastic talent attracted attention of swimming coaches from Zhejiang Province. Soon, he was chosen as one of the members of the provincial swimming team, made a big difference thanks to his talent and hard training and won the second place in national competition.

Since 1980, as a coach, Zhu has devoted himself wholeheartedly to his work. Even in the tough time of Zhejiang and China's swimming, Zhu, bursting with energy, vowed to adhere to his chosen road to bring credit to Chinese male swimming. In order to achieve the dream, he worked with all his efforts and won praise from his colleagues.

In 1996, Zhu put forward a new theory, "to train driven by management", which aims to make breakthroughs by management. In

2001, Zhu advocated "scientific management", of which the most prominent was "physiological and biochemical test". Every Monday, the swimmers' haemoglobin, blood lactate and haemochrome and so on would be tested by medical staff, who would inform their coaches of the testing results timely. Accordingly, their coaches would work out the training plan. Another one was to change the previous big cycle training to a small one, that is, to reduce the distance of 20000 m a day and focus on the training intensity to enhance the efficiency and quality.

Great efforts should be made to recruit potential swimmers in order to ensure the development of the swimming team. More than 80% of swimmers in Zhejiang swimming team are from Hangzhou. Therefore, Zhejiang swimming team has adopted a more scientific training system, that is, sports school could recommend one or two swimmers who are going to undergo half-a-year's observation and test. And the swimming team will make the final decision of their stay or leave. In the past, a large number of students would be recruited. If some of them couldn't meet the demands, they would have to leave. It wasted a lot. The new training system has helped to save a lot and improved the success rate.

It's also necessary to manage scientifically. The swimming team takes initiative to reform the management mode from unified management to group management, which, brings the initiative of the excellent swimmers into full play, and helps to enhance the communication between coaches and swimmers, involve coaches into management and improve their enthusiasm. With scientific management, the training discipline and atmosphere have been improving a lot and the whole swimming team is developing in an all-round way.

With advanced theories and scientific means, Zhu has cultivated many excellent swimmers such as Wu Peng, Chen Hua, Yang Yu, Wang Shun, Shao Yiwen and Sun Yang, who are the representatives in swimming. Zhu has also achieved his dream to bring credit to Chinese male swimming: making a breakthrough and getting gold medals in Olympic Games. In 2014, his athletes took part in the National Swimming Championship, the 17th

Asian Games and National Swimming Championships and achieved great success. Zhu plays a great important role as the meritorious coach in Zhejiang.

【人物启迪】Character Enlightenment

如果说中国游泳队中“浙江军团”是一面旗帜，那么这面旗帜的执旗手就是朱志根。他的激情让年轻教练都感慨万分。朱志根教练的一生让我们想到了美国著名诗人罗伯特·弗罗斯特的著名诗篇《未选择的路》：

“也许多少年后在某个地方，
我将轻声叹息将往事回顾：
一片树林里分出两条路，
而我选择了人迹更少的一条，
从此决定了我一生的道路。”

If Zhejiang swimming team is regarded as a flag among Chinese swimming teams, the standard-bearer must be Zhu Zhigen whose passion has even impressed many young coaches a lot. His life career reminds us of the well-known poem “*The Road Not Taken*” by Robert Frost:

“I shall be telling this with a sigh,
Somewhere ages and ages hence:
Two roads diverged in a wood,
and I—I took the one less traveled by,
And that has made all the difference.”

第二章
守信 Trustworthiness

一　守信内涵
Connotation of Trustworthiness

守信,就是讲信用,讲信誉,信守承诺,忠实于自己承担的义务,答应了别人的事一定要去做。守信是中华民族传统美德的重要规范之一。孔子作为著名的教育家,他认为:在社会生活中,“守信”是一个人的立身之本,是一个人品德修养状况和人格高下的表现,如果没有诚信,也就失去了做人的基本条件。

Trustworthiness means keeping our words, keeping promise and being faithful to the responsibility we take. If you promise to do something, you should keep your promise. Trustworthiness is one of the most important criteria of judging a person with good virtue or not. Confucius, the great educator, holds a view that trustworthiness is the fundamental quality of being a man in social life, which can be used to evaluate a man's morality and personality.

二　守信力量
Force towards Trustworthiness

做人诚实守信,是赢得别人尊重的重要前提条件之一。

A man without trustworthiness can not be called a man. Being trustworthy is one of the prerequisites for winning others' respect.

三 守信名言
Quotations on Trustworthiness

没有比诚实更珍贵的遗产。 No legacy is so rich as honesty.

言行一致。 Match words to deeds.

四 守信故事
Stories on Trustworthiness

故事一 陶晓莺——家政女皇 The Queen of Homemaking Service

【人物介绍】Character Introduction

陶晓莺，杭州三替服务集团有限公司总经理，1963年出生。她曾获得"全国三八红旗手""浙江省劳动模范""全国关爱员工优秀民营企业家"等多个荣誉称号。

Tao Xiaoying, born in 1963, is the General Manager of Hangzhou Santi Service Group Co., Ltd. Tao Xiaoying has been awarded a series of honorary titles, such as the "National March 8th Red-Banner Holder" "Model Worker in Zhejiang Province" and "Outstanding Entrepreneur for Staff-Caring".

【人物事迹】Character Story

在杭州市的主要路口，只要你站几分钟，就能看到身穿绿色工作服的三替员工或者是三替的服务车从你面前经过,他们已成为杭州人生活中的一道风景线。

创办三替公司的就是陶晓莺。三替公司从 1992 年创办之初的十几名员工发展到现在的 800 多名员工,包含 100 多项服务项目,现在已经成为广大市民的好帮手。

三替,顾名思义就是“替你排忧,替你解难,替你受累”。这也是陶晓莺定下的服务宗旨。陶晓莺说:“诚信是三替的灵魂,更是我们的人生品格。”创办三替公司以来,她始终坚持以诚信对待客户、以诚信对待员工、以诚信对待社会,赢得了社会的尊重,创造了良好的社会效益。她始终坚持“标准收费、当面议价、做不好不收费”的服务准则和回访制度,用制度确保对客户的诚信。三替不但建立了培训学校,还解决了 6000 多人的就业问题。“今后,要把三替打造成为中国家政行业的沃尔玛,”陶晓莺说,“实现三替的‘中国梦’。”

Waiting for a few minutes in the main roads in Hangzhou, you will find staff in green work clothes or service vehicles from Santi company passing by. They have become an integral part of local people's daily life.

In 1992, Tao Xiaoying founded Santi Company which has developed from a company with a dozen staff to one with more than 800 staff and 100 products and services. At present, Santi Group has become a good helper of the public.

Santi, just as its meaning of the name, is to relieve your worries, shoot your trouble and relieve your inconvenience, which is the aim of Santi Company. Tao Xiaoying says, “Integrity is Santi's soul as well as our life character.” Since the establishment of Santi Company, she insists on treating her clients, staff and society trustworthily, which helps her to gain the respect from society and social benefits. With her insistence on the service principles of “Direct Deal, Reasonable and Faithful Charges” and Revisiting System, she has ensured the integrity to customers. Not only has Santi set up on-the-job training programs, but she has helped more than 6000 people get employed. “In the future, Santi is supposed to be the ‘Wal-Mart’ of the homemaking service in China,” Tao Xiaoying says, “aiming to realize my China Dream.”

【人物启迪】Character Enlightenment

一个企业能够受到一个城市上百万人的喜欢和信任,绝对是一件难事。三替的成功源自于企业对社会的诚信。诚信是一朵玫瑰,传递着我们散发的芳香;诚信是一座大桥,架起了你我沟通的桥梁。

It's a difficult task for a company to blend well and gain love and trust in a city with millions of people. The success of Santi lies in the integrity to the society. Integrity is a rose, giving off our beautiful fragrance; integrity is a bridge, bridging the gap of our communication.

故事二 吴乃宜——诚信老爹 The Trustworthy Dad

【人物介绍】Character Introduction

吴乃宜,农民,1929 年出生,浙江温州人。他被人们誉为"诚信老爹",被评为"2010 年感动温州十大人物"和"最美浙江人——2012 年度浙江骄傲",2012 和 2013 年入选"中国好人榜",是第四届"全国道德模范"候选人和"感动中国 2013 年度人物"候选人。

Wu Naiyi, born in 1929, was a farmer from Wenzhou, Zhejiang Province. Known as "the trustworthy dad", Wu Naiyi was also honored with one of "Top Ten People who Moved Wenzhou City in 2010" and "The Most Beautiful Zhejiang Citizen—the Pride of Zhejiang in 2012". He also had been selected as a candidate on "Chinese Good Fellows" in 2012 and 2013, "The 4th Session of the National Moral Models" and the "People who Moved China" in 2013.

【人物事迹】Character Story

海边长大的吴乃宜老人,祖祖辈辈都从事渔业捕捞。他原本有一个幸福的家庭,膝下四个儿子,家境虽然贫困,但子从父业,都娶妻生子。吴乃宜老人享受着天伦之乐,一大家子的生活也很美满幸福。

之前，他的四个儿子靠一条小渔船在近海捕鱼为生。后来，兄弟四人见虾皮捕捞效益较好，就拿出多年积蓄的40多万元，并从信用社借款18万元及从亲戚朋友处借款凑齐70万元买了一艘钢质渔轮，又从各渔需品商店赊来各种渔具近30万元，共凑集一百多万，成为霞关镇第一批拥有钢质渔轮和先进捕捞工具的渔民。正当兄弟四人雄心勃勃准备靠这艘新渔轮发家致富时，梦想和希望却在瞬间被“桑美”台风撕碎了。2006年“桑美”台风夺走了他三个儿子的性命，同时也让他背上了儿子们欠下的80多万元债务。

噩耗传来，犹如晴天霹雳。两位已经70多岁的老人老泪纵横、悲痛欲绝，体弱多病的吴乃宜老人更是悲到极点，几度晕厥。三个儿子去世后，吴乃宜曾一度陷入绝望，对生活失去了信心。一位朋友的话惊醒了沉浸在绝望中的他：“你不能这样，那些借钱给你的人日子也不宽裕，难道你不管他们了吗?”从法律上讲，老人没有替子还债的义务。但是，这个正直的的老汉面对债务，强忍悲痛向债主们做出承诺：“做人要讲信用！是我儿子的欠条我都认，我一定会想办法还钱。”吴乃宜说到做到，三个儿子人身及船只保险赔款的24万元，及卖掉打捞上来的渔船的钱，全部用来还债。

体弱多病的吴乃宜和他的老伴还得担负起照顾两个未成年孙女的重任，靠着每月200元的低保金相依为命，他们生活极其清苦。当记者问起每月200元，一家人如何过日子时，老人说，够了够了，凑合凑合。然后一个劲地感谢政府。多么朴实的老人，邻居们都知道老人还债不容易，舍不得吃穿，当面给他钱他也从来不收，所以就会在他家门口放些吃的，想退还也找不到人。每当这时，他心里都暖暖的，也有了坚持下去的信心。妻子告诉记者，老夫妻俩平常帮人织渔网，一个月也有30来元的收入。另外，家里再种些瓜果蔬菜贴补家用。6年来，他和老伴省吃俭用，终于还清了所有的债务。

2014年1月19日，“诚信老爹”吴乃宜因病医治无效，在浙江省苍南县老家去世。

Wu Naiyi grew up by the seaside, and his family had been engaged in fishing for generations. Wu had four sons who all got married and had their own children. Poor as he was, Wu enjoyed family happiness together and lived a comfortable and happy life.

The four sons made a living on a small fishing boat by fishing offshore. Later on, they found it profitable to fish shrimp. So they loaned 180 000 RMB from the local credit cooperative and some from their relatives and friends, together with their savings 400 000 RMB, to purchase a steel fishing vessel over 700 000 RMB. They bought on credit some fishing tackles worth 300 000 RMB from the local fishing stores. With the large number of money of more than one million RMB invested, they became the first group of fishermen who had the steel fishing vessel and advanced fishing tackles in Xiaguan Town. But unfortunately, when they were ambitious and ready to build up a family fortune, their dreams and hopes were torn to shreds by "Sangmei" typhoon disaster. In 2006, three of them lost their lives in "Sangmei" typhoon disaster, leaving their father 800 000 RMB in debt.

The grievous news came like a bolt from the blue. The old couple who was over 70 years old were in tears and deeply grieved all day long. Wu even fainted away several times with the shock of the news. After three of their sons passed away, Wu fell into despair and lost all hope. One of his friends said to him, "You can't do like this. Those who have lent you money are not rich. Do you want to leave them alone?" Wu, in deep sorrow, was awakened by what his friend told him. In terms of law, the father is not liable for his son's debts. However, facing the huge debts, the righteous old man kept promise with great grief to creditors, "We should be trustworthy. I will try my best to repay my sons' debts." Wu did what he had promised. He sold the salvaged boat and put 240 000 RMB insurance to pay the debts.

Although in poor health, Wu, together with his wife, still took care of two young granddaughters. The government gave them 200 RMB as the minimum living security monthly. Since then, they had been dependent on each other for survival. When a journalist asked him how life was going on with only 200 RMB monthly, Wu said it was enough and showed great gratitude to the government. The old couple lived fairly frugally. Their neighbors knew it was not easy to repay the debts, trying giving them some living expenses but refused by Wu Naiyi. Then the good neighbors brought some food, secretly leaving them on the door, which made the old couple unable to refuse. Wu felt warm and had the confidence to hold on. His wife told the journalist they usually have woven fishing nets to earn 30 RMB monthly. Besides, they planted some fruits and vegetables. In the successive 6 years, the couple scrimped on food and clothing to pay off all the debts.

On January 19th, 2014, Wu Naiyi, the trustworthy dad, failed to respond to any medical treatment and passed away at home in Cangnan, Zhejiang Province.

【人物启迪】Character Enlightenment

吴乃宜老人用老百姓最朴素的方式,告诉我们"诚信"的含义。他很贫穷,也很富有。诚信,就是他最大的财富。无论在哪个年代,坚守承诺是支撑人性的基石。

As a farmer, Wu Naiyi was interpreting the connotation of "integrity" by means of the simplest way. Poor as he was, he was a man of inner wealth. Integrity was his most precious treasure. Whenever we are, integrity is the cornerstone forever upholding our humanity.

故事三　杨冬林——开锁大王 The King of Locksmith

【人物介绍】Character Introduction

杨冬林,通信器材经营部负责人,1962 年出生,浙江安吉人。他曾先后被评为"五好经营户""文明经营户""残疾人个体就业十佳先进个人""残疾人之友""十佳自强标兵""市劳模",并获得全国"光彩之星"荣誉称号。

Yang Donglin, born in 1962, is the manager of communications equipment business from Anji, Zhejiang Province. Yang Donglin has been awarded the titles of "Excellent Businessman" "Civilized Businessman" "Ten Excellent Disabled Individuals of Self-employment" "Friend of the Disabled" "Ten Excellent Individuals of Self-reliance" "Labor Model" in the city and the national "Bright Star".

【人物事迹】Character Story

杨冬林是“开锁大王”，身怀绝技，不管多么精密的锁具，他也能凭一根细铁丝打开；他是安吉公安的“编外 110”，常常救人脱困，甚至擒获小偷；他是竹乡热心人，开着一间小店却成了许多人的“心理顾问”。然而，他说自己只是一个普通的生意人，赚点小钱，恪守着这份手艺活最后的底线。

两岁时，杨冬林因为摔了一跤，跌成重伤，落下了终身残疾，从此不能像正常人一样直起身板。18 岁高中毕业后，杨冬林先学习修钟表，后来开了一家钟表修理店，同时开始自学修锁具。他明白，开锁是一个高危行业，一不小心就有可能触犯法律。“该开的锁可以开，但不该开的锁，就坚决不能开。”杨冬林说。正是凭着诚信的原则，他得到了社会的信任。

对于要杨冬林开锁的顾客，他要求对方必须出示相关证件，能证明自己的身份，否则坚决不开。要是有人把钥匙不小心锁家里面了，没有证明，他会先开锁，然后让顾客自己找到钥匙，当面验证开门。“如果他不能熟练地找出钥匙，熟练地开门，那就说明有问题，我们会及时报警。”

如今，杨冬林已经有了自己的店面和小车，还前前后后带了 40 多个徒弟。虽然广收门徒，但是他每收进一个徒弟，都要先立规矩，教会他们做这一行的基本准则。“人在做，天在看，没有不透风的墙。要知道，我们修锁的，靠的就是诚信。如果贪小便宜撒谎的话，那是十分危险的，也会砸了我们辛辛苦苦打下的招牌。”

杨冬林不仅在县城站稳了脚跟，而且生意兴隆，口碑良好。在自己富起来的时候，没有忘记社会对他的帮助，他常常无私地为社区群众、残疾人服务，先后帮助 50 多名残疾人走上了工作岗位。在杨冬林经营部的墙上有一条横幅：孤寡老人、下岗工人以及残疾人一律免费。他用 20 余年的恪守，诠释了“诚信”二字。

Yang Donglin is the Locksmith King with unique skills. No matter how sophisticated the locks are, he is able to unlock them with a piece of thin iron wire. Yang Donglin is always ready to help others out of trouble, even to catch thieves, playing the role of a supernumerary of Anji's public security. Warm-hearted as he is, he is a mental counselor when running his business. He takes himself as a serious businessman to live his life.

Yang had a fall and got seriously injured when he was two years old.

What's worse, the accident left him disabled for life. He was completely different from those physically healthy people. After graduation from junior high school at the age of 18, Yang Donglin started to learn to repair watches and ran a clock and watch repair shop. Meanwhile, he started to learn the trade of unlocking. He knows unlocking is a dangerous profession. It's easy to break the law unless the regulations of the craftsmanship are strictly observed. "Unlock those that could be. Never unlock those that couldn't be." Yang Donglin insists, gradually gaining the trust from the society.

Yang Donglin will often ask his customers to show their documents to verify their identities. Otherwise, he would refuse to provide his services. If some customers accidentally leave their keys at home, unable to show their identities, Yang Donglin will unlock first and ask the customers to find the keys as quickly as possible. "There must be something wrong if the customer fails to find the key to open the door. We will call the police immediately in that case."

Now Yang Donglin has been running his own business and purchased a private car. He has more than 40 apprentices these years with whom he is strict. He has his own principles to each apprentice and teaches them to learn the basic rules of this trade. "What is done by night appears by day. You know, what is the most important for us is integrity. It is very dangerous to tell a lie for gaining petty advantages. It will ruin our business."

Not only does he settle himself in the county, but his business becomes prosperous and prestigious. After becoming rich, Yang Donglin bears the help from the society in mind so he selflessly gives service to the community and the disabled, helping more than 50 disabled people be employed. On the wall posts a banner: Free for those who are old, laid-off and disabled. Yang Donglin took his promise for over 20 years to interpret the connotation of "integrity".

【人物启迪】Character Enlightenment

这个身残志坚的山里汉子，用一颗火热的心，不仅创出了许多健全人都无法成就的事业，还能做到回报社会，主动助学帮困、捐钱捐物。从一个需要别人帮助的人到自食其力，再到帮助别人，杨冬林做着他认为应该做的事，不断追求着他的完美人生。

Disabled but determined, Yang Donglin, with a fervent heart, has accomplished what is even beyond the reach of physically healthy people. He doesn't forget to return to the society, taking the initiative in helping poor students and those who are in trouble, and donating money and goods. From being a person who needs help to becoming a self-reliant person who helps others, Yang Donglin has been doing what he thinks he should do and pursuing his perfect life.

故事四　陈金英——奶奶商人 Grandma in Business

【人物介绍】Character Introduction

陈金英，退休人员，1929 年生，浙江丽水人。她 49 岁退休，53 岁办羽绒服厂，至今还在为自己的企业奔波忙碌。陈金英的创业史，是“老骥伏枥，志在千里”的励志故事。

Chen Jinying, born in 1929, is a retiree from Lishui, Zhejiang Province. Retiring at the age of 49 and establishing her own down jacket corporation at the age of 53, she has been still working for her corporation by far. Her story illustrates an old saying: an old steed in the stable still aspires to gallop a thousand Li. It means an old hero still cherishes high aspirations.

【人物事迹】Character Story

2012 年年底，在丽水中山街，很多人都看到过一个鹤发鸡皮的老人，在摆摊叫卖羽绒服。还有人以为,她肯定是老无所依,给自己赚养老钱。这位老人就是陈金英,49 岁从丽水一家卫生院退休后,想干点事业,本打算开诊所,但没批下来。

53 岁时,她发现丽水市场上中老年羽绒制品很少,就在城郊租了一栋 300 平方米的民房,买机器招工人开始创业。她的产品专攻中老年人市场,她说:"老人家买东西,几块钱都是算起来用的,所以我们的价格也定得比较低,一般都是在 100 元到 200 元之间。"十几个工人一年生产 4 万多套羽绒服。一进入丽水市场,这些羽绒服就受到了青睐。她一度把生意做到了杭州、金华等地。2004 年,陈金英达到事业高峰期,手下有五六十个工人,产值高达千万元。

办厂 30 多年,陈金英在 2012 年遇上了大麻烦,公司资金吃紧,银行又贷不出款,羽绒服销路不畅,产品积压,200 多万的存货无人问津。为给员工发薪水过年,老人横下心来,在丽水中山街摆摊低价抛售厂里生产的羽绒服。"50 元一件、70 元一件这样卖出去,尽管这些衣服的成本都要 90 元。"最终,她为 12 名员工筹得 12 万元薪水,让员工过了个安心年。更让人尊敬的是,办企业 30 年,她已捐助善款 57 万多元,包括捐助汶川地震、印尼海啸、丽水贫困生上学、福利院老人生活费等。

一个八旬老人,何以有这么旺盛的精力?陈金英说,除了注重身体保养,她还注重养心,也就是心态好。"对人家好,助人为乐,能帮到人家的就帮一帮。除了把自己身体照顾好,还要懂得谦让,吃亏是福。"

At the end of 2012, lots of people saw a grandma, with grey hair and wrinkled skin, sell down jackets in Zhongshan street, Lishui City. They had thought her as a homeless one who wanted to earn her own living. The grandma is Chen Jinying who retired from a hospital at the age of 49. She had planned to run a clinic but didn't get approval.

At the age of 53, she noticed there was few choice of down jackets for aged citizens. She decided to rent a 300m^2 house in the suburb to establish her own down jacket corporation. Her target customers were these citizens. Chen Jinying said, "Aged citizens are good at careful calculation and strict budgeting. In order to satisfy their need and appeal to them, the prices of our down jackets are fairly low, ranging from 100 RMB to 200 RMB." Soon, dozens of workers were manufacturing more than 40000 down jackets yearly, which gained great popularity in the market in Lishui. Chen Jinying once expanded her business in other cities, such as Jinhua and Hangzhou. By the year of 2004, she had reached the summit of her career with more than 50 workers and an output value of as much as 10 million RMB.

During the 30 years since she set it up, she encountered the first big trouble. her company had suffered from the lack of grant, lack of support from the bank sponsorship and poor selling result in 2012, leaving more than 2 million jackets in the storehouse. In order to pay salaries to the staff, she chose to set a stand in the street. She made up her mind to sell the down jackets at fairly low prices in Zhongshan street. Chen Jinying said, "The cost prices of these down jackets are basically 90 RMB. Now they are for sale, 50 RMB or 70 RMB each." She eventually collected 120 000 RMB for her 12 staff, in hope that they could have a peaceful new year with their salaries. Furthermore, what arouses more respect from people is that she has donated more than 570 000 RMB in the 30 years to help the victims from Wenchuan Earthquake and Indonesia Tsunami, the poor students in Lishui and the elderly in nursing homes.

We can't help asking why Chen Jinying, over eighty years old, is so energetic and enthusiastic. She said, "Not only should we keep our physical health, but we should pay more attention to our mind. We are supposed to have a healthy state of mind. We should be kind and helpful to others. We should take care of ourselves. Meanwhile, we need to be modest. Suffering a loss is a blessing."

【人物启迪】Character Enlightenment

陈金英老人的事迹让我不禁默默吟诵:“青春不是年华,而是心境。……无论年届花甲,抑或二八芳龄,心中皆有生命之欢乐,奇迹之诱惑,孩童般天真久盛不衰。人人心中皆有一台天线,只要你从天上人间接受美好、希望、欢乐、勇气和力量的信号,你就青春永驻,风华常存。”

The story of Chen Jinying reminds us of the prose, "Youth isn't a time of life; it is a state of mind.... Whether 60 or 16, there is in every human being the lure of wonder, the unfailing childlike appetite for what's next and the joy of the game of living. In the center of my heart and your heart there is a wireless station: so long as it receives messages of beauty, hope, cheer, courage and power from men and from the infinite, so long are you young."

故事五　吴斌——最美司机 The Most Virtuous Driver

【人物介绍】Character Introduction

吴斌,司机,1965年出生,浙江温州人。他曾获"全国五一劳动奖章""浙江省劳动模范""浙江省五一劳动奖章""杭州市道德模范"等荣誉,中央文明办授予他"时代楷模"荣誉称号。

Wu Bin, born in 1965, was a bus driver from Wenzhou, Zhejiang Province. Wu Bin had been awarded a series of honorary titles, such as "National May 1st Labor Medal" "Labor Model of Zhejiang Province" "May 1st Labor Medal of Zhejiang Province" "Moral Model in Hangzhou" and "The Times Model" by the Central Committee Spiritual Civilization Construction.

【人物事迹】Character Story

2012年5月29日中午,吴斌在驾驶大客车行驶于沪宜高速时被迎面飞来的铁片砸碎前窗玻璃后刺入腹部致肝脏破裂、多根肋骨骨折。然而虽身受重伤,他却忍着剧痛完成了靠边停车、拉手刹、打开双闪灯等一系列令人难以置信的动作,并提醒车内24名乘客安全疏散及报警,后被送往医院抢救。2012年6月1日,吴斌因伤势过重抢救无效死亡。

吴斌是杭州长运客运的司机。据安全科长陈一波说,吴斌驾驶客车已经安全行驶100多万公里,从来没有发生过一起交通事故和旅客投诉。吴斌与爱人汪丽珍结婚18年,他们的女儿今年16岁,正在读高中,他的父母已是古稀之年。

吴斌的英雄事迹深深感动了社会各界。车上监控拍摄的1分16秒的视频在网上流传开来,数百万网民表达了敬意。在论坛、微博上,网民自发为他祈福、送行。吴斌的遗体在警车的护送下被送往当地一家殡仪馆火化，成千上万的杭州市民前往殡仪馆为他送行。

时任浙江省省长的夏宝龙于2012年6月4日主持召开省政府第94次常务会议，批准省总工会关于建议追授吴斌同志"省劳动模范"荣誉称号、评定其为烈士的请示，以表彰他无私的舍己救人行为。吴斌用生命践行了"一切为了顾客"、"诚信、爱岗、敬业"和忠于职守的职业道德观，他被人们誉为"最美司机"。

无锡警方确认铁片系一辆红色东风大货车的车辆制动毂残片。经过一系列深入的调查，此次事故定性为意外事故，所以不会对肇事司机进行处罚。

It was in the afternoon on May 29, 2012. When Wu Bin was driving an intercity bus on Huyi Expressway, a metal chunk suddenly flied directly through the windscreen and hit his abdomen, lacerated his liver and caused a severe bone fracture. Suffering from the fatal pain, Wu Bin still went on to pull over, put on the parking brake, turn on the hazard lights, evacuate 24 passengers safely and report to the police. Wu was quickly sent to a hospital but died of the severe injuries on June 1.

Wu Bin was a bus driver working for Hangzhou Long-Distance Transport Group. Before the tragic accident, he'd had a spotless driving record of more than one million km, according to Chen Yibo, the chief of security section. Wu Bin got married to Wang Lizhen 18 years ago, with whom he has a 16-year-old daughter. His parents are over 70 years old.

Wu Bin's heroic actions have deeply touched the whole public. The video lasting 76 seconds shot by the surveillance camera system in the bus was widely spread on the Internet. Millions of citizens spontaneously prayed for him and saw him off on the forums and micro-blogs. His body was sent to a local funeral home under a police escort for cremation. Thousands of Hangzhou citizens attended his funeral and gave him their best wishes.

During an executive meeting of the provincial government on June 4, 2012, the original Governor Xia Baolong announced that the government had conferred the honorary titles of "model worker" and "martyr" upon Wu Bin in order to commemorate his acts of selflessness. Wu Bin sacrificed his life to confirm the professional ethics including " all for customers" "integrity, dedication and loyalty". He was praised as "the Most Virtuous Driver".

The Wuxi police confirmed that the piece of iron which hit Wu Bin was part of a brake pad of a red Dongfeng truck and announced that the event was an accident after further investigation.

【人物启迪】Character Enlightenment

吴斌在千钧一发的紧要关头,在生命的最后一刻,用超人的冷静和勇气,保障了全体乘客的生命安全,展现了乘客至上、忠于职守的职业道德,闪耀着普通劳动者身上的人性光辉,给我们这个时代留下了宝贵的精神财富,值得我们永远怀念。"平民英雄"值得我们尊敬。

At the crucial moment, and the last moment of his life, Wu Bin ensured the safety of the passengers calmly and bravely which illustrated such professional ethics as "Customers First" and "Loyalty", spreading the glory of inner beauty of human nature and leaving us the most precious spiritual wealth. Wu Bin deserves our eternal memorial. "Common heroes" deserve our respect.

故事六　蒋引娣——一诺千金的农家女 Promise is Debt

【人物介绍】Character Introduction

蒋引娣,农民,1950 年生,浙江德清人。2007 年,蒋引娣被评为"感动湖州——2007 年度最具影响力人物"和"感动德清十大女性"。2009 年 9 月,她被评为首届"浙江省诚实守信道德模范"。

Jiang Yindi, born in 1950, is a farmer from Deqing, Zhejiang Province. In 2007, she was awarded the title of "The One who Moved Huzhou City—the Most Influential in 2007" and "The Ten Women Who Moved Deqing County". In September, 2009, she was awarded the title of "The 1st Session of Moral

Model for Integrity in Zhejiang Province”.

【人物事迹】Character Story

1995 年,蒋引娣和丈夫在镇上经营一家大型副食品批发部,谁知批发部的生意每况愈下,短短 1 年零 4 个月,不但赔光了本钱,还欠下 24 万元外债。这突如其来的打击,让全家人陷入了绝望。蒋引娣咽下泪水,决心和意志消沉的丈夫一起还债。她和丈夫借了 1500 元钱,买了 7 头猪,凭借以往的养猪经验,开始了养猪过日子还债的生活。红酒渣是饲养生猪的好饲料,蒋引娣每个月都会从酒厂买便宜的红酒渣给猪当饲料,节衣缩食努力还钱。有债主主动减免债务,但她谢绝债主的好意,坚持诚信绝不赖账。

1996 年至 2006 年,为偿还总计 24 万元的债务,蒋引娣将债权人的姓名和债务一一记在了香烟壳上,每还清一笔就勾掉一个名字。十年来,蒋引娣养过猪,开过小吃店。其间,她被诊断出患有子宫肌瘤,必须动手术。手术后,她马上开始干活。再苦再累,蒋引娣也从未放弃过还钱的念头。每天晚上睡觉前,她都要在脑子里琢磨一遍,欠香烟店王老板的债还了,接下来该还哪一笔。就这样一分一厘地扣,香烟壳上剩下的债务也终于一天天少了下来。苦难终将过去,2006 年,蒋引娣到达了漫漫还债路的最后一站。在菜场开小店的王女士拿到钱几乎都不敢相信,本以为借了十来年,当时也没有写过借条的 5000 元肯定是打了水漂,一去不复返了,没想到还能回来。接过蒋引娣所还的最后一笔钱,王女士感慨地说:“这 5000 元没有打欠条,都这么多年了你还记得。”

“我的承诺我都会记得,我的承诺我都要去兑现!”蒋引娣掷地有声。蒋引娣,用行动书写了“诚信”二字。从王女士家出来,已是正午时分,春天的阳光在这时格外温暖,蒋引娣深深地吸了口气,眼眶湿润了,十年艰辛,终于还清了所有债务。

In 1995, Jiang Yindi and her husband ran a large-scale wholesale food department. Unfortunately, the business went increasingly worse. Within one year and four months, not only did they lose all of their capitals, but they owed 240 000 RMB debts. As the strike came unexpectedly, the whole family fell into despair. Jiang Yindi held back her tears and made up her mind to pay their debts with her husband who became depressed and lost all hope. They borrowed 1 500 RMB and bought seven pigs, hoping the traditional way of farming pigs to help them bring home the bacon and pay the debts. Jiang Yindi bought bags of distillers' grains with low prices from the local brewery monthly to feed pigs. Jiang Yindi scrimped on food and clothing. The creditors initiatively relieved their debts, but Jiang Yindi declined their kindness and insisted on repaying the debts.

From 1996 to 2006, Jiang Yindi wrote down the names of the creditors and the amount of the debts on the cigarette case. She would tick one off after paying. Over the ten years, Jiang Yindi has raised pigs and run snack bars. Unfortunately, she was diagnosed with the illness as myoma of uterus and went through a surgery. Soon after the surgery, she plunged herself into work without enough rest. No matter how hard and tired she was, she never gave up the idea to pay the debts. Every night before going to bed, she would ask herself the similar question, "Who would be the next one since the debts owed to Boss Wang in the cigarette store has been paid?" With her careful calculation and strict budgeting, she eventually paid most of the debts. Let the hardest time go. In 2006, Jiang Yindi came to Mrs. Wang's home to pay the debts. Mrs. Wang ran a store in the food market, and she was also the last creditor on the cigarette case. When she received 5 000 RMB, she couldn't believe it for Jiang Yindi borrowed the money ten years ago and they didn't write a receipt for the loan at that time. Mrs. Wang sighed with emotion, "There is no receipt for the sum of money, but you still remember after so many years."

"I remember my promise and I will make it true," Jiang Yindi said firmly. She earnestly practiced what she advocated—integrity. It was high noon and the sunshine in the spring was very warm. After coming out from Mrs. Wang's home, Jiang Yindi took a deep breath and her eyes were moist with tears. With ten years of hard work, she eventually paid all debts.

【人物启迪】Character Enlightenment

欠债还钱,天经地义。一个本就不富裕的家庭面对 20 多万巨额债务时,蒋引娣用顽强的毅力和惊人的坚持,感动了许许多多的人,那张用来记账的香烟壳诠释了她身上最美的人性光辉。

It's right and proper that we should pay our debts. However, not rich as the family was, Jiang Yindi moved a lot of people with her strong will and amazing determination to pay the heavy debts which reached as much as 200 000 RMB. The cigarette case with creditors' names has well illustrated her inner beauty of human nature.

故事七 董忠岳——心中没有欠条 No Wage Strips in My Hands

【人物介绍】Character Introduction

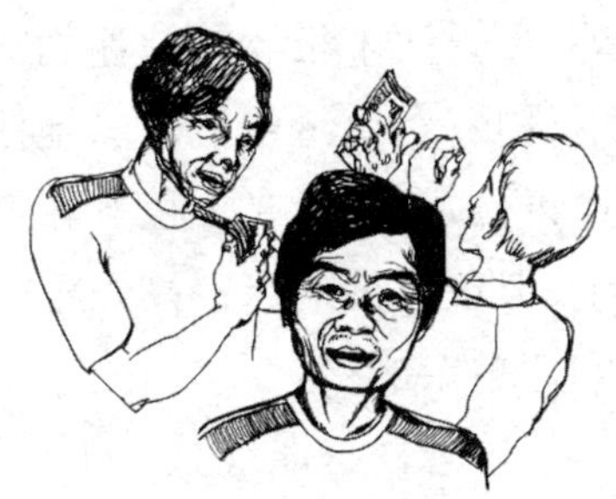

董忠岳，农民，1959 年生，浙江嵊泗人。董忠岳先后被评为"2007 浙江骄傲"候选人和"浙江省首届道德模范"，获第二届"全国道德模范"提名奖和"浙江骄傲——2009 年度最具影响力人物"荣誉称号。

Dong Zhongyue, born in 1959, is a farmer from Shengsi, Zhejiang Province. Dong Zhongyue has been awarded the titles including the candidate of "The Pride of Zhejiang in 2007", "The 1st Session of Moral Model in Zhejiang Province", nomination for "National Moral Model at the 2nd Session" and "the Pride of Zhejiang—the Most Influential People in 2009".

【人物事迹】Character Story

董忠岳有着一手过硬的爆破技术。在家乡，他经常带着乡亲们走南闯北揽活儿干。1999 年，经人介绍他认识了葫芦岛市的张某。不久，董忠岳与张某签订了一份葫芦岛市填海工程的爆破合同。合同签完后，董忠岳召集了 82 位熟悉爆破技术的老乡和 19 位农民工来到葫芦岛开始施工，然而让他万万没想到的是，不到两个月，填海工程因款项未到位而被迫停工，董忠岳带来的工人一共被拖欠了 114 万元工钱，他前期垫付的 61 万元工程款也没了踪影。年关将近，为了凑足工人回家的路费，他不得不让家乡的老父亲去向民间借贷。2002 年春节前夕，董忠岳拿着 101 张欠条，拍着胸脯对大家说："你们放心吧，这工钱我一定会还你们的。"有人劝他说，你也是受害者，可以不用还那些民工的工钱。他却说："我有我的良心，那些钱我一定得还。"

在追讨欠薪一年无果后,他对妻子说,自己要出去打工挣钱来还债,因为欠债还钱是天经地义的事,如果不还,怎能对得起农民工兄弟,又怎能对得起自己的良心。2003 年春节刚过,董忠岳就在异乡当起了打工仔,早出晚归四处打工。为了多节约一分钱,多还上一分债,他与妻子省吃俭用,但董忠岳说,这不算什么,让他最苦闷的就是牵挂和思念,牵挂的是何时能把农民工兄弟的钱还清,思念的是家乡的亲人。每逢佳节倍思亲,每年春节,董忠岳非常想回家与亲人一起团聚,但董忠岳告诉自己:“等到还清所有的债,再回家与你们团聚。”

为了早日还清农民工兄弟的工钱,身处异乡的董忠岳每天除了打工挣钱外,还奔波于相关部门追讨欠薪。2006 年 4 月,在当地一位好心律师的帮助下,抱着一丝希望他向当地法院提起了诉讼,希望通过法律途径要回工钱。经过诉讼,法院判决工程方张某须支付给董忠岳工程款共计 175 万元,官司胜诉了,但董忠岳一点都高兴不起来,因为张某只给了董忠岳 3000 元钱,还说没法归还剩余的钱。

董忠岳只能继续打工。每次他一拿到打工挣来的钱,除了留下一点生活费外,都立即通过邮局汇给了那些农民工兄弟。靠着自己的手艺和业内的口碑,找他干活的人慢慢多了起来。从 2001 年到 2008 年,董忠岳信守自己对民工兄弟的承诺,在 7 年时间里,依靠自己外出打工和法律途径追讨,终于让 101 位民工兄弟拿到了被拖欠的 114 万元工钱。

With his proficient blasting skill, Dong Zhongyue often takes his fellow villagers to seek for jobs everywhere. In 1999, introduced by others, Dong Zhongyue got to know Mr. Zhang from Hulu Island, with whom he signed a blasting contract about reclamation works. Later, Dong Zhongyue assembled 82 fellow villagers who were proficient in blasting and 19 migrant workers to come to Hulu Island. But unexpectedly, they were forced to stop within no more than two months because the capital was not in place. His fellow villagers' wages were delayed in total of 1.14 million RMB. There was also no trace of 610 000 RMB, the amount invested in the construction project himself. As the Chinese New Year was approaching, Dong had no choice but to ask his father to do private lending to cover the travelling expenses for fellow villagers going home. On the eve of Spring Festival in 2002, holding the 101 wage strips in his hands, Dong Zhongyue boldly promised to them, "Don't worry. I will pay back the wages to you." Some people advised him that he shouldn't pay them since he was also a victim. But he said, "I have my conscience. I will pay the wages. I promise."

After one year of demand of wage owed didn't get for him, he said to his wife that he would go out to work to pay off the debts. It's right and proper that they should pay off their debts. He was reluctant to let his fellow villagers and his conscience down. In 2003, soon after the Spring Festival, Dong Zhongyue and his wife left their hometown to earn money. The couple scrimped on food and clothing in order to pay off the debts as early as possible. Dong Zhongyue said the hard life didn't matter at all, but what worried him most was the time by which he could pay off all the debts and what he missed most was his family members in his hometown. There is a Chinese saying, "On festive occasions more than ever we think of our dear ones far away." When it was approaching the Spring Festival, he was eager to reunite with his family members in his hometown to observe the New Year. But Dong Zhongyue made a promise, "I will not go home until I pay off all the debts."

In order to pay off the debts as early as possible, not only did Dong Zhongyue do manual work every day, but he shuttled back and forth between some relevant departments to demand wages owed. In April, 2006, with the help of a kind-hearted lawyer, he took legal channel against Mr. Zhang, hoping to demand wages owed. After the litigation, the court convicted that Mr. Zhang was required to pay RMB 1.75 million in full to Dong Zhongyue. Although winning the lawsuit, Dong Zhongyue was not happy at all, for Mr. Zhang just repaid him 3 000 RMB. Because Mr. Zhang had no money and Dong Zhongyue couldn't get back the money.

There's nothing for him to do but work. Once he earned money, except a small sum of living expenses, he would post the rest of money to his fellow villagers. With his proficient skills and public praise in this field, it's easy for him to find a job. From 2001 to 2008, in order to keep his word, Dong Zhongyue obtained the wages eventually by means of law and work in the seven years.

【人物启迪】**Character Enlightenment**

"人活着就要有诚信,欠别人的钱就要还。"这是董忠岳始终坚守的人生信条。诚信是做人的基本准则,如果把诚信看作一种精神、当成一种力量,那么一个人就会得到认可,也就会受到人们的敬佩。

Dong Zhongyue insists on his life motto that people should keep their words and pay back what they owe to others. Integrity is the basic moral. Regarding integrity as the spirit and the power, you will have public praise and gain respect.

故事八　陈林——诚实立身 信誉立业 Being an Honest Man and Establishing a Trustworthy Enterprise

【人物介绍】**Character Introduction**

陈林,1973年出生,浙江温州人。他曾多次获浙江省"诚信工商户"、温州市"文明市民"、龙湾区"诚实守信道德模范"等荣誉称号。

Chen Lin, born in 1973, is a businessman from Wenzhou, Zhejiang Province. He has been awarded a series of honorable titles such as "Trustworthy Businessman in Zhejiang Province" "Civilized Citizens in Wenzhou City" and "Moral Model for Integrity in Longwan District".

【人物事迹】**Character Story**

作为温州市龙湾区永中镇陈林家电维修部负责人,陈林始终坚持"诚实立身、信誉立业"的信念。为保证服务质量,陈林积极引进各种硬件设施,一直坚持24小时的上门维修服务,且做出第一时间为顾客维修的承诺。有一次,龙湾区沙城街道七甲村,因电压不稳定烧坏了几十户居民的家用电器,严重影响了居民的正常生活。在接到求援电话后,陈林第一时间组织人员上门调查、修理,他们放弃了休息的时间,经过二十多个小时的抢修,终于让这几十户家庭的电器重新投入使用。精良的设备、优质的服务为陈林家电维修部赢得了良好的口碑。

凭着诚信经营，依法纳税，坚持维护消费者的合法权益，陈林家电维修部连续二十多年没有发生过一起侵害消费者权益的事件。陈林积极参与“青年文明号”创建、诚信评选、“守合同，重信用”等各种评优活动，并引导其他商户也踊跃参与到诚信经营的行列中来。他所在的服务部已成为辖区近 30 万人口维修家电首选的维修部，国内外的众多知名企业也慕名与之签约，如樱花卫厨、松下、海尔、长虹等。该服务部已成为各大品牌企业首屈一指的授权特约维修服务中心和维修服务站。

从事家电维修服务二十年来，陈林自愿积极组织维修工作人员进入龙湾区永中养老院、龙湾区消防队进行义务活动。为了进一步在全区倡导“奉献、友爱、互助、进步”的志愿精神，陈林维修服务部经常组织人员参加龙湾区青年志愿者便民服务活动，推行上门维修等便民服务项目。陈林说：“作为个体劳动者，作为一名党员，能以自己的一技之长参加志愿者行动是我的荣幸，更是我的职责。”

Working as the household appliance repair service provider in Yongzhong, Longwan District of Wenzhou, Chen Lin insists on his principle of being an honest man and establishing trustworthy enterprise. Chen Lin actively introduces facilities to ensure the quality of repair service. He launches indoor repair services available for 24 hours to make convenience for people and makes a commitment to serve customers in time. An accident once occurred in Qijia Village, Shacheng Street, Longwan District. Because of voltage instability, dozens of civilians' household appliances had been destroyed, severely affecting their daily life. No sooner did Chen Lin get the call for help than he arranged his staff to investigate and offer repair services immediately. Giving up their rest time and spending more than 20 hours repairing, Chen Lin and his staff succeeded in putting the civilian's household appliances back into work. Sophisticated equipment and high-quality repair services won him the public praise.

His trustworthy management, paying tax by law, protecting consumers' rights and interests have aroused good effects, without any violation of customers' rights in the successive 20 years. Chen Lin vigorously takes part in various activities for excellence selections including the construction of

"Youth Civilization" "Excellence for Being Trustworthy" "Recognition of Abiding by Contract and Being Trustworthy", setting a good example for other providers to take an active part in trustworthy management. His household appliance repair service has ranked top in the area in the community where there is a population of more than 300 000. His repair service has signed contracts with some well-known enterprises at home and abroad such as Sakura, Panasonic, Haier and Changhong, becoming the best authorized maintenance service center and maintenance station in the local area.

Over the 20 years of providing household appliance repair service, he has often actively volunteered to organize his staff to provide help for the nursing home for the aged and the fire brigade, appealing to such voluntary spirits as commitment, friendship, mutual help and progress in the whole community. Not only does he often call on his staff to take part in the youth volunteers serving activities, but he also launches indoor repair services to make convenience for people. Chen Lin said, "As a self-employed worker and a communist, it's my honor and my duty to participate in volunteering and unpaid work with my professional skills."

【人物启迪】Character Enlightenment

人们常说机遇都是给那些准备好的人的,其实机遇是给那些准备好且有诚信的人的。创业靠的不仅仅是勤奋,一个诚信对待社会、懂得回馈社会的人,不仅可以创造未来,实现梦想,而且可以造就辉煌的人生!

People often say "God helps those who help themselves." But I want to say"God helps a self-reliant man of integrity". Diligence is not the only factor to lead to success. Those who are trustworthy and learn to contribute to the society can mould their future, realize their dream and create a brilliant life.

故事九　吴岩兴——老吴热线 Lao Wu Service Hotline

【人物介绍】Character Introduction

吴岩兴,退休老人,1948年出生。他是"老吴热线"创始人,曾获得全国"优秀志愿者",是浙江省"优秀共产党员",并当选第二届"绍兴市道德模范"。

Wu Yanxing, now retired, was born in 1948. He is the founder of "Lao Wu Service Hotline" and he has been honored with the "National Outstanding Volunteer" and "Excellent Member of Communist Party of Zhejiang Province", and has been elected as the "Moral Model at the 2nd Session of Shaoxing city".

【人物事迹】Character Story

自1986年搬入塔山街道花园社区居住后,吴岩兴就承诺要利用自己年轻时在部队里学到的水电维修技术,为社区居民提供免费服务。2010年"老吴服务热线"设立以来,吴岩兴主动向社区居民公布他的手机号码方便周边居民求助。他把自己的手机号码印在联系卡上,使得一个普通的手机号码,成了花园社区居民,尤其是独居在家的老人的应急电话。拿出联系卡拨打电话,问题就会迎刃而解,因为老吴马上会到。一个盛夏的傍晚,吴基平老人家里突然断了电,年逾八旬、孤身独居的老人感到特别无助。老人犹豫着拨通了老吴的电话,刚刚睡下的老吴二话不说,拎着工具袋匆匆赶来,在闷热的房间里检修线路、查看故障,一干就是两个小时。老吴一直免费为居民维修照明线路、疏通下水管道、上门换锁等。"我常常劝爸爸,年纪大了就不要再这样劳心别人了,毕竟自己的身体要紧。可他总是不听劝。"儿子吴炯说。"做人最重要的是开心。我出门帮帮别人,心情好了,对身体健康也有好处。"老吴笑着说。

在他的影响下,更多的人加入了"老吴服务热线"花园社区志愿者服务站。服务内容也由免费提供水电维修的服务,扩大到法律咨询、健康讲座、医疗咨询、英语翻译等。

Since he moved in Garden Community of Tashan Street in 1986, Wu

Yanxing promised to use his experience of utility maintenance, which he learned in the armed forces when he was young, to provide free services to community residents. In 2010, Wu Yanxing set up “Lao Wu Service Hotline”, releasing his cell phone number for the community's residents. He printed his cell phone number on the cards, which has become an emergency card especially for the elderly person. Once they call him, all problems will be disposed of because of Lao Wu's arrival on the scene. On a hot summer evening, the electricity was suddenly cut off in Wu Jiping's house, which made this eighty-year-old man depressed. He hesitantly called “Lao Wu Hotline” without expecting him to come because of the extremely hot weather. Lao Wu, who was just falling asleep, got up immediately and rushed to this old man's house. It was indeed an extremely humid and hot room where Lao Wu had to work for two hours checking circuitry and breakdown. He has helped residents repair lighting circuits, clear drains, and change door locks all the time. Lao Wu's son said, “I have always dissuaded my father from doing it as from my perspective, his health is the most important thing in our family. But he never follows my advise.” Lao Wu smiled and replied, “The most important thing for a man is being happy. It is good for my health when I go out to help people, because it brings me a beautiful mood.”

Influenced by him, more people joined the “Lao Wu Hotline” volunteer service station. Services provided include free water and electricity maintenance services, as well as legal advice, health lecture, medical advice and translation service.

【人物启迪】Character Enlightenment

多数人在劳碌了几十年后,常常想拥有一个安静和快乐的退休生活,不再让紧张、焦虑继续缠绕着自己。但这位老人不同,虽然退休了,他身上的正能量却没有退休,他还在继续为身外事发挥自己的余热。他值得我们去尊重他。高尚道德的体现并非得做出惊天动地的事情,而往往是在我们的日常行为中。我们播下一个动作,便收获一个习惯;播下一个习惯,便收获一个品格。希望我们每一个人都能成为道德的传播者、践行者和受益者。

Most people are willing to live a peaceful and joyful late-life after several decades of toil, not wishing to be harassed by nervousness and anxiety. But this old man is quite different, because his positive energy has not retired. He has been devoting his remaining energy and taking too much care of others. He deserves our respect. The noble moral doesn't necessarily require doing a dramatic thing but lies in our daily life. We gain a good habit after we start doing good things; We gain a good personality after we have a good habit. Hope all of us can be the disseminator, practitioner and the beneficiary of moral.

故事十 周言松——百姓的好干部 People's Good Cadre

【人物介绍】Character Introduction

周言松,干部,1964 年出生。生前为横山镇人大主席。他是衢州市共产党员的先进代表,是基层干部模范人物。

Zhou Yansong, was born in 1964. He was the Chairman of the People's Congress in Hengshan Town of Zhejiang Province. He is a representative of the communists of Quzhou and a model figure of grassroots cadres.

【人物事迹】Character Story

自 1984 年参加工作后,周言松先后在 8 个不同的乡镇工作。无论工作岗位如何变动、条件如何艰苦,周言松从来没有向组织部门提出过进城或其他调动的要求。他无怨无悔,自始至终服从党组织的安排,一心扑在工作上,信守一个共产党人的誓言。他经常揽下本不属于自己负责的工作,把公家事当成自家事。2009 年 2 月,周言松提出的改善横山镇 4 万农民饮用水条件的议案,被龙游县人大列为一号议案。不久,工程进入实施阶段。按照镇党委的工作分工,作为镇人大主席的周言松欣然接受,主抓工程实施工作。在周言松的影响和带动下,横山饮用水工程顺利推进,不到两年,近四万群众喝上了甘甜清冽的自来水。不想 2011 年 5 月的一天,第一批通上自来水的农户反映水质异常。“水质有问题?!”最让周言松揪心的事情还是发生了,本准备外出的的周言松二话没说,驱车直奔村里。走访农户、了解情况、取样观察直到问题浮出水面。周言松完全忘记了要陪女儿去看外婆的承诺,而是带着从水库不同部位取出的三瓶水样,连夜赶到水利设计院。他常年不辞辛劳为基层群众奔走,直到累病,倒在了工作岗位上。老百姓夸赞他:言松是百姓值得信赖的好干部。

Zhou Yansong worked in eight different small towns since he began to work in 1984. No matter how hard the working conditions were, nor what kind of post he had been assigned, Zhou Yansong had never made an application for personal transfer to the big city from the higher authorities. He showed his loyalty to the Communist Party and put all his efforts into his job without regrets, representing the best qualities of a Communist by living simply. He often took over other people's work as his own business. In February 2009, Zhou put forward a proposal of transformation project of drinking water for 40000 peasants in Hengshan Town, which was treated as the top priority of all proposals by Longyou County. Soon the project came to the implementation phase and Zhou was in charge of the main task. Influenced by Zhou, the project was implemented smoothly. Less than two years, this project has provided clean and sweet running water for over 40 000 peasants. One day in May of 2011, some farmers, who were the first ones enjoying the tap water, reported that there was something wrong with the water quality, which was the most serious matter Zhou cared. Zhou drove to the village and forgot his former promise of visiting her daughter's grandmother. He went to farmers' houses and got samples when he talked with them. As the investigation continued, the problem began to be clear. With three water samples extracted from different places of the reservoir, Zhou rushed to Zhejiang Hydraulic Design Institute at that night. He was someone who worked tirelessly for the grassroots all the year round. Finally he died in his boots because of years of overwork. People praised him as a great and trustworthy cadre.

【人物启迪】Character Enlightenment

基层条件差,待遇低,城里的人才不愿来。但在群众眼中,任何一个基层工作人员都是整个政府形象的代言人。周言松活着是为了多数人更好地生活,群众把他抬得很高,很高。一个共产党员应该更关心党和群众而不是个人,更关心他人而不是自己。对人民守诺,人民敬之。对有些人而言,奉献是一种与生俱来的本能,而周岩松便是其中一员。

People in cities are unwilling to work at grassroots level for the poor conditions and the low salaries. But people hold a view that every grassroots worker is a spokesman of the whole government. Zhou Yansong is the one who lives to make others live better, accordingly, people have always regarded him highly. A Communist should be more concerned about the Party and the people than about any individual, and care about others than about himself. People who do not keep their promises will not win the respect of others. Dedication is like an innate instinct for a group of people and Zhou is one of them.

故事十一　田思嘉——烈火青春 Burning Youth

【人物介绍】Character Introduction

田思嘉,消防员,1986 出生。他生前多次因工作中的英勇表现受到部队嘉奖。2012 年 3 月 13 日被追授“浙江青年五四奖章”。同年,公安部追授田思嘉为烈士。

Tian Sijia, born in 1986, was a firefighter. He was awarded for his bravery performance many times when he was alive. He was posthumously awarded “Zhejiang's May 4th Youth Medal” in March 13, 2012. In the same year, he was officially recognized as a martyr by the Ministry of Public Security of China.

【人物事迹】Character Story

2012 年 3 月 10 日凌晨,义乌小商品市场发生火灾,现场日用化妆品罐装产品发生爆炸,正在大火中搜救被困群众的田思嘉被气浪冲倒,空气呼吸器损坏,受伤严重。他被送往诸暨市第一人民医院,经全力抢救无效,田思嘉光荣牺牲,年仅 26 岁。“指导员非常注意战士安全,每次有危险都是自己上,我们都习惯了。如果知道他是最后一次和我们一起救火,我绝不会同意让他冲进去。”战友骆少飞至今仍非常后悔。骆少飞回忆道:“当时火场温度已经 500 多度,常人不用说进去,连站在旁边都不行。田思嘉冲进去很久都没出来,我们急了。忽然间,一阵爆炸声传来,一下子我整个人都懵了。”当他们找到田思嘉时,他脸上的呼吸器已经炸裂,脸上还在流血。他们知道他的指导员不行了……

所有人都会记得这个伟大的人——那个把自己的呼吸器给孕妇、民工、老人的人,把生的希望留给他人的田思嘉;那个在三年中经历了 500 多次救火和救援,救出数百百姓,为群众挽回亿元损失的田思嘉。他用短暂的生命实现了自己入伍时对人民的承诺——人民利益高于一切,用火热的青春谱写了一曲新时期消防官兵的壮丽凯歌。

It was in the early morning on March 10th, 2012, when Tian Sijia was rescuing the trapped people in a fire in the small commodity market, he was knocked down by a heat blast from a sudden explosion caused by some canned cosmetics. Meanwhile, his air respirator was damaged which resulted in severe injury to him. He was then sent to the First People's Hospital of Zhuji to receive emergency treatment, but unfortunately he died. He was in his youth, only 26 years old. Tian's comrade Luo Shaofei regreted that he did not keep him from entering the fire, "Our instructor, who paid great attention to the safety of soldiers, was always at the frontline in the fight against danger. If we knew it was the last time we fought together, we would never let him go inside." Luo told us the temperature of the fire reached as high as over 500 degrees Celsius, which kept people from approaching, let alone entering inside. "We got anxious as it was for too long Tian stayed inside the burning supermarket. Suddenly, that a deafening explosive sound and I knew that something very bad happening to Tian," Luo also said. He knew his instructor was dying when they found him, as his face was bleeding and his air respirator was damaged.

People will never forget this great man, who gave hope to others by giving his own air respirator to the pregnant, peasant laborers and the elderly. He was the one who experienced over five hundred times of fire fighting and rescue mission within three years, saved hundreds of people and millions of properties. Though his life was short, he had not only realized his promise to the people when he enlisted in the army—the interests of the people are the highest, but also wrote a magnificent song of triumph about the fire brigade, which inspired by his burning youth.

【人物启迪】Character Enlightenment

荣誉和牺牲是一对孪生兄弟。当人们的生命安全面临威胁时,有几人有田思嘉的胸怀——把生的机会留给战友,危险留给自己。田思嘉给我们留下了宝贵的精神财富,他的生命虽然短暂,却绽放出了无比璀璨的光芒,他用行动诠释了当代青年人的人生价值。为了表扬他舍己为人的精神,浙江省委发了文章报道他的事迹。这种用生命践行自己对人民的承诺的精神让人震撼。田思嘉一生信奉"为了大家的利益可以牺牲自己",他做到了。许多年纪轻轻的烈士为人民献出了生命,难道他们不爱人生?不,他们对人生也充满了眷恋与渴望。但是,他们为了更多人的生,面对死亡毅然决然。他们的光辉形象将永远屹立在人们的心中。他们死得光荣,死得伟大。

Honor and sacrifice are twins. When we are facing the danger of our life security, who will have the same choice like Tian Sijia, leaving chance to live to others, facing dangers by himself? Tian left us the precious spiritual wealth. Though his life was very short, his spirit shone extremely bright. He interpreted the contemporary young people's life values with his heroic action. Zhejiang Provincial Party Committee published a special report with a whole page about his deeds, to praise his spirit of sacrifice for the sake of others. His virtue of trustworthiness with his life for the people and himself is inspiring. The faith Tian always held is that we must do everything even to sacrifice for the people. And he did it. In our life, we can see many martyrs die young for the people. Don't you think they don't cherish the life? Yes, they do. They are sentimentally attached to life and they are full of hope and desire. But they confront the death bravely and resolutely in order to let much more people live. Their brilliant image will be impressed on the hearts of people. They died a great and worthy death.

故事十二　郑樟瑞——一个50年的承诺 A 50-Year's Promise

【人物介绍】Character Introduction

郑樟瑞，退休老人，1930年出生。2012年4月他入围了“中国好人榜”，成为嵊州市第一个入围该榜单的好人。

Zheng Zhangrui, born in 1930, has retired from his post. In April, 2012, his name was on the shortlist of "Chinese Good Fellows". He is the first person whose name appears in that honor roll in Shengzhou city.

【人物事迹】Character Story

50年前，郑樟瑞借用当时好友俞玉兔30元钱急用。50年后，一直惦记着债务的郑樟瑞“以一倍百”将3000元钱还给俞玉兔，但俞玉兔只肯收当初借走的30元钱，在郑樟瑞的一再坚持下，才收下了这笔饱含50年情谊的钱。郑樟瑞提到他一辈子都带着一份扔都扔不掉的愧疚。这是为什么呢？原来在1959年，虽然自己不想离开学校，但为了能让家人过好日子，郑樟瑞响应国家号召要去宁夏“支边”。因家里太穷了，他只好四处借钱，但借了好几次都没有借到。村里的小学老师俞玉兔看在眼里，主动把存折交给他，让他自己去取。当时俞玉兔存折上只有35元钱，本来郑樟瑞向她借20元，可计算后发现自己需要30元，于是多取走了10元，他觉得很难为情，于是不辞而别。年轻的郑樟瑞没想到，这件事让自己背了半个世纪的思想包袱。梦想很美，现实很残酷，此后郑樟瑞的生活一直过得很清苦，没钱还债，心里还压着一个包袱，他没有主动和俞玉兔联系，但一直记挂着这笔债。直到这几年他在儿子的帮助下生活好起来后，攒足 3000 元立即与俞玉兔联系还债。他说："一个人的信用，是比黄金还贵重的东西，无法用金钱衡量，是花多少钱也买不来的。在我有生之年，能够用自己的积蓄把这笔债还清，我觉得心安理得。"当有人询问他为什么偿还 3000 元时，郑樟瑞说，他参考了黄金和粮油的价格，在两者之间折中了一下，定下了以借 1 元还 100 元的比例，来还这笔半个世纪的债。于是，他向俞玉兔寄出了一张 3000 元的汇款单。他的这种诚实守信的好品德受到了社会的关注和好评。

Fifty years ago, Zheng Zhangrui borrowed 30 RMB from his friend Yu Yutu for emergency usage. Zheng couldn't get his mind off the matter, and after fifty years, he repaid Yu 3 000 RMB. Yu, who initially refused to accept this large repayment, finally took this sum for Zheng's insistence. He mentioned that he had been carrying an unshakable sense of shame and guilt for the rest of his life. Why? In 1959, in order to earn a better life for his family, Zheng Zhangrui decided to leave for Ningxia to answer the call to assist the frontier. He tried to borrow money from others as he was too poor, but failed and got nothing. Yu Yutu, a primary school teacher in the village, voluntarily gave Zhen her bankbook and asked him to draw money by himself. At that time, there was only 35 RMB in Yu's account, so he asked Yu for 20 RMB. But after calculating the expenses he would spend on the way, he withdrew 30 RMB without Yu's permission. Because of the guilt feeling for Yu, he left there without telling her. The young man didn't know that it would become a great mental burden for him for half a century. Dreams are nice, but life is realistic. Zheng had been living in poverty since he arrived in Ningxia and had no money to pay off the debt, which made him dare not to contact with Yu. But he didn't forget the debt he owed Yu. Fortunately, he lived a better life with his son's assistance in recent years. When he saved enough money, he managed to find Yu Yutu. He said, "A person's credit is something more precious than gold, and cannot be measured in monetary terms; it cannot be bought during a lifetime. I feel justified and contented for using my savings to pay off this debt." When asked why he repaid Yu 3 000 RMB, he said he got the compromised price of the gold and the grain and oil, and finally decided to mail Yu a money order at a rate of 1∶100. His virtue of trustworthiness and honest character have earned him the social attention and praise.

【人物启迪】Character Enlightenment

欠债还钱是对诚信最好的诠释。有时候有些人欠债还不认账，还想扛债不还，明明欠人的债，却不承认。如此不讲道理，所以世界上有种种麻烦的事。然而与此同时，我们每个人又都有可能成为他人学习的模范，我们每天都可能是他人的老师，但又每天可能是需要向他人学习的学生。不要低估普通人的能量。文中的郑樟瑞老人印证了中国的一句古语：与朋友交，言而有信。

That those who owe money repayment is the best interpretation of trustworthiness. Sometimes some people don't even acknowledge their debts to others; instead, they try to renege. Such unreasonable actions cause many troubles in the world. Everyone has their own causes and conditions, which are entangled and difficult to separate. But meanwhile, the ordinary people may set examples for others, and we may be the pupils of others as well as their teachers. Do not under-evaluate the power and energy of ordinary people. The old man Zheng Zhangrui has proven the old proverb in China, "To keep a friend, you should keep your words."

故事十三　邵宝林——诚信商家 A Trustworthy Businessman

【人物介绍】Character Introduction

邵宝林，企业家，1963年出生，现任开化县宝林山珍总行总经理，开化县诚信商会会长，开化县食用菌协会副会长。他先后被评为"浙江省绿色公益使者"和"开化诚信优秀商家"，并获得开化县"希望工程个人贡献奖"和第二届浙江省"道德模范"称号。

Shao Baolin, born in 1963, is an entrepreneur. He is now the general manager of Baolin Delicacies in Kaihua County and holds posts as the Chairman of the Trustworthy

Chamber of Commerce in Kaihua and the Vice Chairman of Edible Fungus Association in Kaihua. In recent years, he has been honored with "Herald of Public Welfare in Zhejiang" "Trusted Store in Kaihua" "Individual Contribution Award for Hope Project in Kaihua" and "The 2nd Session of Moral Model in Zhejiang".

【人物事迹】Character Story

1996 年从商以来,"诚信经营、持续发展"的理念是邵宝林始终不变的信念。当时,有些"聪明"的商家为了多赚钱,玩起花样儿:卖香菇时,上面是大的,卖相很好,底下却是一堆小的。事实上这些卖家利用了不正当的手段来对付生活,他们是毫不超脱的,更是不体面的。邵宝林觉得:"这样搞下去,肯定不行。"他认为,应该把产品质量控制好。诚信的人,确实不会吃亏。一开始,他卖的山货因为价格高,顾客很少。但是,一段时间后,大家觉得虽然贵一点儿,但是东西很实在,于是回头客慢慢多起来,生意也越做越好。随着自己的企业发展壮大,本着"让商家诚信经营,让消费者买得放心、用得舒心"的宗旨,他于 2005 年创立了"开化县诚信商会",同县城商贸界一起打造诚信经营环境。早在 2003 年他就有这样的念头,尝到了诚信经营甜头的他与自己的商店所在的城南社区负责人商量,提出组建开化县城南诚信商会。邵宝林上门做商家工作,还现身说法,说明诚信经营的好处。尽管这样,效果还是不佳,他们游说了好几个月,只有 18 家商户答应"试试"。参加的商户虽少,但商会的会规却很"重":如果会员商户卖的东西质量不好,被投诉 3 次以上,就会被除名。渐渐地,商会企业信誉被越来越多的消费者所接受。如今在他的领导下,160 多位个体私营企业主都诚实守信,合法经营。每年商会都会组织评选出"明星企业",让会员企业接受全社会的监督,在消费者中形成良好的反响。"我最大的心愿就是希望能为促进社会诚信尽绵薄之力。"邵宝林说。最近,开化县诚信商会给 82 名贫困学生送去了 8 万元助学款。对这些学生,他只提了一个要求:"将来完成学业后,要做一个有诚信的人。"因为在他看来,在人的一生中,我们会得到许多,也会失去许多,但守信用却是我们时刻所坚守的。如果我们以虚伪、不诚实的方式为人处世,也许能获得暂时的"成功",但从长远看,最终是失败者。这种人就像山上的水,刚开始的时候,高高在上,但渐渐地它就越来越低,再没有上升的机会。

Since 1996, Shao Baolin has started his business on the ideas of management with integrity and development with sustainability. At that time, some cunning businessmen played tricks on selling to make more money, showing the customers good-looking and big mushrooms and hiding the malformed and smaller ones in the bottom. In fact, it often happens that they are not enriching themselves by dishonest means, which would make them disreputable. Shao thought that a trustworthy businessman should not be like that and he decided to attach primary importance to the quality of his products. What is true is that an honest man will not lose. Indeed, at the very beginning of his business, he got few customers because of the high price. But as time went on, customers were returning increasingly—a sure sign that he was on the right track. With the development and expansion of his business, and in order to allow businesses to operate in good reputation and allow consumers to buy products surely, he founded the Trustworthy Chamber of Commerce in 2005. This is a county business community for the purpose of building credibility in a business environment. In 2003, Shao proposed to set up Trustworthy Chamber of Commerce, and discussed with the people who were in charge of business in Chengnan Community. Shao visited commercial tenants and persuaded them to join the Commerce. But after several months' endeavor, there were only 18 commercial tenants showed their inclination to have a try. Though the number of the Commerce members was few at that time, the principles of the Commerce were stern. The members of the Commerce would be removed their names from the roll if they were complained over 3 times by the customers. Gradually, the trustworthiness of the Commerce was increasingly accepted by the people. Today, under his leadership, more than 160 individual and private business owners are honest and trustworthy. Now the Chamber of Commerce selects annually a "Star Enterprise" from member companies accepting the supervision of the whole society in order to strengthen consumer confidence in those businesses. The Chamber of the Commerce has gained a solid social reputation. Shao said, "My greatest wish is to try my best to popularize the idea of being a trustworthy man in society." Recently, the Trustworthy Chamber of the Commerce has donated

80 000 RMB to help 82 students for their study. Shao Baolin has one request for those students who received the subsidies, "I do hope you can be a trustworthy person in the future." Shao holds a view that through our lifetime, we can gain a lot and lose so much, but being honest should always be with us. If we live our life in a deceptive and dishonest way, we may succeed temporarily. However, from the long-term view, we will be a loser in such a way. Such kind of people are just like the water on the mountain. It stands high above the masses at the beginning, but gradually it comes down inch by inch and loses the chance of going up.

【人物启迪】Character Enlightenment

约瑟夫·巴伯·莱特福特曾说过:"没有什么比纯净的心、真诚的生活更有说服力的了。"没有正确的观念,就如同走在漫长的黑夜中,走错了也不知道。我们惊讶于他居然可以这般地说真话,做实事,提倡"诚信",一点也不从众媚俗。这在谎言日增的社会里,已经愈来愈少见了。面对金钱诱惑,不怦然心动,不为其所惑,虽平淡如行云,质朴如流水,却让人领略到一种山高海深。这是一种闪光的品格——诚信。

Joseph Barber Lightfoot once said, "There is no persuasiveness more effectual than the transparency of a single heart, of a sincere life." Without right values, it would be like walking in endless darkness; we won't even know when we wander onto the wrong path. We are amazed by the way he spoke the truth and promoted the deeds of integrity, without following traditional customs just to please people. Living in the society where truth is becoming rarer while lies are increasing daily, our respect for Shao Baolin arose naturally. People appreciate those who can keep their inner peace without vacillation when facing money temptation. It is trustworthiness that makes them more peaceful and respectable.

故事十四 汪南南——眼盲心不盲 A Blind Man with a Clear Heart

【人物介绍】Character Introduction

汪南南，盲人推拿师，1986年出生。中央电视台的《新闻联播》栏目播出了汪南南的诚信故事。2013年，他荣获“最美衢州人”的称号。

Wang Nannan, born in 1986, is a blind massager. CCTV News had broadcasted his trustworthy story in 2013. He was named “The Most Beautiful Man in Quzhou City”.

【人物事迹】Character Story

2013年1月11号中午，在浙江省衢州市人民医院的手术室里，汪南南正进行心脏手术，手术室外20多位市民等待着手术结果。自14岁失明后，汪南南潜心学习推拿，并在2009年开了一家推拿店。2013年年初，当南南被查出疾病时，他发誓即使失去生命，也要通知顾客前来退会员费。忍住剧痛，南南用盲人手机编写短信通知他的60多位顾客。“爸，我上手术台可能就下不来了，在我这里办卡做推拿的60多个顾客，留了联系方式的我都用语音手机发短信通知他们来退钱了，还有个顾客没留手机号，你帮我在店门外贴张告示，通知他来退钱，总共的退款大概7000多元。”即将上手术台的汪南南再三叮嘱父亲。但没人来索款，大家还自发给他捐了7000多元。手机不能准确识别语音，汪南南编辑了半个小时，原文还是错字连篇。但大家都看懂了，纷纷回信，只字不提退款的事情：“有什么我能为你做的，就告诉我”“你在哪家医院，我来看你”……汪南南被顾客的热心回应深深打动，却也了然其中的缘由。有时候，顾客会把一些东西落在店里，物品便宜的几百元，贵的上万元，有时候是一只手镯、一根项链，还有时候是一个苹果手机或者钱包。汪南南就根据顾客留下的电话拨过去。甚至有一次，有顾客在他店里落下一枚贵重的玉佩，却没有登记联系方式，汪南南就把它收好，等到第三天她找上门来，才完璧归赵。汪南南的诚信行为在衢州市引起了强烈共鸣。1月15日，衢州市区19家盲人推拿店在《衢州晚报》联合刊登各自推拿店的联系电话和地址，决定无偿接管汪南南的60多位办卡顾客。作为发起人,盲人推拿师夏高旺说:“党和政府以及社会对我们残疾人一直很关心,我们也想用自己的方式回馈社会。南南的诚信让我们感动,帮助他正是我们盲人间的爱心传递!”这种诚信精神值得大家的肯定。

On January 11th, 2013, more than 20 people waited outside the operating room at the People's Hospital of Quzhou City, Zhejiang Province, while Wang Nannan underwent heart surgery. Blind since 14 years old, Wang Nannan devoted himself to learning massage, and in 2009 opened his own shop. Earlier this year, when he was diagnosed with the heart disease, he vowed to return his customer's membership dues, as he might lose his life. Wang Nannan, using a phone for blind persons, sent text messages to more than 60 customers, informing them that their membership dues could be refunded. Wang left strict orders to his father before he went to the operation room, “Dad, I am not sure if I can survive after this operation. I did inform all the customers of coming for their membership fees, but there is still one customer I cannot contact as he did not leave me his telephone number. Please help me and paste a notice on the door to ask him getting back his money.” However, no one came to demand returning, and actually 7 000 RMB was donated by customers and others. His telephone cannot recognize accurately his voice, so there were still many wrong characters in the text. But everyone understood and responded, “Where are you? I want to go to the hospital to see you.” “Do not hesitate to tell me what I can do for you.” Wang was deeply moved by the responses of his customers and he knew they were more than his customers but friends. Wang returns everything to the owners who lost things in his massage shop. Sometimes it was a bracelet, a necklace or an IPhone or a wallet. Wang tries to find the owners when it happens. Once there was a customer left her jade pendant in his shop but did not write down her contact information. Wang kept it and waited the owner to get it back. Wang Nannan's behavior strikes a great chord with other blind massagers in Quzhou City. On January 15, 19 blind massage shops announced in *Quzhou Evening Paper* that they were willing to voluntary take over the service job for Wang Nannan's customers and published their telephone numbers and shop addresses. Xia Gaowang, originator of this movement, said, "The development of our handicapped people cannot be separated from the concern and support of the Party, the government and the whole society, so it is time we shall do something paying back them. We are deeply touched by Wang's trustworthiness and regard this movement as a transmission of love." Wang Nannan's spirit of honesty is worthy of recognition.

【人物启迪】Character Enlightenment

其实这个故事里还有一群人也在给我们传递着正能量,那 60 多位交了会员费的顾客收到短信后都没有前去索款,反而给汪南南捐款。我们的世界,每天都有不幸发生,车祸、疾病、生离死别……命运有时仿佛把我们当作唐僧,安排我们历经九九八十一难,却又要求我们像孙悟空一样会七十二变,勇敢地站起来。自助者天助。不要追求华丽的外表,外表常常具有欺骗性。不要追求万贯家产,财富也会散尽。守住内心最真诚的自己,只有真诚才能使黑暗的日子变得光明。"没有完美的人生,心灵美才是真的美。"汪南南平静朴实的话语,道尽了人之立世的哲学。

The customers of Wang, who didn't ask for money from Wang but made a donation to him. in this story conveys strong positive energy. Various misfortunes occur every day in this world, such as traffic accidents, diseases, death and parting... We are required to be Tang Monk as well as Sun Wukong, as our destinies give us variety of difficulties and need us to start over bravely. God helps those who help themselves. Don't go for looks; they are deceptive. Don't go for wealth; even that fades away. To be the real one who makes you smile because it takes only a honest heart to make a dark day bright. Wang Nannan has given the definition of philosophy being a human being in life: life is not perfect. Those who owns a beautiful heart is the real beauty.

故事十五　胡惊雨——支教教师 A Volunteer Teacher

【人物介绍】Character Introduction

胡惊雨，曾为支教教师，1990 年出生。国内各大媒体包括中央电视台对她帮新疆孩子圆“看海梦”做了全程报道。她当选了 2012 年“最美宁波人”。

Hu Jingyu, once being a volunteer teacher, was born in 1990. Many major media, including CCTV had reported her story of helping her students from Xinjiang Province realize their dream of seeing the sea. She was honored as the “The Most Beautiful Ningbo Citizen” in 2012.

【人物事迹】Character Story

2010 年，胡惊雨放弃待遇不错的工作只身前往千里之外的新疆支教。这是她 2003 年对支教的新西兰老师做出的承诺。那位在新疆支教的外教告诉她：“新疆很需要英语教师，如果你以后有机会，可以来新疆支教一段时间。”胡惊雨心想：外国人都能到中国支教，我是中国人，更应该去！于是她毫不犹豫地回答：“我会去的。”支教期间，她一学年至少上课 40 周，一周至少 12 节课。在达浪坎乡支教的日子里，她感受最深的除了当地人的善良和淳朴外，就是水资源极度匮乏。那一年，胡惊雨支教所在地只下过一次雨。孩子们对水的渴望可想而知。一次，她与孩子们谈梦想时，孩子们都有一个共同的愿望，就是想“看一次大海”。她当即答应他们：“我一定要带你们去看大海。”孩子们听了非常兴奋，立即把这一消息告诉了爸妈。“既然已答应他们，那就一定要做到，像当初我答应外教老师来新疆支教一样。”于是她在网上发起了倡议。在广大网友和社会各界爱心人士的支持下，胡惊雨陪同她的 25 个新疆学生来到宁海一圆“看海梦”。然而，到了宁波，带着这群年龄最大只有 15 岁、最小 13 岁的半大孩子旅行，保证 25 个孩子的衣食住行无忧的这份压力很大。胡惊雨以女性独有的细心周到地一一安排，考虑了方方面面的问题。为此，她亲自策划、安排、落实孩子们的每一项行程,确认各个细节。孩子们在来宁波前,胡惊雨就向当地教育部门承诺:一定会让孩子们在 7 月 12 日前返回新疆。但由于时值暑假,是高校放假、假日外出旅游的旺季,火车票都所剩无几,很难在同一车次凑齐 25 张票。于是,胡惊雨决定将乘坐火车的计划改为乘飞机,但光飞机票一项预算就需要 7 万余元。可公益金也只剩 3 万元了,还差 4 万多元。于是,她向妈妈提出“借”4 万元钱,答应上班后,挣工资还“账”。在妈妈的帮助下,胡惊雨帮孩子们购买了由上海飞往乌鲁木齐的飞机票。当看到孩子们顺利登上飞机时,胡惊雨紧张的心情一下放松了下来,脸上露出了笑容。因为,她没有失言,履行了让孩子们看海并准时返回的承诺。

对将来的事情不轻易许诺,但说到就一定做到。胡惊雨就是这样一个诚信的人。

In 2010, Hu Jingyu gave up a well-paid job in city and worked as a volunteer teacher in Xinjiang Province thousands of miles away, thus keeping a promise she made to her volunteer teacher from New Zealand in 2003. The volunteer foreign teacher in Xinjiang Province told her, “Xinjiang needs English teachers, if you have opportunity in future, you could come here as a volunteer teacher for a period of time.” Hu thought that even foreigners can do it, so as a Chinese, She should take more responsibility for it and do it much better. So she made a promise to the volunteer foreign teacher, “Yes, I promise I will come here some day.” During the teaching period, she took 12 classes per week and 40 weeks in an academic year at least. What struck her most is the serious scarcity of water resources when Hu Jingyu taught her students in Dalangkan village. It rains only once during that year! The desire for seeing the sea for students there, as we can imagine, was very strong. One day, Hu discussed with her students about “Dream” and it was that time that she knew all the students had got the same dream—seeing the sea. She promised them, “I will take all of you to see the sea.” The children got extremely excited about the promise and they told their parents immediately the news. Hu thought, “Since I do promise them, I will do it just as I keep my promise to my foreign teacher.” So she launched a proposal on the Internet. With the support of the warm-hearted people, in the beginning of July this year, Hu Jingyu and her

25 Xinjiang students were able to realize their dream of seeing the sea in Ninghai. However, Hu took a great pressure when she took these 25 students to Ningbo City, as among them, the eldest student was 15 years old, and the youngest was 13 years old. It required patience and consideration of the organizer. During those days, Hu did detailed plans for every aspect to ensure everything would go smoothly. She did not get enough sleep and always got busy with her two cellphones as she had to check every detail by herself. Before the students came to Ningbo, Hu Jingyu promised to the local educational department that she would let every student go back to Xinjiang before July 12th. But the problem was that it was the peak time for people traveling around and the colleges began summer vacation. Hu could not buy 25 tickets in the same train and she decided to book flight tickets which required over 70 000 RMB. All these flight tickets came to more money than she had, and she asked her mother to help her. With her mother's help, all the students flew home on time. Hu relaxed and smiled when she saw the children off in the airport as she had a feeling of being trustworthy to the children.

Do not make promise easily. If you make a promise, keep it. By keeping this promise, Hu Jingyu showed her integrity and beautiful character.

【人物启迪】Character Enlightenment

很多这个年纪的女孩子都想留在父母身边,留在自己的故乡,但她却为了一句承诺只身到千里之外的新疆支教,并帮新疆孩子实现了看海的梦想,她的青春是靓丽的。要悟透自己就要欣赏自己。无论你是一棵参天大树,还是一棵小草,都有自己存在的价值。只要你认真地欣赏自己,你就会拥有一个真正的自我。只有自我欣赏才会有信心,一旦拥有了信心也就拥有了守护诺言的动力。

Girls at her age prefer to stay with parents in their hometown, but Hu Jingyu chose leaving alone to teach in Xinjiang Province and helped her students realize their dream of seeing the sea. We can say her youth is flamboyant. To get a thorough understanding of oneself needs self-appreciation.

Whether you liken yourself to a towering tree or a blade of grass, you should value of your being. If you earnestly recognize yourself, you'll have a real sense of self-appreciation, which will give you confidence. As soon as you gain full confidence in yourself, you'll be able to fight and keep any promise you make.

故事十六　梅光汗——重情守信 An Affectionate Man Who Keeps His Promise

【人物介绍】Character Introduction

梅光汗，台州农民，1948 年出生。2014 年他被评为“最美浙江人——2014 年度浙江骄傲人物”。

Mei Guanghan, a peasant from Taizhou, was born in 1948. He was honored with “The Most Beautiful Zhejiang Citizen—the Pride of Zhejiang in 2014”.

【人物事迹】Character Story

1990 年，梅光汗的妻子任春爱有一天外出买粮食，在回家路上发生车祸，从拖拉机里面被甩了出去。抢救后她胸口以下瘫痪了，后续治疗还需要 7 万元。7 万元在 25 年前对一个农民来说无异于天文数字，而且梅光汗家庭负担本来就很重，当年家里的 3 个孩子，最大的才 15 岁，最小的也只有 9 岁，突然间家里所有重担都落在了他一个人肩上。为了尽快筹到足够的钱给妻子治病，梅光汗无奈之下，带上夫妻俩的身份证，村里开的家庭困难证明以及妻子的病历，步行赶往一个个陌生的乡镇，走进上百个村庄、上千户人家，挨家挨户乞讨借钱。接受了许多好心人的资助，也忍受了数不清的冷眼与怀疑，但为了救妻子，梅光汗默默忍受。

当有人给他钱，梅光汗都会将热心人的名字与资助的金额认真地记录下来。遇到不愿意留姓名的热心人，他就把门牌号抄下来，或者去问他的邻居。为的就是以后还钱方便。他说，这些钱都是借的，以后一定要还。很多人只是一笑而过,根本没想过他会还。梅光汗一边起早摸黑干农活,一边悉心照顾妻子。随着妻子的病情逐渐稳定,儿女渐渐长大,还钱的念头也在梅光汗的心里一天天强烈起来。梅光汗翻开珍藏的记着姓名和地址的账本,决定重走当年的乞讨路,上门还清债务,虽然最少的一笔只有两毛钱,但对梅光汗来说,哪怕是一分钱,也是救活妻子的生命钱,更是一份必须永远铭记的善心。

当年的热心人收到梅光汗的还款时,很多都早已记不得当年的情景了。村民丁兴广,当年曾随手给了梅光汗两元钱。“那时他说借钱给妻子治病,会还的。我根本没在意,就当好心送给他,没想他真的上门还钱来了,”丁兴广说,“这么讲信用的人真少见,真后悔当时没多借些钱给他。”多年过去了,很多村民已经很难找到,还钱的路并不顺利。“还一笔钱,我可能要跑好几次。”时至今日,除了实在找不到的三四户人家外,债已经全部还清。

那本已基本还清的旧账本,梅光汗仍然细心收藏着。“钱虽然还了,但每一份恩情都不能忘。我对别人说,当年的两角钱也是一笔不小的数字。我同他们既不是亲戚,也不是邻居、朋友,他们都是好心的恩人,”梅光汗说,“这本账本是传家宝,要留给后代。”

It was in the year of 1990. Mei Guanghan's wife Ren Chunai, had a serious accident when she had finished shopping foods. Mei's wife was threw away from the tractor and got hurt badly. The accident paralyzed her that she lost her esthesia below chest. After resuscitation, the trouble was that they were still short of money, around 70 000 RMB. This cost was tremendous for Mei Guanghan. There was already a heavy family burden for the poor peasant with three dependants, the eldest one being only 15 years old and the youngest 9 years old. In order to raise money to cure his wife, he decided to borrow money from his friends, relatives and even strangers. Taking their ID cards and official certificates, he went out to beg from door to door and visited over a hundred different villages. Some people might roll their eyes and doubt him which he suffered for a long time with tremendous courage. But meanwhile, he received lots of charity.

Mei recorded clearly all information of the warm-hearted people, including their names and family addresses. Sometimes he needed to get these people's names from their neighbours when they wished to remain anonymous. Mei worked from dawn to night on the farm and took well care of his wife. The idea for paying back the money came to him when his wife's condition was beginning to stabilize and their children were growing up. Mei opened his account book and decided to follow his route he had taken many years ago. Reviewing his account book, he was touched by every sum of money, even touched by the smallest charity which was only twenty cents. For Mei, every cent was vital for saving his wife's life.

Most people had forgotten the story when they received Mei's repayment. Ding Xingguang, a peasant who had lent Mei 2 RMB, recalled, "I remember he said that he needed the money to cure his wife and promised to pay back one day. I didn't take it to my heart, but unexpectedly he really come here to pay me back. It's rare to meet such trustworthy person in my life. If I believed him at that time, I would lend him more money." Because many villagers moved away from the original addresses, sometimes he needed to go for them several times to pay back the money. Till now, all the debts are paid back except four villagers whom are really hard to find.

Mei collected the old account book and said, "We cannot forget those people who gave me a hand when my family was in trouble. They are neither my relatives, neighbours nor friends, they are strangers who have kind heart. This account book will be my family heirloom."

【人物启迪】Character Enlightenment

也许有人认为欠债还钱,本是天经地义的事情,不值得大力宣扬。但我们之所以为梅光汗感动,是因为他做出的诚信之举超出了我们的想象。他让我们读到了一个人的信义,也让公众体会到了社会对于诚实守信的敬重。

Maybe some people hold a view that we needn't praise Mei's story as repaying debts is a natural part in this world. However, we are touched by his story not only because of his repaying, but also because of his story beyond our expectation. His story offers us a chance to know what the deepest trustworthiness and let us know the respect for a trustworthy man from the society.

第三章
崇学 Studiousness

一　崇学内涵
Connotation of Studiousness

崇学向来是我国传统,《礼记·学记》就明确记载:"君子如欲化民成俗,其必由学乎!"意思是君子想要教化百姓,并形成良好的风俗,一定要设学施教。又说:"玉不琢,不成器;人不学,不知道。是故古之王者,建国君民,教学为先。"意思是人不学习,就不明白做人的道理;古代君王建立国家,首先要做的事就是设学施教。可见学习之重要。

Studiousness has always been our tradition. *The Book of Rites* clearly says, "If you wish to educate the vulgar into a group people with good habits and create good customs, you need to set up teaching facilities and teach them." As the old saying goes, "If jade is not polished, it cannot become a thing of use. If a man does not learn, he cannot know his duty towards his people. That is the profound reason why the Kings attached importance to the role of teaching and put education in the first place when they governed the whole country." It is clear to show the importance of studying.

二　崇学力量
Force towards Studiousness

学习促进社会发展,崇学可以营造一个好的社会氛围。

Study promotes the social development. Furthermore, studiousness is able to create a good social atmosphere.

三　崇学名言
Quotations on Studiousness

知识就是力量。　　Knowledge is power.

学无止境。　　There is no end to learning.

四　崇学故事
Stories on Studiousness

故事一　谷超豪——大师的求学路 A Master's Studying Life

【人物介绍】Character Introduction

谷超豪,数学家,中科院院士,1926 年出生。他曾获得 2009 年度国家最高科学技术奖。经国际小行星中心和国际小行星命名委员会批准,编号为 171448 的小行星命名为“谷超豪星”。他于 2012 年去世。

Gu Chaohao, born in 1926, was an mathematician and academician of Chinese Academy of Sciences. He received the "National Top Scientific and Technological Award" in 2009. Approved by the Minor Planet Center, the Nomenclature Committee has named minor planet number 171448, as "Planet Gu Chaohao". He passed away in the year of 2012.

【人物事迹】Character Story

谷超豪五岁入私塾接受启蒙教育,聪慧过人,对各门功课都很有兴趣,数学、语文、历史、地理、自然等课程都学得很好。在课堂上,他思维活跃,喜欢独立思考。谷超豪在温州中学读初中一年级时,吴人鉴先生教他数学。一次吴先生在课堂上问道:"一个四边形,每边边长都是 1,面积是否是 1?"谷超豪想了一想回答说:"面积不一定是 1,把这四边形一压,压扁了,成为直线,面积就变 0 了。"谷超豪就这样开始了解菱形。他记忆力超群,年轻时学过的诗词到了晚年还能背诵出来。当时,有些名家回到家乡温州,温州中学会请他们来校讲课。谷超豪听夏承焘先生讲过两次课:一课是苏轼的词《临江仙》,一课是杜甫的诗《月夜》。这两首诗词到现在他还能背。他从事数学研究 60 余年并取得了举世瞩目的成就。谷超豪情系桑梓,对教育事业尤为关心。在担任温州大学校长期间,他对学校的建设和发展做出了卓越贡献,用在大学任职的所有收入捐资设立了"谷超豪奖学金",激励温州大学学子立志成才。无论什么样的环境,他都努力战胜重重困难,刻苦钻研,并根据国家的需要多次调整自己的研究方向,把自己的知识化作力量造福国家和人民。这位 84 岁的老人每天依然工作 8 小时以上,当人们问他最近正在思考的科学问题时,他眼睛发亮:"现在每天的重要功课是思考爱因斯坦的广义相对论,里面可有不少值得探究的好东西。"我们国家正是因为有了这样的大师,科学技术才会突飞猛进。

When Gu Chaohao entered school at the age of 5, he immediately showed extraordinary talents, and he was interested in all subjects. He learned mathematics, Chinese, history, geography, and natural sciences very well. He thought actively, and liked to think independently. When he studied in Wenzhou Middle School, his mathematics teacher named Wu Renjian asked the students in class, "There is a quadrilateral with each side of 1, can I say its area is 1?" Gu thought for a while and responded, "I don't think so. If it is squashed into a line, then the area is zero." From that moment on, Gu started to know what rhombus was. His faculty of memory impressed others a lot as he could recite the poetry he learnt in his youth. At that time, Wenzhou Middle School often invited masters returning to their hometown to give lecture to the students. There was a master, Xia Chengtao, who taught the students two classes, one was the analysis of *Lin Jiang Xian* written by Su Shi, the other was *Moonlit Night* written by Du Fu. Gu could recite them when he was in his old age. He engaged in mathematical research for more than 60 years and had achieved remarkable scientific achievements. Gu Chaohao had emotionally tied to his homeland and was particularly concerned about the cause of education. During the construction and development of Wenzhou University, he made several outstanding contributions to the university, including donating to establish the "Gu Chaohao Scholarship" with his all income during his presidency to support students of Wenzhou University. He had experienced a lot in the past. No matter what the difficulties and hardships, even himself remaining, he had always tried to study hard to overcome various difficulties and adjusted his research area several times in accordance with the demands of the state. He turned his knowledge into the driving force benefiting the people and the country. He worked over 8 hours per day at the age of 84. When he was asked what he thought recently, he replied firmly with bright eyes, "Recently I am thinking over General Relativity Theory of Einstein, in which There are many things worthy researching." Owing to such great masters like Gu, our country's science and technology have been advanced by leaps and bounds.

【人物启迪】Character Enlightenment

他一步一步地走向科学殿堂,登上科学高峰;他给人类造福,让世界欢呼。我们应该立下雄心壮志,像谷老先生那样爱科学、学科学、用科学,促使自己成为建设国家的栋梁之材。我们每个人都是农夫,若种下好种子,就会有丰收。倘若种子不良且长满杂草,我们就会徒劳无获。如果我们什么也不种,就根本不会有收获。

Step by step, Gu Chaohao went to the science hall and stood in the scientific summit, benefiting people around the world and letting the world cheer up. We shall set a high ambition to be the backbone of our country, just like Gu, to love science, to learn science, and to use science. We are all in the position of the "farmer". If we plant a good seed, we reap a good harvest. If our seed is poor and our land full of weeds, we reap a useless crop. If we plant nothing at all, we harvest nothing at all.

故事二　杨晓丽——不言放弃 Never Give Up Studying

【人物介绍】Character Introduction

杨晓丽，公司职员，1988 年出生，优秀大学生代表。她曾获得"2007 中国大学生十大年度人物""2008 年中国大学生自强之星""2008 浙江省十佳大学生"以及"浙江省道德建设先进个人"等荣誉。

Yang Xiaoli, born in 1988, is an office worker and an outstanding college representative. She was awarded the titles "Chinese Top Ten College Students in 2007" "Chinese College Students Self-Improvement Star in 2008" "Top Ten College Students in Zhejiang Province in 2008" and "Advanced Individual of Moral Construction in Zhejiang Province".

【人物事迹】Character Story

"叫你别来，怎么又来了！"看到女儿杨晓丽又风尘仆仆地出现在自己面前，躺在丽水养老院床上的吴火梅边努力尝试着坐起来，边忍不住唠叨着。晓丽熟练地打来热水，给妈妈擦好身子，又挨着她在床边坐下，开始每天例行的头部按摩，"想你了，来看看你嘛。"晓丽撒着娇。这个时候，母女俩一脸幸福。很难看出这个坚强乐观的晓丽，其实经受过同龄人难以想象的磨难。1996 年的一天，向来体格健壮的父亲的猝死使杨晓丽的幸福生活画上句号，那年她才 8 岁。殊不知之后的打击接踵而来。18 岁时又接连遭遇继父去世，母亲因过度劳累患急性脊髓炎而瘫痪的厄运。家庭的重担，全部压到了杨晓丽和姐姐的身上。面对生父猝死，继父病死，母亲高位截瘫的重重打击，杨晓丽没有低头。为了给上大学的姐姐减轻负担,18 岁时她开始照顾生活无法自理的母亲;一边学习,一边捡废品,用以支付母亲的医药费和自己的学费。她每天早起,伺候母亲洗漱,做饭,下午定时回家给母亲翻身,弱小的她要把比自己重的母亲翻个侧身实在不易。正是她对母亲的爱赋予了她耐心,使她在别人可能会放弃的时候继续坚持,并且无怨无悔地照顾自己的家人渡过难关。晚自习结束给母亲擦完身才算结束了一天的生活。面对艰难境遇,她积极乐观,自强自立,在照顾母亲的同时勤奋学习。尽管压力大,但杨晓丽的学习成绩却一直名列前茅。因为她抓住每一个空闲时间学习,从不浪费时间。在得到学校和社会的大力资助后,她努力回报社会,资助其他贫困学生。在学校创建"晓丽爱心传递站",以一颗感恩的心回报社会。杨晓丽以非凡的毅力坚持着自己的学业和理想。无论干什么事,她总是准时到,从不轻易请假。这种精神值得我们学习。

"You needn't come here. Why you come again?" Trying to get up from her bed in the rest-home, Wu Huomei had been jawing at her daughter, Yang Xiaoli. Yang Xiaoli expertly prepared hot water and began to clean her mother and massage on her head. "I come here because I miss you!" Yang said in a spoiled manner. The mother and the daughter smiled and their faces alighted with happiness. We could hardly know it was this smiling girl who had lived through unimaginably awful tribulation. One day in the year of 1996, her natural father's sudden death terminated her happy life when she was only 8 years old. She had no idea there was a series of great misfortunes waiting for her. When she was 18 years old, her step-father died and because of overstrain, her mother had acute myelitis and finally became paralyzed. The heavy burden of the family fell on her and her elder sister. She suffered through the sudden death of her father, the death of his step-father, and caring for a paraplegic mother. In order to alleviate the burden of her sister who was in college at that time, Yang began to take care of the whole family life and take care of her mother from the age of 18. In order to pay for her mother's medical bills and her own tuition, she was picking up the waste, while she also continued to study. Every morning she got up quite early as she had to serve her mother's morning toilet and finished the preparation of breakfast and lunch before she went to school. In the afternoons, she came back home from school at a regular time to help her mother turning over in bed. It was indeed an extremely difficult task for such a thin girl to do it, for her mother was much heavier than she was. The love for her mother gave her patience that allows her to keep going when everyone else would give up, and take care of her family through hardship without complaining. After evening study, she washed and cleaned her mother before she called it a day. Faced with such a difficult situation, she remained positive, optimistic, self-reliant and hard-working, taking care of her mother and studying all the time. Even under such great pressure and tension, Yang did exceedingly well in her studies, and had always among the best performance in her class as she was good at grasping every narrow chance to study and never wasted her time. Since her study and life was heavily subsidized by society, she wanted to give back to the community, so she tried to finance other poor students. She had set up a "Xiaoli Love Transfer Station" in school showing her gratitude to the society. Yang Xiaoli persists in her study and dream by her extraordinary perseverance. Whatever she does, she is always punctual and never asks for leave rashly. Her learning attitudes deserve our emulation.

【人物启迪】Character Enlightenment

没有一条人生路是平坦的。杨晓丽是就读于中国一所普通大学的极其普通的女生,她经历了同龄人不曾经历过的痛与悲,同时也成了一个坚强、理智和成熟的人,她让我们懂得了一个人只有自强才能对外事事强。面对挫折你会怎么做?很多人可能会选择放弃。然而,要想成功,最可靠的方法就是坚持你的方向和目标。生活时而无比顺畅,时而倒霉透顶,好坏参半。生活就像来回晃动的钟摆。读懂生活的常态需要时间和阅历,也正是这样才练就了杨晓丽面对未来荣辱不惊的生活态度。把生活想象成一个在空中抛接五只球的游戏,这五只球分别被称为:工作、家庭、健康、友谊和精神,你要努力不让它们从空中掉下来。马上你就发现唯有工作是一个橡皮球。如果你将它掉到地上,它还会弹回来。但其他四只球——家庭、健康、朋友和精神都是玻璃球。如果你把任何一个掉到地上,便会不可挽回地留下疤痕、裂缝,甚至摔得粉碎,永远也无法恢复原样。你必须懂得这一点并在生活中努力保持平衡。

There is no easy way in our life. Yang Xiaoli, who is a common girl in a common college, has experienced the pain and sorrow that others have not experienced at her age, however, she also has become a person with the quality of strong-willed, intellectual and mature. Her story tells us a truth that only by strengthening ourselves, can we be powerful when handling every difficulty. What would you do when you face frustration? Many people may choose to give up. However, the surest way to success is to keep your direction and stick to your goal. Half the lifetime things are better than normal; the other half, they are worse. Life is a pendulum swing. It takes time and experience to understand what normal is, and that gives Yang Xiaoli the perspective to deal with the future. Imagine life as a game in which you are juggling five balls in the air. You name them: Work, Family, Health, Friends, and Spirit. And you are keeping all of these in the air. You will soon understand that work is a rubber ball. If you drop it, it will bounce back. But the other four balls—family, health, friends, and spirit, are made of glass. If you drop one of them, they will be irrevocably scuffed, marked, nicked, damaged or even shattered. They will never return to the original ones. You must understand it and strive for balance in your life.

故事三　许欢——困境中寻出路 Seeking Way Out of the Difficult

【人物介绍】Character Introduction

许欢，工厂的电工，1990 年出生。2011 年他被评为第二届“浙江孝贤”十大人物，他是十位获奖者中唯一的“90 后”。

Xu Huan, born in 1990, is an electrician. In 2011 he was named the “Top Ten Filial People at the 2nd Session in Zhejiang Province” and he was the only one who was born in the 1990s of the ten people.

【人物事迹】Character Story

2010 年,一边是梦寐以求的象牙塔,一边是医生宣布得了卢伽雷氏病的父亲。在天平的两边,许欢面临人生的一大抉择,最终他选择了后者。由于父亲得了卢伽雷氏病,母亲因患小儿麻痹症行动不便而无法照顾生病的伴侣,许欢毅然放弃了上大学的机会。当 2010 年宁波轻纺学院的录取通知翩然而至的时候,许欢含泪撕掉了手中的通知书。家里经济条件差,如果他上大学,父母谁来照顾?为了父母,为了这个家,他决定放弃到外地读大学的机会,担起家庭的重担,陪伴在父母身边。"我只是放弃到外地读大学,但我并不是要放弃读书。"许欢认真地对妈妈说。他要一边打工赚钱,一边在长兴读电大,这样既能照顾父母,又能继续学习。从那一刻起,许欢如同换了一个人。虽然家里的生活依旧,但他的生活确实发生了变化。他发现自己不仅能够学习,而且能够学得很好!他发现,自己能够理解并牢牢记住知识,还能将学到的知识运用到自己的生活中。他开始变得优秀。为了照顾父母,他留在自己的家乡成了一名电工。面对生活的艰辛、工作的劳累,他并没有放弃梦想,仍坚持利用业余时间读电大,选择攻读计算机专业以圆自己的大学梦。每天他很早起床,为父亲擦身子,背父亲上厕所,喂父亲吃早饭,然后去上班;中午,工厂只有 1 小时休息时间,他骑着自行车赶回家,为父亲揉身体,喂午饭,然后再去上班;到了晚上,他每晚都要起床两次,背父亲上厕所。等到夜深人静了,许欢总要打开台灯,温习功课。他说为了这个家庭以后能过上好日子,他必须坚持学习。许欢的父亲已经去世了,现在的他仍然每个周末都去电大读书,提及当年的决定,许欢说这是值得的。

In the year of 2010, Xu Huan faced a dilemma in his life, going to the college he desired or taking care of his sick father. He made his final decision and chose the latter one. Because of his father's Lou Gehrig's disease, his mother's inability to care for a sick partner for her polio, he then gave up the opportunity to go to college. In 2010, Xu Huan tore the College Admission Notice into pieces with tears as he could not ignore the reality that no one would take care of his parents, if he chose to leave for college. For his parents, he gave up the opportunity to study in college and turned around to take over the responsibility for the family. He told his mother very seriously, "I just give up studying in another city in the college, and it does not mean I will give up studying." Since then, he worked in the local town as well as studied at an open university in Changxing. From that moment nothing was the same for Xu Huan. Life at home remained the same, but life still changed. He discovered that not only could he learn, but he was good at it! He discovered that he could understand and retain knowledge, and that he could apply the things he learned to his own life. He began to be excellent. In order to take care of his parents, he stayed in his hometown and became an electrician. Facing the hardships of life, and tired of his work, he did not give up on his dream, spending his spare time reading, studying computer science, and continuing to pursue his college dreams. He got up quite early in the morning as he had to serve his father's washing and carry his father on his back to the toilet; after he fed breakfast for his father, he rushed to the factory for working. At noon, though there was just one hour for the workers to take a rest, he always rode back home to give his father massage and feed him lunch. He got up twice to carry his father on his back to the toilet every night. When everything was settled down, he would turn on the table lamp to study and review the course books in every late night. He said that he had to struggle hard to learn in order to provide a better life for his family. Now his father passed away and he still studied in college every weekend. When mentioning his decision of giving up the opportunity to study in college, he said he would never regret and it was worthwhile.

【人物启迪】Character Enlightenment

父母是我们最温暖的依靠。小时候我们爱和父母一起玩耍,等我们长大后为了生存离开了他们,只有在我们困难的时候我们会再回来找他们,向他们索取所需的一切,而父母总是竭尽所能地为我们提供一切。当父母需要我们时,我们是不是也可以做到这一点呢?许欢做到了。从某种意义上讲,当我们失去了一些东西时反而感到更加完整。一个拥有一切的人其实在某些方面是个穷人。他永远也体会不到什么是渴望、期待以及对美好梦想的感悟。他也永远不会有像许欢这样的体验:他的父亲对自己意味着什么。年轻的许欢很会调节自己,没有让家庭的压力成为他求学路上的负担,他把一切的压力化为自己前进的动力。这个故事让我们再一次思考这个问题:我们为了什么而学习呢？可以为了国家和人民的利益,也可以为了我们的小家庭和个人。

When we were young, we loved to play with our parents. When we grow up, we leave them, and only come to them when we need something or when we are in trouble. No matter what happens, parents will always be there and give everything they can do to make us happy. Can we do the same thing if our parents need us to help them? Xu Huan did it. In some sense, we feel more complete when we lose something. The man who has everything is in some ways a poor man. He will never know what it feels like to yearn, to hope, to nourish his soul with the dream of something better. He will never know the experience, like Xu Huan, of what a father meant to him. This young man is adept in adjusting himself, not viewing his family troubles as the burden in his studying life, but viewing it as the driving force to move on. This story made us think over the question again, "What are we studying for?" We study for the interests of our country, for the people, and for our family and our own benefit as well.

故事四 陈宇峰——科研达人 A Master of Scientific Research

【人物介绍】Character Introduction

陈宇峰,教师,1978 年出生,浙江金华人。他 2003 年毕业于浙江大学管理学院,2006 年毕业于中国人民大学,成为浙江省内最年轻的副教授之一。

Chen Yufeng, professor, was born in 1978 in Jinhua, Zhejiang Province. He graduated from School of Management Zhejiang University in 2003, and in 2006, he graduated from Renmin University of China. He is one of the youngest associate professors in Zhejiang Province.

【人物事迹】Character Story

2006年,陈宇峰毕业于中国人民大学,获得经济学博士学位。同年,他破格晋升为副教授,成为浙江省内最年轻的副教授之一。2006年至2007年,他赴日本早稻田大学担任国际研究员,2011年又晋升为经济学教授。2012年他被评为博士生导师。获得经济学博士后,他回到浙江工作,现任浙江工商大学现代商贸研究中心副主任。凭借对科研工作的热爱和执着,陈宇峰每周在办公室和研究所的工作时间长达100小时,并取得了丰硕的科研成果:共发表高质量的科研学术论文30余篇,主持国家自然科学基金等国家级科研项目4项、省级项目3项,出版学术著作和译著10余本,获得省部级奖项6项。

In 2006, Chen Yufeng got a Doctorate in Economics from Renmin University of China and was promoted exceptionally to be an associate professor, becoming one of the youngest associate professors in Zhejiang Province. In the years of 2006 and 2007, he worked as an international researcher in Waseda University in Japan. In 2011 he was promoted to full professor of Economics. In 2012 he was promoted as a doctoral supervisor. After getting Doctorate in economics, he returned to work in Zhejiang Province. Now he is the associate director of Center of Modern Trade Research in Zhejiang Gongshang University. Because of his love and dedication to research, he spends more than 100 hours in his office and the researching center every week. In addition, he has made great achievements in scientific research, published more than 30 academic papers with high quality, hosted 4 research projects supported by the Natural Science Foundation and 3 provincial research projects, published 10 scholarly works and translations, of which 6 received provincial and ministerial awards.

【人物启迪】Character Enlightenment

年纪轻轻就成了教授,是什么造就了他的成功?努力钻研?坚持不懈?我想这都需要,但更重要的是兴趣。兴趣是最好的老师,是学习的最大动力。

What brings about the great achievement and success of him to be a full professor at such a young age? Study hard? Persistence? I think we need both, and another factor is as important as the former ones—interest.

Interest is the best teacher and the strongest driving force in our learning process.

故事五　曹秋芳——侍孝学习两不误 Neglecting Neither Filial Piety Nor Study

【人物介绍】Character Introduction

曹秋芳，职员，1992 年出生。2011 年 1 月 13 日，曹秋芳当选“浙江骄傲——2010 年度最具影响力人物”。2011 年她获得第三届“全国道德模范”提名奖。

Cao Qiufang, born in 1992, is an office worker now. In 2011 she was named “The Pride of Zhejiang—the Most Influential Character in 2010” and nominated for “The 3rd Session of National Moral Model”.

【人物事迹】Character Story

在上虞，有两件孝事几乎妇孺皆知：一是二十四孝之首虞舜的孝行，二是孝女曹娥投江救父的故事。如今，在曹娥江畔的上虞章镇，又演绎着感天动地的人间至孝。曹秋芳两个月大时，母亲便在一场医疗事故中丧失了生活自理能力，常年卧病在床。父亲迫于生计外出打工，家里大小事物都压在了留在家中的孩子们身上。从 4 岁开始，曹秋芳就照顾瘫痪的妈妈。到了读书年龄，为了在求学期间不耽误家务，她三度将妈妈带到身边，在校外租房照顾妈妈。放学后，当同龄小朋友在嬉戏玩耍时，曹秋芳便早已回家，利落地做好家务，准备好母亲的晚饭，然后开始预习、复习功课，做作业。对于学习，她始终未敢松懈，尽管照顾母亲有时候会让年幼的她感到力不从心。但是这些反而成了她学习的动力，这样的生活让她觉得，能读书就很开心。命运让曹秋芳多了些艰辛，也让她比同龄人多了一份成熟和坚定。年幼的秋芳便立下志向：通过学习来改变命运，让母亲在今后过上更好的生活。读小学四年级时，她伸出脖颈给母亲借力支撑起上身；读初中时，她用腰背撑着母亲站立；在读高中时，她坚持撑着母亲站立,14 年后母亲终于能站起来了。尽管要照顾妈妈,但曹秋芳的学习成绩一直名列前茅。12 岁时,曹秋芳以优异的成绩被章镇中学录取。初二那年,曹秋芳捧回了全市“奥林匹克数学大赛”二等奖。后来曹秋芳又以优异的成绩考入上虞市重点中学的实验班。从初中到高中她多次被评为班级的“三好学生”。有人背后议论曹妈妈拖累了女儿,曹妈妈听了很伤心很自责,几次寻死未果,曹秋芳都用行动告诉她:“妈妈,无论发生什么事,我都会在你身边!哪怕你只多生活一天,这一天也应该活得优雅,有尊严。”她做到了。许多同学都说,曹秋芳是个天才,学习成绩一直在年级段中出类拔萃!曹秋芳解释说:“我不是什么天才,只是因为在家里要做许多家务,耽搁了学习时间,所以在课堂上就听得特别认真,课余时间抓紧复习,成绩自然差不到哪里去。”“虽然我目前成绩在年级段处在第 10 名左右,但我觉得还是不够好,因为我的理想就是要考上重点大学!”既要照顾好母亲,又要努力保持学习上的好成绩,这需要很大的恒心和毅力。曹秋芳做到了。她不光专注于学习,也积极参加课外活动,获得了大大小小多种奖项和荣誉,如数学竞赛三等奖、古诗文阅读竞赛一等奖、优秀学生、优秀团员等。经过初中三年的努力,她以不错的成绩顺利考入东关高中。读高中了,课程骤然加多,让曹秋芳应接不暇。如何处理好照顾母亲与不影响学业成了曹秋芳的头等大事,但她还是取得了令人满意的成绩。“因为要做家务,我好多作业都做不完,只能晚上加班。晚上睡得迟,感觉有点累,老师在上面讲课,我斜在课桌上想睡觉。”曹秋芳坦言。不能睡着!她就是这样坚持,时刻提醒着自己,继续自己的学业。

In Shangyu, there are two things that everyone knows. The first is the story of “Yu Shun with Filial Piety” and the second is the legend of “Cao E Saved Father in River”. Now, along the same river bank of that legend, Zhangzhen Town in Shangyu, there is another girl giving the interpretation of her filial piety. A serious medical accident incapacitated Cao Qiufang's mother and since then she was laid up in bed when Cao was a baby only two months old. To support the family and earn more money, Cao's father had to leave for the city, leaving all the housework to his children. From the age of 4, Cao Qiufang began to take care of her paralyzed mother. At the age for school, in order to take care of her mother, she with her mother rent a room three times, near school during the school days. In her childhood, she always went back home as soon as the class was over while her peers were playing together. After finishing the preparation of supper, she began to preview or review the knowledge she learnt and do assignment from her teachers. Though sometimes she had a feeling that she was exhausted by taking care of her mother and study, she never gave up. She took the heavy housework as her studying motivation. She felt deeply that her life would be happy as long as she could study. The destiny put her through the difficulty and meanwhile gifted her firm and mature character. The young girl aimed at letting her mother enjoy a better life by knowledge. Only knowledge can change her family's fate. When she was in the fourth grade of primary school, she stretched out her neck to her mother to support the upper body; junior high school, she used to stand back propped up her mother; When she was in high school, after her 14 years persistence, her mother was finally able to stand up. Even under such great pressure and tension, Cao did exceedingly well in her studies, and had always among the best performance in her class, as she treasured every narrow chance to study and never wasted her time. She was enrolled by Zhangzhen Middle School with an excellent score at the age of 12. In the second year of the middle school, she won the Second Prize of Olympic Mathematics Contest of Shangyu. Later Cao successfully entered the key high school with good scores and studied in an experimental class. She was successively elected as "Excellent Student" many times from junior middle school to high school. Cao's mother prepared to suicide for several time as she was so upset at the gossip that she was the burden to her daughter. Everytime Cao told her mother with her action, "No matter what happens, I'll always be there with you! Even if you live for only one day more, that day deserves to be lived graciously and with dignity." And she did so. Lots of her classmates praised Cao Qiufang as a genius for Cao's grades were always at the top in their class. Cao said, "I am not a genius. I am just very conscientious and earnest in class, as you all know, I need spend a lot of time doing housework, so I have to treasure every minute to study." She did an incredible job in balancing her study and her life. She won numerous prizes and honors during her studying in junior middle school, such as the Third Prize for Math Competition, the First

Prize for Reading Ancient Poetry, Excellent Student and Excellent League Member, etc. When Cao studied in high school, she faced more courses which made her too busy to balance well her study and life. But finally she got satisfactory scores in the exams. She told us she often stayed up very late to study and finished all her homework assigned by her teachers. Sometimes she was on the verge of falling asleep in classroom, but she told herself that she could not do it and refreshed herself to further her study.

【人物启迪】Character Enlightenment

曹秋芳的事迹给人们留下了深刻的印象。我们或许也会扪心自问,当学习遇上孝心,该怎么选择?古人说"百善孝为先",曹秋芳怀着一颗孝心努力学习。她做到了两不误,因为她知道还有一句话也是真理:"知识就是力量。"只有知识才会帮助她改变家庭命运。如果你觉得心有余而力不足,觉得缺乏前进的动力时,只需要改变思维的角度。

People are impressed by the kindness of Cao Qiufang. We may ask ourselves a question from time to time: Which will be my choice, continuing studying or staying at home to look after our family members? We Chinese people believe a saying: Filial Piety comes first. Cao did balance the two sides well, as she believed another saying: Knowledge is power. Only knowledge can change her family's fate. If your life feels like it is lacking the power that you want and the motivation that you need, sometimes all you have to do is to shift your point of view.

故事六　洪佳琳——钻研弱智教育 Studying on Education for Mentally Retarded Children

【人物介绍】Character Introduction

洪佳琳,校长,1950年出生。她曾被评为"浙江省特级教师",同时她也是"全国优秀特殊教育工作者"和"杭州市十佳校长"等荣誉称号的获得者。

Hong Jialin, principal, was born in 1950.

She was awarded "Special-Grade Teacher" in Zhejiang Province, "National Outstanding Special Education Teacher" and "The Top Ten Headmasters" in Hangzhou.

【人物事迹】Character Story

洪佳琳把特殊教育作为自己一生奋斗的事业。近20年来,她带领全体教师努力为智障儿童提供无障碍的教育环境和公平发展的机会,刻苦钻研智障人群的教育,先后创办了全国首家弱智教育职业高中部,首家弱智青年康复培训托管中心,建立了弱智人群"学龄前教育—九年义务教育—职业教育"的纵向教育系列和集"教育康复—医疗康复—训练康复"为一体的横向教育体系,形成了独树一帜的弱智教育模式。根据多年的工作经验,她系统地、有条不紊地进行科研工作,所撰写的论文多次在全国、省、市获奖。她对特殊教育的摸索和研究为后来进一步的探索打下了坚实的基础。洪佳琳任杭州扬绫子学校校长时的办学理念与做法得到了专家们的赞同和响应。该校不仅仅针对智障残障儿童,而且面向所有有特殊教育需求的孩子,包括有行为障碍、学习障碍和情绪障碍的孩子。弱智孩子由于大脑发育不全,动作协调性差,所以,他们大多数走路不稳,严重的甚至无法独立行走,每天要父母接送上学。学校除了每天早上进行走路训练外,还特地开设了一间康复室,针对孩子们的这一缺陷进行矫正。经过学校的训练后,多数孩子进步都很大。别看他们中有些人的走路姿势还很不规范,但对于这些孩子来说,能这样走路,已是很了不起的了。学校是一所特殊教育学校,学生大多是残疾人,有学生学的是面点。四年前有一位学面点的学生毕业时,洪佳琳很担心,怕他找不到工作,没想到新侨饭店招工时要了他,安排他在餐饮部工作。"饭店总经理、餐饮部经理都很照顾他,还派专人带他。"洪佳琳感到非常激动和欣喜。这里确实有太多的"特别",而这每一个"特别"中,又都凝聚着一个共同的东西——对弱智儿童诚挚的爱。大家被这些"特别"深深地感动了,也被这些特别的爱震撼了。

Hong Jialin spent her life pursuing the career of special education. For the past two decades, she made efforts with all staff to provide access to education for mentally retarded children, and provide opportunities for equitable development for them. She has been made a research continuously for the education of people with intellectual disabilities, and has founded the first high school for the mentally handicapped vocational education, the first caring center for mentally handicapped youth with rehabilitation training; established the longitudinally educational series of preschool education for mentally retarded children, as well as a nine-year compulsory education program and vocational education, and the horizontally educational system including education rehabilitation, medical rehabilitation and rehabilitation training. Therefore, she has formed a unique educational model for the mentally retarded. She has written lots of articles which got the national, provincial and municipal awards. She carried on her research work in a systematic and well organized manner based on her work experience. Her researches and experiments have laid a solid basis for further research. Many experts in this field are in full agreement with the principles of the school and the method of the work, when Hong Jialin worked as the Principal in Yanglingzi school. Her school enrolls not only mentally retarded and disabled children, but also enroll anyone who needs special education, such as behavioral disorders, learning disability and mood disorders. these children cannot walk well and need to be sent to the school by their parents, because of the hypoplasia of their brains which bring about the deficiency of motor coordination. The school arranges the children to do walking training every morning. Besides, there is a function rehabilitation room in the school for these children to correct their walking posture. Most students studying here are disabled and some of them learn baking. Four years ago, Hong once worried about a student when he graduated, but fortunately the student was successfully employed by Xinqiao Hotel and the student was sent to work for the food and beverage department. "Everybody here including the general manager takes good care of him," said Hong with proud and excitement. There are too many special things in this school and every special love for the disabled children, which has touched everyone.

【人物启迪】Character Enlightenment

我们学习的目的是什么？这是个复杂的问题。动机和目的因人而异，而简单的回答就是用知识去改变需要被改变的。这个社会有很多值得我们去研究的领域,献身于自己的研究事业,至少会造福一部分人群。洪佳琳这些努力改善弱智儿童生活的教育者,值得大家学习。教育的长河绵延不绝。一代代的教育人犹如不歇的河工,维护着教育之河奔涌前行。

What is the purpose of study? This is a complicated question for us to answer. The motivation and purpose of study varies from individual to individual. Briefly speaking, the purpose is to change whatever need to be changed. There are still numerous fields waiting for us to research. Devoting yourself to your study, you will benefit a group of people. Hong Jialin has made a great improvement for the intellectual disabilities' study and life, which is well worth studying. Educators are like river engineers who service and maintain the river going unobstructed.

故事七 束沛如——教与学相结合 Combining Teaching with Learning

【人物介绍】Character Introduction

束沛如,教师,1948 年出生。他创立了"束沛如烹饪技能教学法",荣获浙江省"首届优秀职教教学成果一等奖"。2004 年他被评为"杭州市十佳教师"。

Shu Peiru, teacher, was born in 1948. He created "Shu Peiru's Teaching Methodology of Cooking Skills". He won "The First Outstanding Achievement Award for the 1st Session of Vocational Teaching of Zhejiang Province". In 2004, he was named as one of the "Top Ten Excellent Teachers" in Hangzhou.

【人物事迹】Character Story

束沛如从 1981 年参与创立杭州第一个烹饪专业班开始,徒手创业,为全市烹饪专业教育的发展奠定了基础。20 余年来,他进行了以学生为本位,以技能训练为核心,以优化教学内容、教学方法和组织形式为途径的烹饪技能教学法的实践和研究。培养的人才不仅具有一技之长,还具有较强的思维能力。他创立了"束沛如烹饪技能教学法",并荣获浙江省首届优秀职教教学成果一等奖。目前，他正着手制定《烹饪专业教学大纲》《烹饪专业教学计划》和《烹饪操作设备标准》，统一全市烹饪专业开办模式。束沛如回忆道："办学之初条件十分简陋。第一是缺教材，当时没有现在这么多书和菜谱。第二是缺设备，学校只有煤炉，没有煤气灶。第三是缺技术，我们自身的烹饪水平也不高。怎么去教学生呢？我几乎放弃了所有的休息时间，业余时间四处拜师，到饭馆劳动学艺，自学专业理论，在家苦练技术。我们当时也请了一些退休的烹饪师傅来教我们。退休的师傅们有水平，会做菜，但不会讲，他们做一桌菜是很轻松的一件事，但要他们讲菜为什么这样做，就不行了。我们只有边听边自己总结一些规律性的东西出来。以前我们的老师都是'教菜为主'的，一个菜一个菜地教。这个教法不大合适。我们中国有八万多个菜，一天教一个菜也要两百多年才能教完。按照这个教法教完显然是不现实的。我在教学中就改'教菜为主'为'教技法为主'，教学生以技法为主，以菜为载体，用菜来学这个技法，举一反三，学生就会'精一通十'了。"束老师最高兴的事就是看到自己培养的学生能够得到社会的承认。他在烹饪领域成了大师，于是有很多企业都开出诱人的条件想聘他做餐饮顾问，但他都拒绝了各种各样的诱惑，还是选择留在职业学校，他认为他的主阵地就是在职业教育这块热土上。

From 1981 Shu Peiru participated in the establishment of Hangzhou's first professional cooking class, and laid the foundation for the development of the city's culinary professional education. During the 20 years, he has studied practical and student-centered skills training, in order to optimize the teaching content, teaching methods and organizational forms to cook. Trained people not only have cooking skills, but also higher thinking skills. He created "Shu Peiru's Teaching Methodology of Cooking Skills" and won "The First Outstanding Achievement Award for Vocational Teaching". Currently, he is working to develop "professional syllabus on cooking" "culinary professional teaching plan" and "standards for cooking equipment" to offer a unified model for the city's culinary specialties. He recalls, "The conditions were so simple and crude during those years we start running the school. We faced three main problems. Firstly, there were no course books teaching us how to cook; unlike today, there are many books in the bookstores. Secondly, there were short of equipment and device. There was only coal furnace but no gas cooker in the school.

Finally, we were not skilled in cooking and how should we teach our students? I gave up almost all my spare time to learn cooking skills from different masters in different restaurants. When I came back home, I studied specialized theoretical knowledge by myself and practiced over and over again at home. At that time, we did invite some retired cooks who were really talented and skilled to teach us. But there was still one big problem that those gifted cooks could not figure out the reasons why they cooked in that way, though they could easily prepare a table of dishes. We had to find out the regular patterns and summarize what the cooks taught us by ourselves. At that time, teachers taught their apprentices one dish after another, which was not good for the teachers and the apprentices. As we know, there are over 80 000 courses in our country, which requires over 200 years to finish learning them all if our teachers taught us in that way. It is unpractical. I adopted to teach my students the skills of cooking instead of teaching them the steps of cooking the courses. Students could draw inferences from their own experience by this learning method." The greatest pleasure for Shu Peiru is that his students are acknowledged by the society after they graduate from school. Being a master in this field, he inevitably faces many temptations that lots of enterprises want to employ him as their restaurant consultant with high pay. But he refuses them and stays in the vocational school where he believes his life battle is.

【人物启迪】Character Enlightenment

束沛如的教师生涯是从 1970 年开始的,最初他是原杭州五四职业学校的一名体育教师,1981 年才转到烹饪来。从此在烹饪教学领域收获了很多荣誉。正所谓兴趣是最大的老师。三百六十行,行行出状元。只要肯钻研,什么事情都能干好。学习不怕苦,就怕有心人。

Shu Peiru began his teaching career as a physical education teacher in Hangzhou Wusi Vocational School in the year of 1970. In 1981, he started to study cooking. Since then, in his new career he has harvested many awards. Interest is the best teacher. There are masters in every walk of life. One who fears the uneven paths can never reach the summit of a high mountain. Nothing is impossible to a willing heart.

故事八　张献斌——农业技术推广者 Agricultural Technology Disseminator

【人物介绍】Character Introduction

张献斌，农技站站长，1958年出生，“三农”模范人物。2009年，他因劳累过度突发心脏病去世，《人民日报》等几十家媒体先后对他的事迹进行了报道。

Zhang Xianbin, born in 1958, was the head of agro-technical station. He was named as "The Model of Agriculture". In 2009, he died of a sudden heart attack because of excessive working, and his stories were reported in many major media, including *People's Daily*.

【人物事迹】Character Story

张献斌扎根基层、爱岗敬业，三十年如一日，奋斗在条件艰苦的山区农业生产第一线；他心系群众、服务群众，无偿垫付资金和物资帮助农户发展生产。赵友好是丽新乡双坑村党支部书记，他说村民们柑橘卖得困难让张献斌揪心不已，也让张献斌操了不少心。后来，在张献斌的指导下，村里开始进行产业结构调整，控制椪柑种植面积，新发展了400多亩上市较早、价格较高的瓯柑。赵友好说：“为了帮助村民种好瓯柑，张献斌又是技术指导，又是送化肥农药。张献斌总说让农民过上好日子是天大的事，在他眼里这些瓯柑比什么都金贵！”为了帮助销售滞销的柑橘，他将自己生命累垮在了为农民卖柑橘的路上。多年前，丽新乡就有农民种茶叶，可效益一直不好。1998年，茶农钟凤鸣在自家的老茶园里，意外发现了几株发芽特别早、茶味特别香的茶树变异单株。他马上去找茶叶技术员张献斌。凭着敏锐的专业眼光，张献斌断定这茶树有培育价值。于是，他陪着钟凤鸣一家，一头扎进了茶山，一枝枝地教他们修剪，一株株扦插，一棵棵移植。每天早上，家人还在睡梦中，他就早早地上山了。整整3个多月，女儿只见过他两次。张献斌给这个新品种取名“丽早香”，意思是产自丽水、发芽早、茶味香。几年后，钟凤鸣家茶叶年收入 30 多万元，他们逢人便说，张献斌是他们的大恩人。张献斌与时俱进，刻苦钻研业务，练就了过硬的指导服务技能，并把知识和经验毫无保留地传授给身边的农技人员和农民群众，带出了一批熟练掌握农业生产技术的农技员。他与袁隆平等人被农业部授予新中国成立 60 周年“三农”模范人物。

Through three decades of dedication to the grassroots, Zhang Xianbin has struggled to improve agricultural production in difficult conditions in the mountains. He has cared for people and served people by helping farmers to develop production. Zhao Youhao, the Party branch secretary of Shuangkeng village, Lixin Town, told us that the difficulty of selling oranges was a sore point for Zhang Xianbin, who was anxious about it for a long time. Under the instruction of Zhang, the village began to readjust the industrial structure. The village developed a new 66 acres to plant a kind of orange which could come into the market earlier with higher price than others. Zhao said that in order to help the peasants, Zhang worked for them as their instructor as well as their carrier. Helping the peasants get well and make a good living was the top priority for Zhang. Oranges were more valuable than the gold in his eyes. To help sell unsalable masses of oranges, he died of excessive working on the way selling oranges for farmers. There were some peasants in Lixin Town planting tea but they earned little. In 1998, Zhong Fengming, a tea planter, claimed that he found one variant tea plant with special fragrance in his own tea plantation. He rushed to Zhang Xianbin and told him the surprising finding. With his professional judgement, Zhang concluded that this kind of tea tree was worth planting. He taught Zhong Fengming the skills to cultivate, prune and the method of transplantation. He went to the tea mountain very early every morning that his daughter met him only twice in 3 months. Zhang named this new kind of tea “Lizaoxiang” which indicated its place of origin and its features—sprouting early and having a special fragrance. Several years later, the income of the kind of tea reached 300 000 RMB for Zhong Fengming, who viewed Zhang Xianbin as his benefactor. Zhang Xianbin kept upgrading his professional technical skills and did sophisticated researches on agriculture issues. Meanwhile, he acquired a strong guiding service skills and taught agricultural workers and peasants around him without reservation. Under his guidance, a group of agro-technical workers had been grown up. Zhang Xianbin and Yuan Longping were honored as "The Models of Agriculture Since the Establishment of PRC for 60 Years" by the Minister of Agriculture.

【人物启迪】Character Enlightenment

张献斌学习时,把全部精力倾注进去;工作时,就像雷锋同志一样尽自己的努力为人民服务,并努力把工作搞好。

When Zhang Xianbin was studying, he put his heart and soul into the research. He was just like Comrade Lei Feng, who made every effort to serve people and carry the work through.

故事九 徐业——坚持自学的维和警察 A Peace-Keeping Police Persisting in Self-Studying

【人物介绍】Character Introduction

徐业,维和警察,1980 年出生。2011 年,联合国驻利比里亚代表团为徐业所在的中国第九支维和警队举行了隆重的授勋仪式,他被授予"联合国维和勋章"。

Xu Ye, a member of the peace-keeping police, was born in 1980. The delegation of United Nations in Libera held a great ceremony for Xu's group and he was honored with the "United Nations Peace-Keeping Medal" in 2011.

【人物事迹】Character Story

翻开徐业的个人履历,你会惊奇地发现徐业并非毕业于名门院校,也不是英语或警察专业出身。虽然第一学历仅为中专,但徐业却十分勤奋和刻苦,通过自学考试顺利取得了大专文凭。2002年12月更是凭着扎实的功底，通过公务员考试进入公安系统，完成了自己人生的转变，成为一名人民警察。在基层派出所工作时，虽然工作量大，但他仍刻苦钻研公安专业知识，虚心向老同志请教。在分局组织开展的知识学习考试结束后，他还被评为“十佳学习型公务员”。业余时间他还自学法律和英语。更难能可贵的是，从学校毕业至今，徐业一直没有放弃英语学习。虽然没有英语专业系统学习的经历，但他仍将学好英语作为自己的追求和爱好。平时，不管工作如何繁忙，徐业总是千方百计挤出时间学习英语。几年来，通过短期培训班、英语角、观看英文电视电影等方式，徐业的英语阅读、口语能力得到了快速提高。学到的知识很快就有了用武之地。2007年的一天，新桥派出所接到一位外国人的报警，接警民警由于外语基础差，无从下手。见状，徐业立即上前与外国人对话，询问案情，受理案件，制作笔录。老外惊喜不已，向他投以赞赏的目光，这更坚定了徐业继续学好外语的决心。机会总是垂青有准备的人，徐业一路过关斩将，经过层层考核，脱颖而出，终于成为一名维和警察。很快他被派往廊坊集训，时值我国三十年一遇的寒流天气，北方各地普降大雪，廊坊市的气温骤降至零下16摄氏度，这给徐业带来了重大的考验。他没有被寒冷、干燥和水土不服等困难所击倒，而是积极地迎难而上。每天早上6点10分起床集合，安排8节至10节的课程，徐业不曾皱过眉头。徐业回忆起了这样一个模拟训练场景：叙利亚发生一起杀人案，他和相关人员接警后赶赴现场处置。当时徐业等3人乘坐一警车，携带指北针和地图自行搜查目标。他们驱车数十千米进入一片荒原，照地图上所标注的方位查找了半个多小时，发现一条小道，进入后出现一个村落。道路越来越窄，陷阱越来越多。突然闯出3个蒙面人，将徐业等3人劫持到一片树林里。之后，徐业等3人和蒙面人斗智斗勇，终于跟对方谈判成功，脱离了困境。通过这次训练，徐业的谈判技巧和口语水平有了很大提高。

Looking at Xu Ye's curriculum vitae, you would amazedly find that his graduate school was not a prestigious one and his specialty was not English, nor police. Though Xu Ye only received polytechnic school education, he diligently studied on and successfully obtained a college diploma. Then, through civil service examinations, he became a member of the people's police in December, 2002. When he was working in local police station, although there were heavy workload, he still assiduously studied professional knowledge of public security, humbly asking to the experienced colleagues. After an examination held by the branch of the police station, he was also named the "Top Ten Excellent Learning-Type Civil Servant". In his spare time he also studied law and English. It is indeed something rare and deserving praise that Xu Ye has never given up learning English after he left school. Though he had no systematic English learning experience, he still took it as his pursuit and interest. No matter how busy he was, he tried to set time for learning English. His reading skill and spoken English had been improved quickly by participating in short-term training classes, English corner and watching movies. His displayed his prowess and abundant energies when a foreigner called the police one day in the year of 2007. His colleague could not understand the foreigner's words. Xu came to help to ask the details of the case, record and handle it. The foreigner was pleasantly surprised at Xu's language skills, which inspired Xu's determination of learning English. Chance always favors the prepared mind. Through all the levels of assessment, Xu Ye stood out, and finally became a peacekeeping police officer. Soon he was sent to Langfang to start training when it was the coldest winter in recent 30 years. It was a big test for him! However, he was not defeated by the unbearable cold and dry weather and he was not feeling sick during that harsh time, on the contrary, he kept moving without any frown. After he got up at 6:10 every morning, there were about eight or ten classes for him. There was a simulation training impressed Xu Ye a lot. The setting was set in Syria and the mission for him was to be in the spot of a murder. With the help of compass and map, Xu drove in a police car with another two policemen to search the target criminal. They entered into a wasteland after they drove around ten kilometers. Half-an-hour's search with the help of map, they found a path then in a short while they found a village. The path narrowed with more traps. Suddenly Xu and his fellows were set upon into a forest by three masked men. Xu battled with them with his fluent English and finally he won the negotiation and escaped the danger. Since then, Xu's oral English and negotiating skills had been improved even more.

【人物启迪】Character Enlightenment

英雄不问出身,只要你有一个清晰的职业规划和人生规划,成功并非遥不可及。牢牢铭记于心:成功的关键在于自己,在于自己的智慧,自己的雄心,自己的勇气和决心。对困难有充足的思想准备,努力战胜它们,让艰难的经历成为未来的竞争资本。

Many great men have arisen from humble beginnings. As long as you have a clear career planning and life planning, success is achievable. To remember that success lies in yourself, your own brain, your own ambition, your own courage and determination. To prepare for difficulties and force your way through them, you will turn hard experiences into the capital for struggles in the future.

故事十 朱佳龙——把优秀当成一种习惯 Taking Excellence as His Habit

【人物介绍】Character Introduction

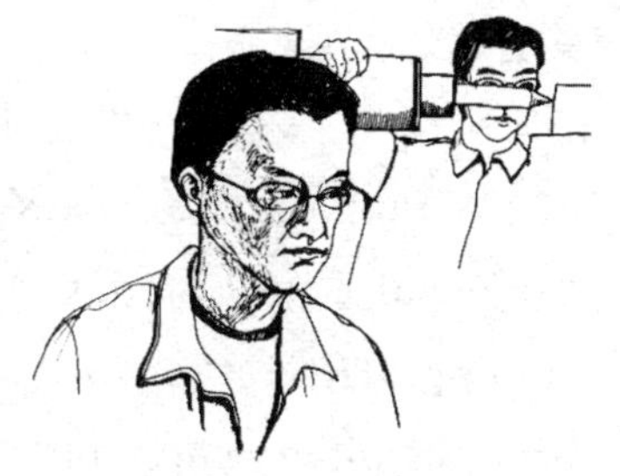

朱佳龙,公司员工,1985 年出生。他于 2006 他获得“杭州市技术能手”的称号,2008 年被评为“全国优秀农民工”,2011 年获得“浙江省五一劳动奖章”。

Zhu Jialong, worker, was born in 1985. In 2006, he was honored with the “Technical Expert of Hangzhou” and in 2008 he was named the “National Outstanding Migrant Worker”. In 2011, he won May 1st“Labor Medal of Zhejiang Province”.

【人物事迹】Character Story

这个 1985 年出生,没有显赫学历的农村青年,工作短短 5 年后就成了省级劳模。他是怎么做到的?朱佳龙出生于海宁农村,父亲是村里的能工巧匠,开了家农机店,朱佳龙从小在父亲的农机店里长大。他说,他对机械的特长和兴趣来自父亲的遗传和这一段经历。朱佳龙小学和初中时,除数学稍好外,其他功课都成绩平平,唯独对机械最感兴趣。在父亲的建议下,他读了海宁轴承专业学校。“把优秀当成一种习惯!”这是朱佳龙刚参加工作时书记对他说的一句话。他牢牢地记住了,把这句话作为自己的人生格言。第一次到车间时,面对一排排大型先进设备,他完全不知所措。于是他诚恳地向自己的师傅求教,晚上对着书进行强化学习。白天师傅在操作时,他跟在后面,目不转睛地看着每一个步骤、每项程序的输入、每种刀具的选用,甚至每一个动作手势……到了晚上别人漫步西湖,欣赏美丽的夜景,他却待在宿舍,把白天所学的在脑海中过一遍,记在本子上,把技术要领、工艺线路和程序运行结合理论形成自己的知识网络。为了精通数控机床的操作,朱佳龙下决心自学数控专业英语。他通过实践摸索专业词汇的意思,在说明书上做了详细的备注解释。就这样,通过刻苦的学习,他掌握了这些机械设备的相关理论知识和实践操作技能,迅速成为厂里的技术能手。他不断追求技术上的新突破,自制加工工具,成功地克服了技术瓶颈,大大提高了效率。培养这样一个熟练的操作工,一般需要 3 到 4 年时间,而小朱只花了一半的时间,就能独自操作如此大的机器了。“在数控加工领域,我需要学习的知识实在太多了。”2013 年,朱佳龙入选浙江省“金蓝领”高技能人才,获得了去新加坡学习的机会。28 天的海外“留学”生活,再次给这位年轻人打开了一扇窗,他每一天都如饥似渴地学习到深夜。“成功是靠一点一滴的努力积累起来的。我就是要证明,我们这一代年轻人一点都不逊色!”朱佳龙说。

Within only 5 years after Zhu Jialong began to work, he won a Provincial Labor Medal. How did he make it? Zhu was born in a village in Haining. His father was a skilled craftsman of that village and owned a farm machinery shop where Zhu often played when he was in his childhood. Zhu said that his interest in machinery profited from father's heredity and that playful time in that shop. He was not a good performer at primary and middle school except his interest in machinery. Taking his father's advice, he studied in a school with a specialty of axle bearing in Haining. “Being excellent is a habit” became his motto for life, which was taught by his Party secretary when he was enrolled in this company. Faced with rows of large advanced equipment for the first time, he was completely overwhelmed. So he asked the master for advice, and spent all night on intensive study. During the daytime, he followed after the master and watched attentively every step, such as how to input every procedure into the system, how to select the knife tools and even the gestures the master made. When others went out walking around the West Lake and appreciated the beautiful night scene, he stayed in his dormitory to review what he learnt in the daytime and wrote down the key points of techniques in his notebook. Finally there came into being his own knowledge network, which he connected theoretical knowledge with the practical operation experience. In order to operate the machines, he decided to study independently numerical control professional English. He made detailed explanations and noted on the books through his experimental practice with every professional word. He became to master the theory of those advanced equipment and the skills operating them. He quickly became one of the factory's technical experts. His constant pursuit of technological breakthroughs, and his ability to make homemade processing tools, successfully helped him to overcome technical bottlenecks, greatly improving efficiency. It required three or four years to cultivate a skilled operator like him. But he reached the same level and could operate such huge machine within only about two years. In the year of 2013, Zhu was sent to Singapore for further study, for he was selected as the member of the high skilled talents in Zhejiang Province. 28 days studying abroad was a precious experience for Zhu Jialong to open a window to know the world. He sat up late into the night and studied every day. He said, "There is still too much I need to learn. Knowledge comes from regular accumulation instead of a gift from God. I want to prove that people of my generation can be good."

【人物启迪】Character Enlightenment

干一行,爱一行;爱一行,干一行。也许后者对每个人来说才是最佳的工作状态。记住,兴趣永远是激发你的潜力的最好的老师。用朱佳龙自己的话说:"劳动创造梦想,我就是要通过努力使自己成为一名知识型、技能型的产业工人,为企业、国家的装备制造业的发展贡献一份力量。"

To love what you do? Or to do what you love? Maybe the latter one is the optimal working condition for everyone. Remember that interest is always the best teacher to motivate your potential. Zhu Jialong said, "Working creates our dream. I am ready to be a knowledgable and skill-based worker with my efforts. I am willing to devote my ability to developing manufacturing industry of our country."

故事十一 慎祖佩——坚守与钻研 Sticking to Her Post and Doing Research

【人物介绍】Character Introduction

慎祖佩,全国优秀教师,1950年出生。她扩大了珠心算这一中国传统文化精粹在国际上的影响力。她使得杭州九堡小学成为珠心算特色学校。

Shen Zupei, a national outstanding teacher, was born in 1950. She has expanded the international influence of the traditional Chinese culture of abacus mental calculation. She makes Jiubao Primary School become a specialty school for its abacus mental calculation.

【人物事迹】Character Story

慎祖佩从1972年开始在九堡小学当教师,一干就是30多年。当时农村的教育条件很差,只有100多个学生,校舍是两间草棚。慎老师和学生在学校里养了七八十只鸭子,养大后卖了钱用作办学经费。那时候,家长还没有那么重视孩子的教育,她经常上门动员孩子来上学。1977年慎老师的哥哥帮她找了一份工作,到丝厂做供销员。当时,做老师一个月只有十几块钱工资,丝厂供销员的月收入有100多元。虽然有这么好的一个机会,慎老师最后还是放弃了,因为对她来说,做一个受人尊敬的教师是她最大的心愿。慎老师很重视自身业务水平的提高,因为她知道,只有把孩子教好,才能实现自己的价值追求。为此,只有初中文化的慎老师,经常挤出时间去几十里以外的师范学校进修业务。她每天总是最先一个到校,最后一个回家。多年来,她精心钻研珠心算教学,作为一名全国优秀教师,她是以珠心算教学闻名的。她常年从事国际文化交流的工作,扩大了珠心算这一中国传统文化精粹在国际上的影响力。慎老师培养了一批又一批的“神算子”;结合教学特点,创造了兴趣教学、游戏教学、鼓励教学、团体教学等教学模式;还自创双手拨珠技法,培养了几百名学生。她鼓励学生努力学习:“这个世界上只有一种东西是别人无法从你身上拿走的,那就是你的智慧。”在学生们努力学习珠算的过程中,慎老师一直分享着他们的抱负,充分理解他们,尽她所能帮助他们。她将刻苦钻研的一套珠心算法毫无保留地传授给她的学生们。慎老师鲜明的教学特色,受到了家长和社区的好评,她的学生经常应邀参加珠心算表演。学校的特色教育引起了社会的关注,浙江电视台、中央电视台等多次报道了学校开展特色教育的情况。因她积极开展珠心算教学研究和推广,使得杭州九堡小学成为珠心算特色学校。

Since 1972, Shen Zupei has been working in Jiubao Primary School for over 30 years. At the beginning of her teaching career, the teaching condition was extremely poor with only 100 students and two huts as the teaching building. To earn funds for teaching, she raised about 80 ducks with her students and sold them after these clucks grew up. She had to visit the students' parents and persuade their parents allowing their children to continue studying. In the year of 1977, her elder brother found another job for her to be a saleswoman, which earned much more than that of being a teacher. But she gave up such good opportunity because being a respected teacher was her dreaming work. Shen had attached great importance to the improvement of her professional skills, as she knew that only teaching the students well, could she realize her value pursuit. So she set aside time to further study far away from the school as she was only with middle school educational background. She was always the first one to arrive the school and the last one to go back. Shen is an outstanding teacher, and is famous for teaching the abacus. Every year she is engaged in the work of international cultural exchanges, expanding the international influence of the traditional Chinese culture. Over the years, she trained many abacus experts. She created a very special teaching method with its features, such as interest-based teaching, game-based teaching, encouragement and group teaching. Besides, she also created playing the abacus with two hands by herself. With these teaching methods, hundreds of people became abacus experts. She encouraged her students to study hard, "there is only one thing that people can't take away from you, and that is your wisdom." In all her students' efforts to learn abacus, Shen Zupei shared fully their ambitions and sympathized with them and aided them in every way she could. Her distinctive teaching characteristics produce students' strengths, which are praised by the parents and the community, and her students are often invited to participate in abacus performances. The special educational features in the school had greatly drawn people's attention. CCTV and local TV station has reported it several times. Because she is active in teaching, researching and promoting the abacus, she makes Jiubao Primary School become a special school for the abacus mental calculation.

【人物启迪】Character Enlightenment

求知的路从来就不平坦,教书育人这条路更需要教师的坚守。面对诱惑时还能守住这份清贫,坚守自己的梦想。没有豪言壮语,慎祖佩用智慧与坚守,为孩子们编织着希望。

There is no easy way for learning. This job requires teachers to stick to their post when facing the lures of life. Without heroic utterance, Shen Zupei made a hope for the students with her wisdom and persistence.

故事十二　徐爱华——政策高参 A Senior Policy Adviser

【人物介绍】Character Introduction

徐爱华,法律援助律师,1958 年出生。她曾获"全国法律援助工作先进个人"称号,"全国三八红旗手"称号,2009 年获得"浙江省劳动模范"称号,2015 年获得"最美司法行政人"称号。

Xu Aihua, legal aid lawyer, was born in 1958. She was once honored with the "Outstanding

Legal Aid Worker in China" and "National March 8th Red-Banner Holder". In 2009 she won the "Labor Medal of Zhejiang Province". In 2015 she was honored as one of "The Most Beautiful Judicial Official of Zhejiang Province".

【人物事迹】Character Story

徐爱华是一位普通的法律援助律师,在舟山市却拥有很高的知名度。在领导看来,她是精通法律的政策高参;在群众心中,她是排忧解困的及时雨;在同事眼里,她是身体力行的带头人。徐爱华从1999年开始每月参与市长接待日,在政策和法律方面为市领导处理信访问题,当好参谋和助手。在参与接待信访的过程中,徐爱华认真引导来访群众通过法律途径维权,为符合条件的上访群众提供法律援助,对无理上访人员做到不歧视、不厌烦,向他们普及法律知识,宣传党和政府的方针、政策,引导他们正确对待改革发展中的利益调整,最终解开他们的心结。徐爱华精湛的业务技能给市领导留下了深刻的印象。为了维护受援者的正当利益,徐爱华反复理解书本中的专业知识,对里面的条文硬是吃了个透。在徐爱华受理的绝大多数案件中,外来民工的案件占了近80%。这些外来民工在很大程度上代表了社会弱势群体。"面对那些人,我总是想,只要我再努力一点点,就一点点,就可以帮到一个人,说不定是挽救一个家庭。"带着这份信念,徐爱华数年如一日地践行着一名法律援助工作者的应有职责,奔波于为弱势群体维权的道路上。有一天,一位白发苍苍的老人找到她,希望她帮自己讨个说法。他儿子在工地遭遇大火,全身烧伤,可责任方想方设法推卸责任。老人拿出一张单子,称是老板写给他的单位名称。徐爱华觉得此事蹊跷:"这家单位连医药费都不愿付,怎么会把单位名称写给当事人?"通过深入调查,徐爱华发现一个大陷阱——单子上写的单位是老人的儿子出事后新注册的公司,注册资本只有100万元,而原来的单位注册资本上千万元,足以偿付相关赔偿费用。徐爱华坚持不懈地奔走取证,最终为老人的儿子争得158万元赔偿款。人们称她一心护弱,是困难群众的"希望之灯"。

Xu Aihua is a common legal aid lawyer but she has a high reputation in Zhoushan. The leaders regard her as the senior adviser who is proficient in articles of the law; people regard her as as friend in need; the colleagues regard her as the foregoer of working. Since 1999, Xu has been participating in the activity of Mayor's Reception Day, handling numerous petition letters with her professional legal knowledge, which gained her good reputation. In the procedure of reception, Xu led the petitioners earnestly to maintain their legal rights in the law courts. She never discriminated those who put forward unreasonable requirements and never felt boring towards them. Instead, she popularized them the law rules and the Party's policies, guiding people to treat the adjustment during the reformation and finally helping them relieve the knots. The leaders are greatly impressed by her professional skills and knowledge. In order to protect the aid-receiving people's legal rights and interests, she made an intensive reading over and over again to understand laws and regulations in the books. The cases from the migrant workers, in total, accounted for about 80% of all cases Xu accepted. As we know, those migrant workers represented the vulnerable members of the society. Xu holds a belief, "looking at them, I am always thinking that if I tried harder, I could help one person, and maybe save a family." Years as one day, she lives up to the responsibilities a legal aid worker should have. One day, a grey-haired old man visited Xu for help, because his son had been burnt terribly in a sudden fire accident in a construction site. The old man felt helpless because the responsible party intended to shirk their responsibility. Xu was puzzled when the old man showed her a sheet with a company name on it. She thought, "how could they offer their company name to the wounded, for they refused to pay the medical expenses?" After further investigation, she found that there was a big pitfall in the whole case. The company on the sheet the old man had shown to her was a new registered one shortly after that fire accident with only one million registered capital, while the registered capital of the primary one was over ten million, which meant that the company was capable of paying the compensation expenditure. Finally, she fought for the compensation expenditure of 1 580 000 RMB for the old man's son with her insistent endeavor. She is the "Hope Light" for the people who need legal aid.

【人物启迪】Character Enlightenment

社会上的律师有那么多,为何徐爱华脱颖而出被大家赏识?没有辛勤的耕耘就没有秋天的收获。她的荣誉离不开她对政策与法律法规的研究。

Why does Xu Aihua stand out among the lawyer group and be appreciated by people? As a man sows, he shall reap. You didn't work, how can you enjoy the fruit? Her research for the policy, the laws and regulations brings her honor.

故事十三 吴文武——技术能手 Technical Expert

【人物介绍】Character Introduction

吴文武,公路站长,1965年出生。曾获"全国交通技术能手"荣誉。通过自学后他成为工作单位里的机械操作的多面手。

Wu Wenwu, the master of highway station, was born in 1965. He has been honored as the "National Traffic Expert". He became a versatile worker in the station by studying on his own.

【人物事迹】Character Story

吴文武参加工作近30年,从养路工到公路站长,从养护一线到养护中心机械队。他知道机械能减小劳动强度,提高工效,所以他买来了很多有关机械车辆方面的书籍,利用休息时间自学,以求把自己学来的机械知识运用到工作中去。多年来,他总是不断地总结学习经验,有所发现,有所创造,有所进步。可谓"功夫不负有心人",他获得了许多县级和省级的比赛奖项。2000年5月调入养护中心机械队当水车驾驶员,他自学压路机、摊铺机操作技术,并获得操作证,成为机械操作的多面手。2009年7月,当得知丽水市公路系统准备开展筑路机械比武消息后,他信心十足地报了名。比赛时,他有条不紊,成功夺得第二名的好成绩,获得丽水市人社局颁发的压路机操作工技师资格证书,并代表丽水市参加全省公路筑路机械大比武。在平常工作中,他服从领导安排，不管是在什么岗位上工作，他都尽心尽职，努力钻研本岗位所要求的工作技能，他说："在公路机械化施工中，我们就要发挥出机械的作用，为公路事业贡献自己的一份智慧与力量。"作为从事技术操作的一线工人，他是这个领域的骨干，在自己的岗位上做出了显著成绩，具备较高技艺并积极向新人传授技术技能。吴文武通过自身努力在同行业中取得了领先的技术能力，在生产工作中总结出先进操作技术方法为企业带来了良好的经济效益。

Wu Wenwu has been working for highway station for 26 years, from a platelayer to a master of this station, from a frontline worker to a maintainer of the central mechanical department. He, who fell in love with machinery, studied hard by himself the operating skills of diverse machinery. As he quite understood the importance of the machinery in the work, which could reduce labor intensity and improve work efficiency, he bought lots of professional books concerning mechanical vehicles to study and hoped he could use his knowledge in his work. For years, he has constantly summed up learning experience and gone on discovering, creating and advancing. He has got a lot of county-level and provincial prizes in competitions. After he was arranged in the central mechanical department being a waterwheel driver, he studied by himself the skills of operating steamroller and pavers and gained operating certificate. He soon became a versatile worker in the station. In July, 2009, he attended confidently to the Road Building Machinery Competition when he got the news from Lishui government. In competition, he won the second without any fluster though he was a little bit nervous. At the same time he also got the Machine Operator Certificate and continued to compete with others as the representative for Lishui. He was obedient to the leaders' arrangement in work. No matter what post he was arranged, he tried to learn by himself the skills the posts required. He said, "we need to make machines playing a major role in the process of mechanized construction and contribute our own power to highway career." As a member of the front line workers, he was the expert and backbone with high skills, who was willing to teach others in his company and made a great achievement for the company. He learnt the latest techniques with diligence and summed up good working methods in the process of production, which brought the company good economic benefits.

【人物启迪】Character Enlightenment

有了准备,我们就能恰当地应对各种复杂的局面。而我们做的准备工作,其本身就是学习的过程。有了学习的沉淀与积累,我们在工作时总是会充满力量。积极的应对是鼓起勇气着手解决。对于看似无法控制的难题,当你能够控制自己的应对方式,那么实际上你就控制了难题对你的影响。你对难题的应对是至关重要的、最根本的。遇到的难题可以使你脆弱,也可以使你坚强;它可以使你痛苦,也可以使你升华。这一切全在于你自己。

Being prepared well, we shall be able to deal properly with all kinds of complicated situations. The process of doing preparation is itself a kind of learning process. The accumulation of years of learning will fill us with power when we are doing our work. The positive solution to a problem may require courage to handle it. When you control your reaction to the seemingly uncontrollable problem, then in fact you do control the problem's effect on you. Your reaction to the problem is the most important part. Difficulty can make you tender or tougher. It also can make you bitter or better. It all depends on you.

故事十四　方重——从中专生到副行长 From a Secondary Technical School Student to Be a Deputy President of a Bank

【人物介绍】Character Introduction

方重,金华银行支行副行长,1980 年出生。他是该行这一级别最年轻的干部之一。他曾获得共青团金华市委 2010 年度"青年岗位能手"荣誉称号。

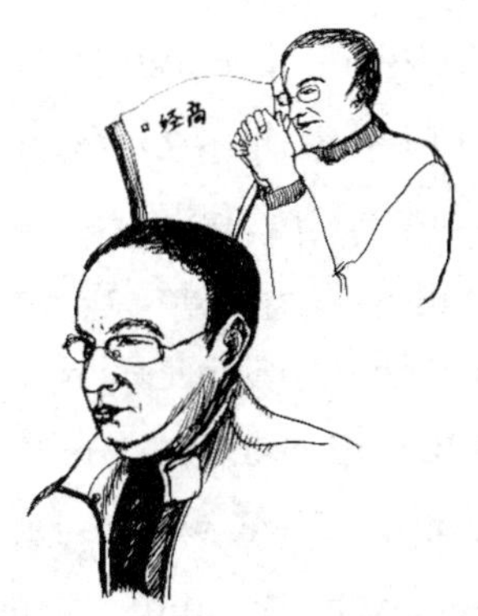

Fang Zhong, Vice President of a sub-branch of Jinhua Bank, was born in 1980. He is one of the youngest leaders with the official title in the bank. He was awarded the "Youth Expert of Jinhua City" in 2010.

【人物事迹】Character Story

方重是金华银行一支行的副行长，是该行这一级别最年轻的干部之一。1995 年，中考结束后自信满满的他，在得知自己的成绩与重点中学失之交臂后，如同跌进了冰窖。他去读了中专。深知考学艰辛的方重在完成中专课程和班级管理工作之外，利用课余的每一个空隙学习。到了工作岗位，在工作之余，他孜孜不倦地埋头于自考书中。这里没有辅导老师，也无人可以请教，但他硬是啃下了一块块硬骨头。他深深地记住了一句话：我们现在播种什么，当我们人生的秋天来临的时候，就会收获什么。如果我们要获取丰硕的收成，摘取珍贵的果实，确保充裕的秋天，那么现在，在这个人生的春天，我们就必须勤勤恳恳、小心翼翼地培育我们的种子。1998 年，他高分通过《基础会计学》，同年，又一举通过了《管理学原理》《国际贸易》《商品学概论》。2002 年，原来 6 个学分的《外贸英语》改为 12 个学分的《基础英语》，学习内容增加了一倍。方重英语基础相对薄弱。“决不能功亏一篑！”方重给自己打气。他用长期自学摸索出的一套学习方法学习，用“悬梁刺股”的典故来磨练自己，终于啃下了英语这块硬骨头。他用了 8 年的时间陆续考完 13 门课。2003 年，方重取得大专文凭。2004 年，方重凭着大专文凭和丰富的实践经验幸运地考取了金华银行。之后他以出色的工作业绩，做到了支行的副行长。即使进入这样一个安稳的工作环境，他还是不忘学习，又取得了本科文凭。“机会总是留给有准备的人。”方重觉得学习让他受益终生。

Fang Zhong is a Vice Director of a sub-branch of Jinhua Bank and he is one of the youngest leaders with the official title in the bank. In 1995, Fang failed to be enrolled by the key high middle school, though he had thought that he would get a satisfactory score. He had no alternative and went to study in a polytechnic school. Knowing the hardness and bitterness of studying, he treasured every narrow chance to learn. Besides finishing all courses the polytechnic school required, he studied the courses the junior college required. Even when he started his career, he still sedulously studied without any help from others. He always remembered that the autumn of life will come on apace; and that what we now sow, so what we shall then reap. If we would reap an abundant harvest, gather precious fruit, and secure an autumn of plenty prosperity, we must now, in the springtime of life, be diligent and careful in the cultivation of our life.

In 1998, he passed examination of *Fundamental Accounting* with a high score and passed the tests of *Management Principles*, *International Trade* and *Principle of Commodities*. In the year of 2002, the credit for the course of Foreign Trade English changed from 6 to 12, which enriched its content as nearly twice as before. English was his weakness. Fang encouraged himself, "it will be a pity if I gave up when it is nearly completed!" Using his own learning method he summed up during his long time self-studying experience, he persisted at his studies and finally passed the English examination. It took him eight years to finish all tests of thirteen courses. In 2003, he gained Junior College Diploma. In 2004, he passed the enrollment examination held by Jinhua Bank and became a bank teller. Step by step, he became the Vice Director of a sub-branch of Jinhua Bank on account of his outstanding achievement. Even he worked in such a steady workplace, he kept studying and gained Bachelor's Degree. Fang thought that the process of studying would benefit him the whole life, and he said, "opportunities are always for those who are well prepared."

【人物启迪】Character Enlightenment

把全部精力倾注到学习中去,学习就会回报你,因为中国有句古话:"书中自有黄金屋,书中自有颜如玉。"有时,一些事情发生了,它们看上去是那么可怕、痛苦和不公;但细想一下你就会明白,如果没有去努力克服这些难题,你将永远也不会知道自己的潜能、力量、意志力和你的决心。

Those who put his heart and soul into the study, the knowledge he learnt will repay him a lot, as there is an ancient proverb in China, "within books, one can find houses of gold. Within books, one can find ladies as fair as jade." Sometimes things happen to you and they may seem horrible, painful and unfair, but in reflection you will realize that without overcoming those obstacles, you would never know your potential, strength, willpower and mind.

故事十五　阮林根——爱钻研的民警 An Assiduous Policeman

【人物介绍】Character Introduction

阮林根，台州民警，1968 年出生。他先后获得“浙江省优秀人民警察”“省模范人民警察”“全国公安机关爱民模范”“全国优秀人民警察”等荣誉称号，荣立个人二等功、三等功各一次。2014 年他被评为“最美浙江人——2014 年度浙江骄傲人物”。

Ruan Lingen, policeman from Taizhou, was born in 1968. He has been awarded a series of honorary titles, such as “The Excellent Policeman” in Zhejiang Province, the “Provincial Model Policeman”, “National Model of Caring about People in Public Security Organization” and “National Excellent Policeman”, a Second-Class and a Third-Class merit citation. He was honored as “The Most Beautiful Zhejiang Citizen—the Pride of Zhejiang” in 2014.

【人物事迹】Character Story

阮林根刚开始做民警时，在一次“警民恳谈”活动中，与老百姓坐在一起聊天不欢而散，因为老百姓把平时对警察的怨气都撒在他的身上，指责警察破不了案，抓不到小偷。阮林根很是郁闷，回去思考了很久，他决定改变方法，做到真正地与老百姓融合在一起。为了抓住小偷，他摸索了很多防盗方法与技巧，找到各类案件的防范技巧，并对辖区发生的盗窃案件逐个进行研究，弄清作案手段与规律，寻找应对措施。对一些自己弄不懂盗窃原理的案件，他就拜小偷为“师”，找犯罪嫌疑人聊天，在聊天过程中，小偷们把他们平时如何盗窃如何诈骗的方法都交代给他，从而一一破解了小偷们的盗窃“秘籍”。那时候，他为了弄清家庭门窗的防盗办法，用自己家的门窗、锁具做试验，使得他家的门窗千疮百孔。

阮林根说：“我们公安干警也要与时俱进，知道现在的小偷惯用的一些手法。目前小偷的手段也是五花八门,我们需要知道他们怎么做,这样才能给老百姓提供更多的安全保障和服务。”为了让群众看得懂,他将这些知识物化为道具,攒下了9箱“宝贝”,里面都是防盗的器材。

通过不断地观察、琢磨、实践,现在他已经成了名副其实的防盗专家。阮林根把自己辛辛苦苦摸索出来的工作经验毫无保留地传授给同事。在他的指导培养下,许多社区民警逐步成长为社区工作的能手。阮林根的事迹得到各级公安机关肯定后,来向阮林根学习取经的人络绎不绝,全省各地乃至全国各地许多公安机关都邀请阮林根上门授课。阮林根只要有空,都会前去授课,倾囊相授。他的经验在全省许多公安机关中已经得到借鉴推广,名气和影响力也不断扩大。阮林根把荣誉当成前进的动力,根据工作经验总结提炼的《阮林根社区警务工作法》,被群众出版社正式出版,成为社区警务工作极有价值的参考资料。

When Ruan Lingen became a policeman, there was an unpleasant conversation between people and him in an activity named “Conversation with People”, as some people complained that policemen were not intelligent enough to catch the thieves. Ruan thought it for a very long time to search for a better way to communicate with people. In order to catch the thieves, he explored various anti-theft methods and techniques by studying burglaries. He sometimes even learnt from the thieves he caught. During their talking, the thieves would tell him how to burgle and he would finally puzzle out. During that period, he did a lot of anti-theft experiments the doors and windows in his own house on which left numerous holes.

Ruan said, “we policemen should keep pace with the times, as the thieves have mastered quite advanced stealing techniques now. We need to know how they steal. Only in this way can we provide people a better security service.” He materialized the anti-theft knowledge into real anti-theft properties which had filled nine boxes.

Now he has already become a veritable anti-theft expert because of his continual observing, thinking and practicing. Ruan passed on all the working and anti-theft experience to his colleagues without any reservation. Many a policeman has become the community working expert under Ruan’s guidance. Ruan gradually becomes popular especially after he got praise from his immediate superior. There was an increasing number of people coming to him and seeking for his experience from various areas. He was invited to give lectures in the whole nation. What's more, most of his anti-theft experience has been popularized among different public security units. Ruan views the honor as the driving force. Meanwhile, according to his own experience, he published a booklet *Ruan Lingen's Community Police Work Service Method* to guide people to keep security.

【人物启迪】Character Enlightenment

阮林根在平凡的岗位上爱岗敬业,为国为民无私奉献,取得了不平凡的业绩,也获得了荣誉。他是我们的好榜样。他不仅在为工作而努力,为群众而奉献,更为信仰而笃行。

Ruan Lingen serves our country and people in such an ordinary position and gets a great achievement. He is a good model for us because he is not only fighting for his job and people, but also for his belief.

故事十六 汪建华——眼神作家 A "Winking" Writer

【人物介绍】Character Introduction

汪建华,《把心捂热》的作者,与其妻子吴梅丽同时荣获"最美浙江人——2014年浙江骄傲"称号。

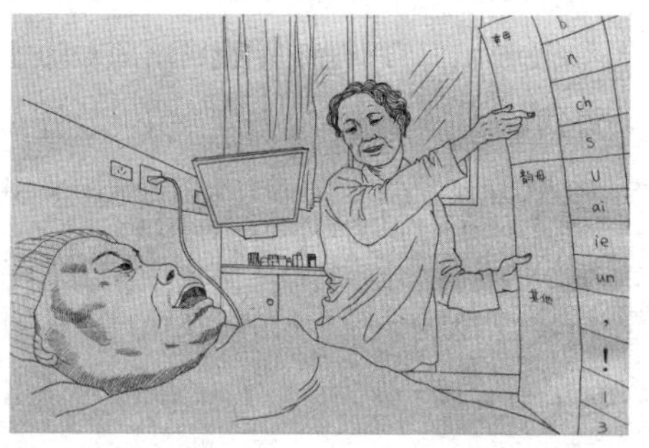

Wang Jianhua, was the author of *Warming the Heart*. He and his wife Wu Meili were honored as "The Most Beautiful Zhejiang Citizen—the Pride of Zhejiang" in 2014.

【人物事迹】Character Story

2006年10月6日,对汪建华夫妇来说,是个难忘的日子。这一天汪建华被确诊为"运动神经元病",全身肌肉逐步萎缩,成为只能用眼神沟通的"渐冻人”。这对他们来说无疑是晴天霹雳。为了支付高昂的医药费，汪建华的妻子背着丈夫卖掉了市区的房子。为了照顾生病的丈夫，她提前从待遇优越的岗位退休，所有心思都系在丈夫身上。肢体训练，吸痰、按摩、换药、挂点滴，甚至换呼吸管、尿管，安插胃管这些颇有技术难度的护理工作都是吴梅丽8年来每天的必修课。

有一天汪建华的女儿汪璐在看一本杂志，汪建华非常激动，眼睛一直转个不停，他女儿十分不解，吴梅丽看到了，就问：“你是否要看杂志？”只见汪建华一只眼闭上，另一只眼继续转动，吴梅丽读出来丈夫在说她只猜对了一半。猜了半天，吴梅丽试探地问：“你不会是想写书吧？”这时候汪建华眼珠子上下飞快地转动，表示她猜对了。不会说话，不会行走，连呼吸都只能依赖机器的丈夫居然要写书！吴梅丽很开心，因为这至少说明她丈夫还有精神上的追求。

吴梅丽买来拼音图，把它贴在一个大纸板上，分成声母、韵母和标点三个部分。汪璐还建议妈妈用手机同步拼写，以尽快找到爸爸想用的字。拼音板上有23个声母和24个韵母，吴梅丽挨个指一遍，每指一次，就看一眼丈夫。如果丈夫的眼球左右转动，就是错了；如果上下转动，就是对的。如此，声母和韵母组合在一起，就可以拼出一个字了。每写一个字都需要花好几分钟，最难的是写诗歌，很多的字词吴梅丽把握不准，于是她把这个字做好标记空在那里，等他们女儿来医院后再确认。汪建华以转动眼球的方式与他的妻子沟通，并在妻子的协助下，用整整四年的时间靠眼睛写出了一本四万余字的生命日记——《把心捂热》。

他用自己的意识创造了人间奇迹，谱写了一曲生命赞歌。这几年，汪建华又开始了音乐创作。吴梅丽最初对音乐一窍不通，到现在能帮助丈夫创作。汪璐为了让妈妈有更直观的感受，建议用电子琴辅助她学音乐。每个旋律，汪建华都要在脑海里琢磨很久。写一首歌需要好几个月。写完之后，不满意，他还要改。第一首歌《秋韵情满》，是他写给女儿的，因为他到不了婚礼现场。第二首歌是《融化吧，渐冻的心》，他想通过这首歌曲，鼓励病友们，不要畏惧，不要放弃，要坚强。尽管他只能无声地和他人交流，但他活出了生命的质量。我们期待生命的奇迹。

An unforgettable date fell on October 6, 2006 for Wang Jianhua and his wife. It was on the day that Wang Jianhua was diagnosed with motor neuron disease, which would gradually cause muscle wastage and finally he would become an amyotrophic lateral sclerosis patient who could only move his eyes. The news was like a thunderbolt out of a clear sky. To pay the high medical expenses, unbeknownst to her husband, Wu Meili sold out their house in downtown.

To take care of her sick husband, Wu Meili decided to retire from a well-paid position in advance. She was committed to look after her sick husband. She assisted him with lots of work, such as body movement training, sputum intubation, massage, changing his dressing, intravenous infusions, even changing breathing and ureter tubes and placing stomach tubes which required very professional training. For eight years, she was always his family nurse.

One day, Wang became extremely excited and rotated his eyeballs very quickly when his daughter Wang Lu was reading a magazine. His daughter couldn't understand what Wang Jianhua's intention was. Neither did his wife. Wu Meili asked, "Do you want to read magazine?" Wang closed one of his eyes and rotated another eyeball which meant Wu had only got half of the information he conveyed. Finally Wu tentatively asked him, "you want to write a book, don't you?" At this time, Wang rotated his eyeballs very fast which meant his wife had got the information. It was this man who cannot speak, nor to walk, even breathing dependent on machine, that unexpectedly wanted to write a book. Wu felt very delighted that her husband still had his spiritual pursuit.

To support Wang's idea, Wu bought a syllable graph with three parts of initial consonant, vowel and punctuation. Wang Lu suggested to use cellphone to assist her mother to confirm the correct characters her father adopted. There were 23 initial consonants and 24 vowels, Wu had to point every single one and turned to look back her husband to make sure which one was what he wanted. If his eyeballs rotated from left side to right side, it referred to NO; If from top to bottom, it referred to YES. In this way, combining the consonants and vowels, they spelt Chinese characters. At the beginning of his book, it required several minutes to find out the correct character. The most difficult for Wu Meili was to assist Wang finding out the character when he wrote poetry. So she left those characters and made marks and discussed with their daughter. They had been astonishingly persistent, and got a good reward. Finally, the book *Warming the Heart* with 40000 characters was published which took four years to compile. Wang created a miracle in this world with his consciousness and a piece of music composed of love echoing in the world.

In recent years, Wang began to compose music with the help of his wife who knew virtually nothing about music at the beginning. Wang Lu suggested her mother using electronic organ to assist. Every single melody that ran through his brain for a long time. It would take several months to compose a piece of music. He had been trying to improve his works if there was any discontent. His first song *Passionate Love in Autumn* was for his newly-married daughter, as he could not be the wedding scene. His second song *Melting*, *the Freezing Heart* was for the patients, encouraging them not to give up and fight for the victory. Though unable to answer, he communicate with other people in silence, he lives an excellent life. We expect the miracle on him.

【人物启迪】Character Enlightenment

或许是老天的安排,在最终找到自我之前,我们总要碰上不尽人意的麻烦。也许只有这样,我们才能对健康这份礼物充满感激之情。一道幸福之门关闭时,另一扇就会打开。成功属于那些受过伤害的人,那些探索的人,以及那些尝试过的人。因为只有他们才懂得珍惜自己与相关的人。真正的美丽源于学习、成长和热爱。这就是生命的艺术。

Maybe God wants us to meet a few troubles before we finally find ourselves. Then we will know how to be grateful for the gift—health. When the door of happiness closes, another opens. Victory lies for those who have hurt, those who have searched, and those who have tried, for only they can appreciate the importance of people who have touched their lives. Real beauty comes from learning, growing, and loving. That is the art of life.

第四章
向善 Kindheartedness

一　向善内涵
Connotation for Kindheartedness

在我国的传统文化中，孔子提出“仁者爱人”，孟子则强调与人为善，其内涵都在于以善为原则帮助成就他人。“向善”价值观一直以来都得到人们的推崇，无论在东方文化还是西方文化中，“向善”都被视为宝贵的美德。

In the traditional culture of China, Confucius put forward, “the benevolent person loves others”. Mencius stressed “helping others”. Their connotation lies in helping others with principles of goodness. Values for kindheartedness have always been worshiped in both eastern and western culture. “Acting for goodness” is considered as a precious virtue.

二　向善力量
Force towards Kindheartedness

“向善”作为一种核心价值观，一方面指引人们人格的完善和公民道德的培育，另一方面引领社会关系和秩序的优化。

Kindheartedness acts as one of the core values. It guides the improvement of people’s personality and cultivation of citizen’s high moral values. In addition, it optimizes the social relations and social order.

三 向善名言
Quotations on Kindheartedness

行善积德。 One good turn deserves another.

善有善报。 Do well and have well.

四 向善故事
Stories on Kindheartedness

故事一 吴菊萍——最美妈妈 The Most Beautiful Mother

【人物介绍】Character Introduction

吴菊萍,阿里巴巴(中国)网络技术有限公司员工,1980年出生,浙江嘉兴人。她于2011年被杭州市总工会授予"杭州市杰出职工"荣誉称号,被全国妇联授予"全国三八红旗手"荣誉称号,并获得2011年"感动中国"人物奖。

Wu Juping, from Jiaxing city of Zhejiang Province, was born in 1980. She works in Alibaba (China) Network Technology Co., Ltd. She was awarded the honorary title of "Outstanding Employee" by the Federation of Trade Unions in Hangzhou and "March 8th Red-Banner Holders" by the All-China Women's Federation. She was one of "The Top Ten People who Moved China" in 2011.

【人物事迹】Character Story

2011 年 7 月 2 日下午一点半，在杭州白金海岸小区，一个 2 岁女童坐在一户人家的窗沿上。不一会儿小孩的哭声从楼上传下来，只见孩子挂在了阳台上，双脚悬空，双手使劲扒住窗台。大约过了一分钟，孩子终于坚持不住从 10 楼窗台上坠落。在危急的瞬间，楼下穿着小格子连衣裙的吴菊萍估摸着小女孩掉落的位置，从人群中健步冲出，张开双臂，在小女孩快速落地的一刹那，用左手臂硬生生接了小女孩一下，“砰”的一声，两人一起重重摔倒在地。小女孩稚嫩的生命得救了，但吴菊萍的手臂瞬间被巨大的冲击力撞成粉碎性骨折。救治医生说吴菊萍是冒着生命危险做好事。因为如果孩子掉落地点稍微有些偏差，假设落在脖子上，她可能高位截瘫；落在头上，就可能当场死亡。当时吴菊萍有一个刚满 7 个月大还没有断奶的儿子，由于治疗需要服用大量药物，她便毫不犹豫地听从医生的建议提前给孩子断了奶。吴菊萍说：“我没有后悔，毕竟我接住的是一条人命，出于本能，这是任何一位母亲应该做的事情。现在最大的心愿是小女孩能够平安快乐成长。”

这一感人事迹在网络上热传，受到海内外的关注，无数网民为之动容，称其为“最美妈妈”。在美国有网民甚至建议授予她诺贝尔和平奖。美联社、法新社、英国《每日邮报》等欧美媒体，巴基斯坦媒体、中东媒体都报道了“最美妈妈”吴菊萍的事迹。世界各地众多网友都赞扬吴菊萍是一个“守护天使”。

At thirty past one p.m. on July 2, 2011, a two-year-old girl sat on the window still. Suddenly people heard a loud cry and saw that the toddler was holding the window still tightly, her hanging feet down. After holding on for about one minute, she fell down from the ten-story building. At that critical moment, roughly locating where the baby might be landing, a woman in grid dress, named Wu Juping, rushed out from the crowd, outstretched her two arms and tried to catch this falling girl with painstaking efforts. With a sound of banging, they dropped to the ground.

This young life was saved by the cushion of her arms. But Wu Juping's arms suffered a comminuted fracture because of the massive impact. The attending doctor said that Wu Juping was risking her own life to save the toddler, if the landing point was not sure. For example, the toddler fell down on Wu Juping's neck may lead to paraplegia. If the toddler fell down on her head, it was highly probable that she would lose her life. Meanwhile, since Juping needs to take large amount of medicine during the treatment process, and she has a 7-month son without weaning, she listened to the doctor's advice and firmly decided to wean her son. She said that she did not regret it as she saved a life and by instinct, that was what she should do as a mother. The only wish she had was that the toddler girl could grow up safely and happily.

This moving event spread over the Internet, affecting people all over the world and touching countless netizens to the heart. Netizens all called her "The Most Beautiful Mother". Some netizens in America even suggested that she should be awarded the Nobel Prize for Peace. *The Associated Press*, *Agence France-Presse*, *Daily Mail* and other media in Europe, Pakistani media and media in the Middle East all reported the story of "The Most Beautiful Mother". Netizens around the world all acclaimed her as a guarding angel.

【人物启迪】Character Enlightenment

我们无法解释这样一种应对突发事件的本能反应。"最美妈妈"吴菊萍的事迹体现了中华民族的传统美德和人性大爱,她不计后果的爱心托举,不仅给坠楼女童妞妞带来了生的希望,也激发着全社会的向善力量。吴菊萍用双手托举起生命、托举出"真、善、美"大爱,她的事迹感动了杭州,感动了中国,感动了世界。对"真、善、美"的追求是我们全人类共有的价值观。

It is probable that sometimes we cannot explain the instinctive response to emergency. The story of "The Most Beautiful Mother", Wu Juping reflected traditional virtues of China and the great love of humanity. Her reckless action of kindness not only saved the toddler's life and brought her hope, but also triggered everyone's power toward goodness. Wu Juping lifted life and held high the banner of "truthfulness, goodness, beautifulness". Her story has moved people in Hangzhou, in China, and in the world. The pursuit of "truthfulness, goodness, beautifulness" is undoubtedly our shared value.

故事二　王海文——南丁格尔奖得主 A Winner of Florence Nightingale Prize

【人物介绍】Character Introduction

王海文,海军第413医院麻醉科护士长,1968年出生,浙江宁海人。她的事迹被中央电视台“小崔说事”、人民网、新华网和《解放军报》等多家新闻媒体报道,2013年被评为“全军巾帼建功先进个人”,并荣获“第44届国际南丁格尔奖”。

Wang Haiwen, from Ninghai in Zhejiang Province, was born in 1968. She is a head nurse in the Anesthesiology Department of the No. 413 hospital. Her story was reported by the CCTV talk show *Stories talked by Cui Yongyuan*, Xinhua net. com, People. cn, *PLA Daily* and many other news media. She was rated as “Meritorious Advanced Individual Female in Army” and won “The 44th Session of Florence Nightingale Prize”.

【人物事迹】Character Story

1989年王海文护校毕业后选择分配到舟山,成为解放军第413医院的一名护士。入院第一年,她就主动申请加入了舟山红十字会千岛巡诊队。怀着对护理这份职业的无限热爱,王海文在每个岗位,从妇产科、门诊部、传染科,再到麻醉科,都争取做到最好。工作中她就像一名敢拼的先锋战士,对待任何一件小事都十分认真。考虑到王海文的出色表现,组织安排她担任要求最严、责任最大的手术室的护士长。期间她所在的麻醉科从未出过一起差错和事故。

24年来,王海文乘小艇、搭渔船,深入56个海岛、120多个哨所、70多个村庄,巡诊送药300余次。她还先后参加“抗击非典”“亚丁湾护航”“和谐使命”等12次重大卫勤保障任务,累计航程近10万千米,足足可以绕地球两圈半。2009年,王海文参加的海军东海舰队首批护航编队从舟山出发赴亚丁湾、索马里海域执行护航任务。除了短暂的停靠补给外,176天的护航几乎都在海上。在大洋上,她克服高温、高湿、高盐、高噪音等恶劣环境,每天巡诊、开展心理疏导,详细记录各种条件下官兵晕船反应的数据和心理变化,为研究远海执行任务官兵的心理、生理健康积累了第一手宝贵的资料。

三个月后她再次主动申请参加为期88天的“和谐使命2010”任务,给吉布提、肯尼亚、坦桑尼亚、塞舌尔、孟加拉等亚非五国提供医疗援助服务。在肯尼亚,一位疟疾病人上吐下泻,病床上到处都是排泄物,家人害怕传染,都不敢靠近。王海文见状后,二话不说就为病人擦洗身体,更换床单,没有一丝恐惧和嫌弃。除了照料患者,王海文还经常给海岛战士邮寄药品、化验单,给内向腼腆的官兵介绍对象,给吵架的夫妻劝和,帮远在外地的官兵看望父母,为即将远航的父亲照顾妻小。在同事眼中,王海文就像一块磁铁,因为她总是能把大家都吸引到一起。她用实际行动诠释了“人道、博爱、奉献”的南丁格尔精神,把中国人民的友谊带到了异国。

In 1989, Wang Haiwen was assigned to Zhoushan, becoming a nurse in the No. 413 Hospital of PLA. In her first year in the hospital, she voluntarily applied for joining Qiandao clinical visiting team of Zhoushan Red Cross. With great passion for the vocation of nurse, Wang Haiwen did her best in every position, from Obstetrics and Gynecology, Outpatient Department, Infectious Disease Department, to Anesthesiology Department. She always works like a soldier and treats every small issue extremely seriously. Because of her extremely serious outstanding performance, Wang Haiwen was assigned to act as the head nurse of the operating room that has the most strict requirement and highest responsibility. When she was in charge of that department, neither one accident or mistake has happened.

For 24 years, Wang Haiwen has taken boats to 56 islands, more than 120 outposts and 70 villages, to make her rounds of visits and send medicine more than 300 times. Also, she has successively taken part in 12 medical support tasks, including fighting against SARS, escorting in the Aden Gulf, Harmony Mission and so on, with total voyage of nearly 1 million kilometers. In 2009, the first convoy of Navy's East China Sea Fleet, which Wang Haiwen joined, departure to Aden Gulf and seas off the Somali Coast to carry out escort missions. Apart from short stop and replenishment, they were on the ship for 176 days in total. She needed to overcome different kinds of severe environment such as high temperature, high humidity, high salinity, loud noise, and so on. Everyday, she made rounds of visits, conducted psychological counseling, and carefully recorded officers' data and psychological change when they felt seasick in different conditions. This information can help to study officers' mental and physical health condition when they are implementing the mission.

Three months later, Wang Haiwen voluntarily applied for participating in the task of "Harmony Mission 2010", which would last for 88 days. They need to provide medical service for five Asian and African countries including Djibouti, Kenya, Tanzania, Seychelles and Bangladesh. In Kenya, a malaria patient's diarrhea and vomiting made excreta all over the bed. His relatives were afraid of infection; thus they dare not get too close to him. Without any hesitation, fear and dislike, Wang Haiwen helped that patient clean his body and change the sheet. Apart from looking after patients, Wang Haiwen regularly sent medicine and laboratory sheets to officers on islands, helped shy officers to find partners, acted as a mediator when couples are arguing, helped officers far away from home to visit their parents and look after their families. In the eyes of her colleagues, Wang Haiwen is like a magnet, because she can always attract people together. She is making a commitment to explain the Nightingale spirit of "humanity, love and dedication", and sowing the seeds of friendship to foreign countries.

【人物启迪】Character Enlightenment

爱与善,并不一定在于悲壮、宏大。"海文姐姐"将随处可见、触手可及的平凡做到了极致,用平凡彰显大爱,用真诚和笑容温暖了身边的每一个人。她的事迹鼓励我们:每一个人,都可以立足自身的工作和生活,用平凡、平淡和奉献,去书写真正的人间大爱。

Love and goodness doesn't always mean something tragically grand or imposingly magnificent. Our elder sister Haiwen made the best of what was within her reach, pervading ordinariness to share her deep love through it, warming everyone around by her sincerity and smiles. Her stories encouraged each of us that everyone, keeping a foothold on his or her own career and life, is able to write out the true love in the world.

故事三　方亚儿——不是亲人，胜过亲人 Not Close Relatives, but Closer than Families

【人物介绍】Character Introduction

方亚儿，宁波市鄞州区高桥镇高峰村人，1975 年出生，获评"最美浙江人——2012 年度浙江骄傲人物""第三届浙江省道德模范"。

Fang Ya'er was born in 1975 in Gaofeng village in Gaoqiao town, Yinzhou district, Ningbo. She was named one of "The Most Beautiful People—the Pride of Zhejiang" in 2012 and "The Moral Model for the 3rd Session of Zhejiang Province".

【人物事迹】Character Story

1991 年，方亚儿与董雪云同厂做工，成为好友。两年后，董雪云患白血病过世。当时还是一个 19 岁少女的方亚儿许诺给雪云的父母做女儿，自愿承担起替亡友照顾家人的重担。20 年的时间，方亚儿一直践行着自己的承诺，无微不至地照顾着雪云的家庭。她帮雪云残疾的哥哥娶亲，给久病的雪云父母看病，接送侄女读书。她用跨越血缘的亲情，撑起了一个饱经风霜的家庭。即使这个家庭接二连三地遭遇变故，方亚儿都没有想过离开，而是主动承担起更多的责任。2011 年春节，董爸爸中风，身体左半部瘫痪。几个月后，董妈妈也被查出患胰腺癌晚期。她在得知自己的病情后彻底失去了信心与希望，打算出院不接受治疗了。但方亚儿却没有一丝犹豫，放下所有家务事，专心在医院做起陪护，悉心照料董妈妈。在董妈妈接受治疗的一个多月里，方亚儿联系了所有的亲朋好友，通过各种途径到处打听治疗胰腺癌的好方法和好医生。那段日子，方亚儿在医院照顾董妈妈，一直陪到晚上她入睡了才匆匆赶回家。同时为了不耽误工作，她常常和丈夫一起熬夜加班到凌晨四五点。第二天早晨天一亮,又赶到病房陪董妈妈。多年来,方亚儿、她丈夫以及他们的亲生父母都一直照顾着董家,三个大家庭亲如一家人。没有血缘,这份情却浓得化不开;不是亲生女,却相守一家亲。

In 1991, Fang Ya'er made a friend with Dong Xueyun when they worked in the same factory. Two years later, Dong Xueyun died of leukemia. Though Fang Ya'er was only 19 years old at that time, she promised to become Xueyun's parents' daughter, and voluntarily shouldered the responsibility of taking care of Dong Xueyun's family. During over twenty years, Fang Ya'er kept her promise and took good care of Xueyun's family. Specifically, she helped Xueyun's brother look for partner and get married; she accompanied Xueyun's parents to see the doctor when they were sick; she dropped off Xueyun's niece outside the school and picked her up. Transcending the boundary of blood affection, she shored up a shattered family. During the twenty years she has never thought of leaving, though misfortunes did always come to this family. On the contrary, she took the initiative to take more responsibilities. In the spring of 2011, Dong Xueyun's father suffered from a stroke which paralyzed the side of his body. A few months later, Dong Xueyun's aged mother was diagnosed with terminal pancreatic cancer. After knowing that, Dong's mother totally lost hope and confidence, and she wanted to give up the treatment and leave the hospital. However, Fang Ya'er put down all household chores without any hesitation in order to take a special care of these two sick and vulnerable old people. During that period, Fang Ya'er called every relative and friend, trying to ask for the best method and doctor for cancer treatment. She took care of Xueyun's mother in the daytime, and rushed home until she went to sleep at midnight. In order to not delay the work, Ya'er and her husband usually burned the night oil to work overtime early in the morning until 4 or 5 o' clock. On the next day, she arrived at the hospital to accompany Xueyun's mother again. Over the years, Fang Ya'er, her husband and their parents all took good care of Xueyun's parents. This large family live together very happily. This affection is too thick to be dissolved, though no consanguinity helps to forge. Fang Ya'er is not their daughter biologically, but closer than a family member.

【人物启迪】Character Enlightenment

在道德观念遭遇冲击和洗礼的时代，人们愈发渴望“善”的能量。“老吾老以及人之老，幼吾幼以及人之幼”，是深植于每个中国人心中的种子。“最美女儿”带给我们的感动会让这颗种子在我们心中发芽、开花、结果。每一个社会中的人，无论身为人子，身为父母，或为任何一个角色，都要学会善待身边的人，社会才会更温馨。

Nowadays people increasingly desire to have energies of kindheartedness in the world in which moral ideas are challenged or even changed towards deterioration. The old saying of “caring the old as they are your own parents and feeding the young as they are your own children” is a seed deeply-rooted in everyone’s heart. What “The Most Beautiful Daughter” has brought us can make this seed rooted in ourselves to sprout, blossom and bear fruit. Every member in our society should learn to be kindly helpful to people around, no matter who he or she is and what role he or she plays.

故事四　周晓丽——光明使者 The Lightbringer

【人物介绍】Character Introduction

周晓丽，现任义乌市残联育智教育中心负责人，1979 年出生，浙江义乌人。周晓丽抛开父辈的生意不做，卖掉机器腾出厂房创办脑瘫康复部和育智教育中心。10 年间陆续接收了 900 多名智障脑瘫儿童。由于媒体的报道，她一夜之间成了名人，有网友甚至称她为“最美富二代”。

Zhou Xiaoli was born in Yiwu of Zhejiang Province in 1979. She currently takes charge of Intellectual Education Center of the Disabled Federation in Yiwu. During 10 years, she accepted more than 900 mentally disabled children with cerebral palsy. The netizens call her “The Most Beautiful Affluent Second Generation”.

【人物事迹】Character Story

2002 年 5 月，周晓丽与丈夫举资创建义乌市首家民办康复机构——义乌市残联脑瘫康复部。2005 年 8 月，她抛开父辈的生意不做，卖掉机器腾出厂房，在市残联、教育局的大力支持下，又成立了义乌市残联育智教育中心，填补了义乌市智障儿童特殊教育的空白。据介绍，智障儿童康复机构现有 30 多位脑瘫儿童，120 多位智障孩子，10 年间陆续接收了 900 余名智障脑瘫儿童，其中大部分困难家庭的孩子都是免费接受治疗。周晓丽发明了一种“千万遍教学法”，每天都教孩子们生活技能和文化知识上百遍，直到这些孩子们掌握。孩子们刚转到义乌智障儿童康复中心时会有些自卑，很少说话，也不愿意与其他孩子一起玩，因为他们很敏感，在之前的学校里常常受到其他同学异样的目光。在康复中心待了一段时间之后，有些孩子学会了写字，甚至还学会了谈恋爱、写情书。这令周晓丽十分欣慰，因为也许孩子们并不知道喜欢的含义，但他们开始知道去关心别人，说明他们的智力已经在慢慢康复。

周晓丽坚持了 10 年，其间的艰辛一般人都难以承受，更何况这个本在温室中生长的富二代，她为残障儿童做出的一切，都是值得肯定的。在每天收获着快乐与成就感的同时，周晓丽也常会担心，害怕孩子们受伤，精神压力非常大。针对全校大约三分之一家庭困难的学生，周晓丽给予了他们减免学费的待遇。这些来自于经济与精神方面的压力曾让周晓丽和她的丈夫产生过要中断办学的念头。最终家人的支持与更多孩子的康复还是使周晓丽夫妻俩坚持了下来。把爱无私地奉献给了这 900 多名残障儿的富二代周晓丽，谁能不爱？她，就是天使在人间。

In May of 2002, Zhou Xiaoli and her husband established and funded the first non-governmental rehabilitation institution—Cerebral Palsy Rehabilitation Department of the Disabled Federation in Yiwu. In August of 2005, she abandoned her father's business and sold the machines to make room for the Intellectual Education Center of the Disabled Federation, which she has just set up under the support of municipal disabled federation and which filled in the gap of special education for retarded children in Yiwu. Based on the data, currently there are more than 30 children affected with cerebral-palsy and more than 120 with intellectual disabilities in this rehabilitation institution. In the past ten years, she accepted more than 900 mentally disabled children with cerebral palsy. Children who came from poverty-stricken family received free treatment there. Zhou Xiaoli has invented the"A Thousand Times for Teaching" method and taught children life skills and knowledge over hundreds of times a day, until they are quite familiar with these aptitudes. When these children at first came to the rehabilitation institution, they suffered from the inferiority complex and were not willing to communicate with other children, since they were very sensitive and suffered from weird looks from other people. After staying in the institution for a period of time, some children learn to write words, and some even learn to write love letters. Zhou Xiaoli is very pleased and delighted. Though these children may not know the meaning of love, they have come to learn how to care about other people, which shows that their intelligence has been gradually recovered.

One can hardly bear the hardships of ten years, let alone a girl who is born to be rich, under the sheltering of her parents. What she has done for retarded children merit our recognition and respect. Though enjoying the happiness and the sense of accomplishment everyday, Zhou Xiaoli fears that bad things may happen and children may get hurt; thus she suffers from high mental pressure. Meanwhile, Zhou Xiaoli lets students from financial distressed families enjoy the tuition waiver, which brings financial pressure to her and the school. She and her husband once had the thought of stopping the school due to these high financial and mental pressures. However, the whole family's support and the hope of more children's recovery encouraged them to stick to it. We love this angel who selflessly devotes affection and love to those over 900 retarded children.

【人物启迪】Character Enlightenment

爱的奉献,爱的传递,是永恒的旋律。周晓丽不光善良无私,更难得的是她的毅力。多少人还没开始就放弃了,又有几个能坚持十年?当今社会方方面面的事都需要去做,周晓丽弯下腰尽心做了自己能做的,为别人点亮了一盏灯,送去了一份希望。如果人人都能像她这样,我们的社会将是充满爱与希望的。

The dedication of love and the transfer of it are the eternal themes. Goodness and selflessness are not the only one by which Zhou Xiaoli wins our admiration and appreciation, but most importantly, her determination, which is hard to come nowadays, moves us to give our praise on her, given that how many people give up even before they set out, and how many people can truly persist in a cause for ten years. It is true that there are so many things and problems which affect every aspect of our society waiting for us to do and address. There is no denying that even Zhou Xiaoli, as an ordinary one, sometimes feels powerless in dealing with problems. But what makes her different from other people is that she really manages conscientiously and persistently to light other people's dark life and send out loads of hope. Our society will be brimming with love and hope if all people can do as she does.

故事五　贾建平——法官妈妈 The Judge Mother

【人物介绍】Character Introduction

贾建平，现任浙江省湖州市南浔区人民法院审判员,1953 年出生，浙江湖州人。她先后获得“全国少年法庭先进个人”“全国巾帼建功标兵”“全国关心下一代先进工作者”“全国优秀女法官”“全国三八红旗手”“全国模范法官”等 10 余项省级以上荣誉称号及立功嘉奖。

Jia Jianping, born in 1953, at present holds the office of a judge of the People's Court at Nanxun district of Huzhou in Zhejiang Province. She has received more than ten honorary titles at or above the provincial level and meritorious service awards such as “The National Advanced Individual of the Juvenile Court” “The National Female Pacesetter ” “The National Advanced Worker for Caring about the Next Generation” “National March 8th Red-Banner Pacesetter” “The National Model Judge”.

【人物事迹】Character Story

贾建平 1990 年调入法院,先后从事经济、民事审判工作,2000 年起一直从事未成年人刑事审判工作。多年来,她以维护社会和谐稳定为职业追求,以未成年人思想道德建设为主线,以教育、感化、挽救失足青少年为己任,结合审判工作实践,不断摸索创新符合未成年人心理特点的审判方式,坚持寓教于审、惩教结合,探索和总结出了一套行之有效的“爱心工作八法”,使青少年犯罪案件从受理、社会调查、法庭教育、延伸帮教,到普法宣传形成了一套操作性较强的工作程序,充分发挥了少年审判的职能作用,取得了良好的法律效果和社会效果。五年里,她审理的案件无一错案,无一发回重审或改判。她不遗余力地帮教了 100 余名少年犯,使一大批失足青少年走向社会、走向新生,她也被群众亲切地誉为“法官妈妈”。

为了挽救失足的孩子,贾建平时常拖着积水的膝盖和疼痛的双腿,在乡间的路上不停地奔波,常年往返于学校和社区之间,调查、走访,做孩子们的思想工作。贾建平自创圆桌审判方法,以平等的视角对待当事人。为了给少年犯今后的改造和漫长的人生道路予以正确的启迪和指引,贾建平仔细剖析每一位少年犯的成长轨迹和个性特点,还增加了附在严肃的判决书后面的法官寄语。为了给所有需要咨询和帮助的人带来便利,她还自己创建了帮教网络和帮教基金,开通了“法官妈妈”热线。同时,为了减少未成年犯罪,五年来贾建平先后与 12 所学校合作建立德育基地,兼任 4 所学校的法制副校长和校外辅导员,为 30 多所学校上过法制教育课,深受学生和家长的喜爱,受教学生、老师和家长 4 万余人。

Jia Jianping was transferred to court and successively engaged in the economic and civil trial work. Since 2000, she has devoted herself into the juvenile criminal trials. She always kept in her mind that to maintain social harmony and stability is a life-long career pursuit, to construct adolescent's ideology is a top priority, to educate, influence, and remedy troubled teenagers is an important task. Over the years, she constantly searches for and innovates the trial mode that is consistent with minor psychological disturbances by virtue of the practice of judicial work. She has explored and summarized a practically effective “eight methods for work of loving”. Through persisting in education in trial, combining punishment with education, she has helped to form a smooth flow of operational procedures such as acceptance and hearing a case, social investigation, the court investigation, the extension of helping and education, the promotion of general law, obtaining good legal effect and social effect. In the past five years, she has never misjudged a case and the cases she heard has never gone through a retrial or commuted. She has spent tremendous effort to help and educate more than 100 troubled teenagers, assisting these teenagers once more to embrace the society or to restart their life. The general public all cordially called her "Judge Mother".

In order to save these young people, Jia Jianping kept running on the road, dragging her painful legs and bearing arthritis. She typically went between schools and community for researching and visiting offenders, their families, and doing careful ideological reeducation. Jia Jianping created the "round table judging method" to treat guilty parties from an equal point of view and guide and inspire young offenders in their future transformation process and new life Jia Jianping carefully analyzed every young offender's growing process and personality, and added her expectations to the end of the written judgement. In addition, to bring great convenience to those who need assistance and help, she established the help and education website and fund, and opened the "Mother Judge" hot line. In the meantime, in order to decrease teenagers' crime rate, Jia Jianping has cooperated with 12 schools to establish moral education bases during five years. As legal vice-president and off-campus counselor, she taught legal classes and all students and their parents quite like her. Totally more than forty thousands students and parents have attended her class.

【人物启迪】Character Enlightenment

未成年人是家庭幸福稳定的基石,是社会和谐安康的希望。贾建平,这位从事少年审判工作的优秀法官,不放弃任何挽救失足未成年人的机会,以"让每个家庭都和谐幸福"作为其崇高的追求,将司法为民的要求落实到本职工作中,行使好手中的权力,履行好自己的职责,实现了不让父母们再哭泣的誓言,为数百个家庭营造了祥和安乐的气氛,为社会奏响了和谐安宁的音符。

Teenagers are the foundation where homely grace is built and the hope of social stability and harmony. Jia Jianping, a good judge engaging in juvenile retrial, has never given up any opportunity which can in any way remedy the troubled teenagers so as to maintain the harmony and bliss in every family. To exercise judiciously her power and to fully perform her duties is central to the realization of not wringing one single drop of tear from parents, which is enshrined in her solemn oath. Her wonderful achievement has created a peaceful atmosphere permeated with happiness in every family and played a fanfare of harmonious notes throughout our society.

故事六　张杰——瘦弱老人造福社会 A Thin Old Man Benefits the Community

【人物介绍】Character Introduction

张杰,1927 年出生,浙江上虞人,1959 年赴香港定居。他因长期捐助家乡教育,1997 年被浙江省人民政府授予“爱乡楷模”称号,2006 年被评为“浙江骄傲”十大年度人物,并被浙江省上虞市人民政府授予“上虞乡贤”的称号。

Zhang Jie was born in Shangyu of Zhengjiang Province in 1927. He settled in Hong Kong in 1959. He was awarded “Model of Loving Hometown” by the People’s Government of Zhejiang Province in 1997, and in 2006 he was rated as one of “The Top Ten Characters—the Pride of Zhejiang”. He was named “The County Sage” by Shangyu local government of Zhejiang province.

【人物事迹】Character Story

张杰,是一位在香港以卖大闸蟹、茶叶蛋谋生的上虞籍平凡老人。关闭了几十年苦心经营的小店后,张杰的生活来源比以前少了许多,只能依靠子女的供养和以前开店积攒下来的钱生活。尽管日子过得并不宽裕,张杰始终非常热切地关注着家乡,每次回乡探亲总想为家乡做点什么。1979 年一次回乡的所见所闻彻底改变了他的生活。那天他走进上虞中学,发现整个学校找不到一个像样的实验室和图书馆,教室光线暗淡。于是,他慷慨解囊,为上虞中学捐建了图书馆、宿舍楼和许多器具。张老先生的人生理想就是以捐资兴学的方式回报家乡。30 多年来,他始终怀着回报家乡、造福桑梓的强烈愿望,节衣缩食,省吃俭用,支持家乡的教育事业,至今已累计捐赠 1200 余万元,让 1.5 万多名学生受惠。除了在教育事业方面的贡献,张杰老先生还捐资改善梁湖镇敬老院贫困老人的生活。八十岁大寿那年,当他得知子女为他准备了一笔祝寿的资金后,想到家乡不少贫困老人的窘境,他马上联系有关部门,委托慈善总会把这笔资金捐给了全市敬老院老人。

Zhang Jie is an ordinary old man who made his living on selling hairy crabs and tea eggs. After closing down his store, his source of income decreased, so he depended on his own saving and children's income to maintain his life. Though he was not rich, he was always concerned about his hometown and was very willing to do something for it. In 1979, he came back to his hometown, which totally changed his life. On that day, he visited Shangyu Middle School only to find a shabby laboratory, a library with few volumes and classrooms with dim light. He was so touched that he donated a large sum of money for the building of library, dormitories and teaching instruments. Zhang Jie's ambition was to serve the hometown through donating the school establishment. In the past 30 years, he tightened his belts in order to donate more money to the education cause in his hometown for he always harbours a strong wish to repay hometown. He donated money totalled 12 million RMB and more, benefiting more than fifteen thousand students. Besides contributing to education, Zhang Jie also made donation to improve old people in the nursing home of Lianghu town. On the birthday of his eighty years old, when he knew that his children prepared a large amount of money to celebrate his birthday, he donated money to all old people living in nursing home around the city through the charity organization. He wanted to use the money to help these old people and resolve some of their difficulties.

【人物启迪】Character Enlightenment

一个靠着卖大闸蟹、茶叶蛋,做小本生意过日子的平凡老人,用自己一分一厘省吃俭用抠出来的钱帮助家乡数千儿童上学,这着实不简单。钱财有价,精神无价。张杰留给我们的,显然不仅仅是几幢楼房,他身上的那种振兴中华的抱负、心系故乡的真情、仗义舍己的美德是更为宝贵的精神财富。

It is indeed extraordinary for an ordinary old man who lives on small business to save every cent in order to ensure that the kids in his hometown will not drop off school because of poverty. The material wealth has its limit but spiritual wealth does not. What he brought us is not just several buildings, but precious spiritual wealth such as the ambition to make China more strong, the unbreakable bond with native soil, and the determination to sacrifice his comfortable life for the sake of others.

故事七　2300 位宁波市民 2300 Ningbo Citizens

【人物介绍】Character Introduction

2300 位宁波市民,6 天内为青海患病女教师罗南英捐出 60 万元。他们是一群充满爱心的无名氏,而无数个这样的群体,构成了真正意义上的"人民"。这 2300 名宁波市民被集体评为 2005 年度"浙江骄傲——最具影响力人物",同时获得了最有分量的单项奖"最具感动奖"。

2300 citizens in Ningbo donated 600 000 RMB within 6 days to a female teacher diagnosed with leukemia in Qinghai. There are so many anonymous people showing the true meaning of "People". The whole group of those 2300 Ningbo citizens was rated as "The Pride of Zhejiang—The Most Influential People" and they are also the recipients of the most significant single award "The Most Moving Prize".

【人物事迹】Character Story

2005 年 3 月,青海乐都高店乡 29 岁的语文教师罗南英被诊断为白血病。她经人介绍来到宁波市第一医院治疗,虽然姐姐可以为她提供骨髓供体,但

60 万元的医疗费用难住了她。她决定放弃治疗,忍着肉体和精神的双重折磨开始给 3 岁的儿子写信。她希望儿子在每个生日都能看到母亲生前预留给他的信。她要给幼小的儿子留下一点什么,让他长大后知道母亲对他最真实的情感,感受到母亲对他深深的爱。同时,她也希望这些信能为儿子在今后生活的每一个关键时刻都带来温暖和力量。信在《宁波晚报》发表后,她对儿子的深沉母爱打动了宁波市民。2300 名宁波市民在一周内为她捐款 60 万元,400 多位市民冒着酷暑到医院看望她。这些人中,既有捐 5 万元的成年人,也有将身上仅有的 1 元钱捐出的孩子。在厚厚的捐款记录本上,留下的捐款人大多是“某小姐”“免姓名”,匿名捐款人数占了 80%,善良的宁波人民都不愿透露自己的姓氏。

在为罗南英捐款的日子里,宁波有无数的妈妈、父亲和孩子为她奔走,发生了许多动人的故事。他们为罗南英那种深深的母爱而落泪,想要千方百计地挽救她的生命。不仅是为一个儿子留住母亲,为一个丈夫留住妻子,为两位老人留住女儿,为学子留住他们的老师,更是要让我们一起来见证爱心的力量。此事经新华社、《人民日报》、中央人民广播电台、中央电视台及各地一百多家媒体报道后,宁波,这座以商业传统而闻名的城市,今天,以爱心而闻名国内。全国各地的读者还给宁波起了另外一个称呼——“爱心城市”。

Luo Nanying, a teacher teaching Chinese living in Gaodian of Qinghai, was diagnosed with leukemia in March of 2005. She was recommended to get treatment in the First Hospital in Ningbo. Though her elder sister can provide matched bone marrow, the cost of six hundred thousand yuan embarrassed her. She made a decision to give up treatment and started to write letters to her 3-year-old son, enduring both physical and mental pain. She hoped that her son would read letters she has written in advance. She wanted to leave something for her son, letting him know his mother's affection and sense a deep motherly love when he grows up. Also, she hoped that these letters could bring warm and strength for her son in every important moment in his future life. The citizens in Ningbo were deeply touched when they read the letters published on newspaper. 2300 citizens in Ningbo donated six hundred thousand yuan to the diseased female teacher within six days, and more than 400 citizens visited her under burning sun. Some of them were adults donating 50000 yuan, and some were children donating the only 1 yuan in their pockets. In the donation list, most of names were like "Miss XXX", "No Name", and so on. These kind of citizens were all unwilling to reveal their names, and the percentage of anonymous people was about eighty percent.

In the process of donating money for Luo Nanying, a lot of mothers, fathers and kids were busy for her, thus a lot touching stories were enacted. They were moved by Luo Nanying's deep motherly love. They aimed to make every endeavor to save her life, not only for Luo Nanying's son, husband, parents, and students, but also for witnessing the strength of love together. Ningbo was reputable across the country after this story was reported by Xinhua News Agency, *People's Daily*, China National Radio, CCTV and others more than one hundred local media. Readers around the country all called Ningbo "the City of Love".

【人物启迪】Character Enlightenment

奉献爱心，为困境中的人点燃希望，是我们中华民族的传统美德。帮助别人解决困难和痛苦是人生最大的幸福和快乐。在改革开放经济高速发展的现在，我们更需要提倡这种奉献精神。现代化的重要标志不仅是物质的充裕，更重要的是精神的高尚，是市民的整体素质的提高。博大的爱，会让一座城市更温馨，更和谐，更亮丽。宁波市民无私大爱带来的爱的冲击波，有助于中国人增强爱的意识，激发爱的激情，提高爱的能力；这对化解矛盾，消除隔阂，减少冲突，增进幸福将产生神奇的作用，使社会更加和谐。

It is our traditional virtue to dedicate love and light up hope for those in trouble. It is the greatest happiness and pleasure in one's life to help others to solve out difficulties and relieve their pains. Nowadays, even with the reform and opening up and the rapid development of economy, we still need to call for the spirit of dedication and kindness. One of the most important symbols of modernization is not the profusion of material, but the noble spirit and the whole improvement on the overall moral quality of the citizens. The expansive loving heart will make a city more harmonious, bright and lovingly warm. Ningbo citizens' story would benefit Chinese people by increasing their sense of love, inspiring their stimulation of love, and enhancing their ability of loving. Furthermore, these can help to resolve antagonisms, bridge the gap, decrease conflicts, and increase the sense of happiness, so as to bring harmony to the whole society.

故事八 黄小荣——最美爸爸 The Most Virtuous Father

【人物介绍】Character Introduction

黄小荣,1963年出生,浙江富阳人,富阳市万市镇众缘村荣腾机械有限公司总经理。他被授予"杭州市见义勇为积极分子"荣誉称号。

Huang Xiaorong was born in 1963 in Fuyang, Zhejiang Province. He is the general manager of Rongteng Machinery Co., Ltd in Zhongyuan village of Fuyang city. He was awarded the title of "Individual for Righteous Behavior in Hangzhou".

【人物事迹】Character Story

2011年8月29日中午12点,万市镇众缘村荣腾机械加工厂厂长黄小荣如往常一样,刚踏出食堂大门,一个有点面熟的小女孩急匆匆地跑过来,喘着粗气大声求救。黄小荣赶紧在求救女孩的带领下赶往事发现场。他眼前的堤坝有足足五六米高,唯一一条通到水渠的小路在另一头,绕过去至少得多花10分钟时间。深水区的水深足有1.5米,要是耽误了时间后果不堪设想,黄小荣果断地从堤坝上跳下去。由于动作过猛,他右脚接触水泥地面时,缓冲不够,后脚跟粉碎性骨折,但他忍着剧痛一步一步爬上前去救人。烈日下,他在粗糙的地面上爬行了十几米,到达小女孩落水处。他慢慢地下水,向前游行,待手够得到小女孩时,一把将她揽入怀里,然后再慢慢地游回堤岸。此时,溺水女童已经失去知觉,身体冰凉,面色苍白,嘴唇发紫,肚子胀起,但仍有气息。凭借自己平时积累的急救知识,黄小荣赶紧拍击女童的背部和腹部,用手指将她嘴里的污物抠出来。在众多好心人的共同努力与帮助下,黄小荣用自己有效的急救方式将女童挽救下来了。

救护车赶到现场之后,急救医生说要是再晚半分钟,孩子的命就没了。女童清醒过来了,但是黄小荣却由于右脚后跟骨折,被转往富阳市中医骨伤医院救治。骨伤科医院张院长分析说,骨折后的疼痛一般是在几分钟后发作,所以黄小荣爬的时候右腿应该是不能动弹,之后很快会感受到剧痛。他给孩子急救的时候,可能是剧痛暴发的时候,这个时候他一定是靠自己坚强的意志力和宝贵的精力支撑着自己坚持给孩子做心脏按压。

At 12 o'clock of August 29, 2011, the factory director, Huang Xiaorong of Rongteng machinery plant, stepped out of the canteen just now, a girl who looked only a little familiar rushed up to him, gasping out for help. Huang Xiaorong hurried to the scene, led by this distressed girl. The height of the dam in front of him was nearly five or six meters, and the only way to the canal was the other side of the road. It may take almost ten minutes to get there. As the depth of the deep end was about one and a half meters and it was really dangerous if they delayed, Huang Xiaorong jumped from the dam without any hesitation. Unfortunately, he found that his heel suffered a comminuted fracture owing to the lack of cushion when he fell to the ground. Under the burning sunshine, he crawled more than ten metres on the rough ground to the place where a girl was supposed to have fallen into the water and entered the water. Slowly he swam forward. He took the girl into his arms with great strength when the girl was reachable. Then he, with the girl in his arm, slowly swam back. After being saved on the land, the girl almost lost consciousness. But she still had a little breathing with her cold body, pale face, cyanotic lip and swelling stomach. Relying on his accumulated first-aid knowledge, Huang Xiaorong clapped the girl on her back and stomach and got the dirt out from her mouth by using his fingers. Finally, with the kind help of the surrounded people, Huang Xiaorong saved the girl from death.

When the ambulance arrived, the doctor said that the girl may lose her life if Huang Xiaorong had taken first-aid measures even late for half a minute. However, though the girl sobered up, Huang Xiaorong was sent to Fuyang Orthopedics Hospital to receive the treatment due to his right foot fracture. According to the president of the hospital, people will feel the pain of fracture after several minutes. So when Huang Xiaorong was crawling, his right leg could not move, and he may feel the pain right away. It is highly possible that it was at the time he was doing cardiac massage that his pain broke out. Therefore, Huang Xiaorong was relying on his strong will and valuable spirit that support him to carry out first-aid measures successfully.

【人物启迪】Character Enlightenment

明知会受伤,面对坚硬的水泥护坝和约5米的高度,他毅然跳了下去;右腿粉碎性骨折的剧烈疼痛让他差点失去知觉,但看着水中的孩子,他毅然爬行十多米后游到水中,救起了溺水的孩子。他的一句话让我们印象深刻:“再晚一分钟可能就来不及了,孩子的一条命和我的一条腿,你说哪个重要?”危难时刻方显英雄本色。黄小荣和“最美妈妈”吴菊萍一样,给了孩子生的希望,让杭州这座“最美城市”时时涌动着爱的暖流。

He jumped down with utmost determination in face of a hard cemented dam over five-meter height, clearly knowing he would get injured. He nearly lost consciousness because of the agonizing pain caused by comminuted fracture, but he still managed to cover over ten-meter length and saved the drowning child, for he couldn't watch a girl who was struggling in the water and desperate for life. What made the most impression on us is that he said the girl would get drowned if he reached for her late for one minute and which is more important, a leg or a life? A hero will truly shows his quality in trying moments. Huang Xiaorong, just like “The Most Beautiful Mother” Wu Juping, gave a hope of life, making the most beautiful city—Hangzhou filled with warm currents of love.

故事九　陈斌强——百善孝为先 Of All Virtues Filial Piety is the Most Important

【人物介绍】Character Introduction

陈斌强,浙江磐安县冷水镇中心学校初中语文教师,1975年出生,浙江磐安人。他日复一日地照顾母亲起床、洗脸、梳头、吃饭,他的形象相继出现在中央电视台的屏幕里:《新闻联播》《焦点访谈》《朝闻天下》。他参加了“五四青年奖章”和“全国道德模范”的表彰会,还荣获了“感动中国”2012 年度人物奖。他的事迹感动了中国,也拨动了我们每个人的心弦。

Chen Binqiang is a Chinese teacher at a junior high school in Lengshui town, Pan'an county in Zhejiang Province. He was born in 1975 in Pan'an County. Day after day, he has looked after his mother around the clock, assuring that his mother gets up, washes her face, and combs her hair. His model deeds sequentially appeared on CCTV's programmes, such as *Xinwen Lianbo*, *Topics in Focus*, *Morning News* and so on. He attended commendation meetings of "May 4th Youth Medal" and "National Moral Models", and also was honored with the award of "People who Moved China" in 2012. His story has moved the whole China, tugging everyone's heartstrings.

【人物事迹】Character Story

2007 年,陈斌强的母亲得了老年痴呆症,丧失了日常生活能力。一天,陈斌强的姐姐无意中提到,母亲最大的愿望就是和儿子住在一起。回忆起多年来母亲对自己的付出,他决定再困难也不会丢下母亲。为了照顾母亲,他硬是把儿子提前一年送进幼儿园。为了能亲自照顾母亲,他每天用一根布条把母亲绑在自己身上,带着母亲去学校上班。陈斌强工作的学校距离县城的家 30 多千米,带着母亲路上骑车要一个多小时。遇上恶劣天气,这个过程更为艰难。一连五年,陈斌强都风雨无阻带着母亲上班。照顾母亲的生活异常辛苦,陈斌强一天到晚连轴转:晚上 9 时,服侍母亲睡下;凌晨 1 时,准时起床抱母亲上厕所;清晨 5 时,闹钟响起,他要赶在师生之前起床,将母亲房间打扫干净,处理好母亲的大小便;早上 7 时喂过母亲吃饭后,开始学校一天的工作。尽管生活上的事儿很多,陈斌强并未耽误教学。他上课风趣幽默,很受学生欢迎,所教的两个班,语文成绩连续多年蝉联当地联考第一。同时,他还负责教初一学生广播体操,总管学校体艺“2+1”活动。他总说:“我是跑着走的。”

陈斌强的孝道,不是只体现在一朝一夕,也不仅限于带着母亲上班的这五年。早在母亲患上老年痴呆症之前,陈斌强就把奶奶照顾得无微不至。陈斌强母子的故事从浙江走到了全国,它温暖了陈斌强的同事、乡邻,以及许许多多的陌生人。这其中最让陈斌强高兴的是,有人寄来治疗老年痴呆症的药,母亲服用后情况有所好转。陈斌强的朴实行为给他的学生,也给整个社会上了极为生动的一课。他是一个真正有师德的好老师。很多学生在周记本上写道:"老师我很佩服你,等我的爸爸妈妈老了,我也会学你,像你一样多陪陪他们。"

In 2007, Chen Binqiang's mother was suffered from Alzheimer's disease which deprived her of the ability of daily living. One day his sister advertently mentioned that the biggest wish of their mother was to live with her dear son. Chen Binqiang recalled years of dedication and hard work by his mother. He made a firm resolve at that moment that he would never leave his dear mother alone and would look after her against all odds. He unwillingly sent his son one year in advance to kindergarten in order to take care of his mother. Every day he ties his mother to himself with a rope and goes to school which is 30 km from his home by electric vehicle. His school is over 30 km away from his home, and it takes more than one hour to ride to the school. They may find it rather difficult if they come across heavy weather. In the past five years, he took her mother to work all the time. One cannot imagine how difficult it is to take care of his mother. He was busy all day long. At 9 o'clock in the evening, he tucks his mother to bed. At 1:00 a.m. of the following day, he picks up his mother and carries her to the toilet on time. Then at 5:00 a.m. with the ringing of the clock, he cleans up her mother's bedroom and disposes of his mothers' excrement before his colleagues and students wake up. At 7:00 a.m. he starts his work of the day after feeding his mother. Though every day he has a lot of irons in the fire, he still fully performs his duty as a teacher. He teaches Chinese classes in a humorous way, which is well popular with students. For many years, his students' Chinese achievement ranked No.1 in their town. In the meantime, he takes charge of radio calisthenics for junior school freshmen. He is the director of "2 + 1" activities of physical fitness. It has become his pet phrase that I always run to walk.

Chen Binqiang's filial piety is not only exemplified in his bringing his mother to work during these five years. Even before his mother suffered from Alzheimer disease, his consideration and caring for his grandmother were also known by many people. His story spreads around colleagues, neighbours and even all across the country. What made Chen Binqiang most happy was that someone sent him the medicine for treating Alzheimer disease and his mother became better after taking it. Chen Binqiang's behavior serves as an active example for students and the whole society. He is quite a good teacher with truly professional ethics. Many students really adore him and regard him as their model. They want to learn from their teacher and frequently accompany their parents when they become old.

【人物启迪】Character Enlightenment

孝敬父母,是一个人最基本的道德底线。一句简短的“我不能丢开她,我一定要把她带在身边”,诠释了他对母亲的感恩之情,孝顺之心。陈斌强只是一个普通的人民教师,身上没有可歌可泣的先进事迹,有的只是五年如一日地背着母亲上班。可就是捆着他和母亲的布条,体现出了博大的爱;一千多个日子的始终如一,让我们看到了陈斌强那颗如金子般闪闪发光的孝心!他的孝心,不仅抚慰了母亲,也抚慰了每一位中国人,这种中华民族朴素而真挚的人性之美,可以作为社会的良药。

It is one's basic moral bottom line to have filial pity for his parents. A very concise word "I cannot abandon her. I must take her by my side" fully reflects his gratefulness and filial piety for his mother. Chen Binqiang is only an ordinary teacher. Perhaps there is nothing about him which is heroically movement, but the meritorious persistence he has shown in the past five years and which drives him to take his mother to work uninterruptedly brought a lot of tears from us. This short story speaks of an unwavering love through which we can see a son's devotion for his mother. His filial piety soothes his mother. But beyond that, such kind beauty of human nature soothes every Chinese's soul.

故事十　石进才——希望老人 An Old Man Full of Hope

【人物介绍】Character Introduction

石进才，1935年出生，浙江乐清人。中国农业银行浙江省乐清市支行退休干部，会计师。从1995年开始，他带领全家三代人，无偿资助151名素不相识的贫困学生，累积金额达52万元。他荣获2006年“感动温州十大年度人物”和“浙江骄傲——2009年度最具影响力人物”荣誉称号。

Shi Jincai was born in 1935 in Yueqing, Zhejiang Province. He is a retired cadre and an accountant in the sub-branch of Agricultural Bank of China in Yueqin. Since 1995, he has led his offspring, which ranges from children to grandchildren, to finance poverty-stricken students without any reward and donated money totaled 520 000 RMB for their education. He has won the title of " The Top Ten People who Moved Wenzhou" and one of "The Pride of Zhejiang—The Most Influential People" in 2009.

【人物事迹】Character Story

在乐清，有这样一位老人，他以“希望”的名义牵线搭桥，组织社会爱心人士和单位328余人(次)，筹集助学资金达419万元，帮助结对贫困学生1130名，使420名贫困学生圆了大学梦。老石随身带着一个笔记本，上面记载着他所资助的学生姓名、地址以及一些小资料。他说：“这样我就能对他们的情况掌握清楚些，也可以随时给他们寄去生活费和学习费。”有人可能认为，石进才一定很有钱，可事实上，他们一家都是工薪阶层。为了省钱，石进才几乎没什么爱好，所穿衣服都很普通，更舍不得花钱去旅游。老两口至今仍住在老房子里，家里的房子实在太破旧了，老伴儿希望装修一下，也让老石给挡了回去。老石自1996年退休后一直不愿休息，到一家花圃打工。他说：“按我现在的退休金，不去打工，对付自己的生活已经可以了，去打工赚钱，为的是能帮助更多的贫困学生上学。”为了教育下一代，老两口经常带领晚辈深入农村、老区了解群众生活,以身边的事例教育晚辈。在老人的带动下,三个子女也加入了捐助的队伍,资助的对象远至云南、重庆等 12 个省(自治区、直辖市)。如今三个子女每人都结对了 5 名贫困学生。汶川大地震那年,全家人又捐资近 2 万元,向灾区人民献出了爱心。

公益做得多了,石进才开始发动社会上更多人扶贫济困。在老石的提议和影响下,2004 年秋,由乐清团市委、希望办、市农行、民革乐清总支倡议"爱心助学"结对活动,在乐清结对贫困大学生 36 名。2006 年秋,帮助结对贫困大学生 34 名完成了四年学业。同时他组织子女在广西壮族自治区结对少数民族小学生 4 名。"希望"的队伍在不断壮大……

There is an old man Shi Jincai in Yueqing, in the name of "Hope Project", mobilized loving people and organizations, the total number of which was about 328 and raised funds, the total amount of which was 4 190 000 RMB. He also helped to make arrangements of pairing between donors and poor students, which helped 1130 students in financial difficulties and enabled 420 students to fulfill their dreams of going to college. Shi Jincai always took one notebook, in which he kept a record of students' names, address and other information. Such habit could help him to learn about students' conditions more clearly, so as to send them necessary fees whenever they need. Someone may think that Shi Jincai must be very rich, but the fact is that he and his wife are just wage-earning class. In order to save money, he and his wife gave up all hobbies. They were frugal in their living and wore just ordinary clothes which were inexpensive and durable, and never spent money on travel. They still lived in an old house. Because the house was too shabby, his wife wanted to fix and decorate it. But Shi Jincai was firmly against this suggestion. After his retirement in 1996, he got a job in garden. He once said it was true that he could live on his pension, but to get a job and earn money is to let more poverty-stricken students go to school. With the hope of educating the next generation, Shi Jincai regularly brought their youngsters to go to the countryside and see other people's life. They wanted to educate juniors by letting them learn about the poor conditions for living. Led by the elders, three children also joined them and they even made donation to students living in 12 remote places. Until now, three children have already paired with five students separately. Additionally, in the year of Wenchuan earthquake, the whole family donated nearly 20 000 RMB to the quake-striken area.

After doing much for the public good, Shi Jincai started to think about how to involve more people in our society in helping the poor. In the autumn of 2004, the paring activities "caring students" initiated by Yueqing's municipal party committee, the office of "Hope Project", municipal agricultural bank of China paired 36 impoverished college students. In the autumn of 2006, the 34 impoverished students finished a four-year curriculum. At the same time, he organized his children to pair with minority students in Guangxi. The team which passes on hope is increasingly expanding.

【人物启迪】Character Enlightenment

石进才的点滴事迹,很难用语言全部概括。这样一位古稀老人,以微薄之力,慈善星火,给了受助者光明!其实我们每一个人都有两只手,一只是用来帮助自己的,还有一只是用来帮助别人的。帮助别人,快乐自己,石进才做到了!

It is hard to summarize Shi Jincai's story by a list of main facts. An old man did his small part to light up the recipients' life, with the philanthropic sparkles. We've got two hands; one is to help ourselves, while the other is to help others. To help people will in turn bring us pleasure, which Shi Jincai has really done.

故事十一　姜伟荣——海盐"保尔热线""Paul Hotline" in Haiyan City

【人物介绍】Character Introduction

姜伟荣,1958 年出生,浙江海盐人。他是省人大代表、海盐县自来水公司"保尔热线"管道抢修工,在"最美浙江人——2012 年度浙江骄傲"的颁奖典礼上被提名。同时,他还荣获 1998 年“嘉兴市职业道德标兵”,2006 年第一届“感动海盐”十大人物,2006 年海盐县“优秀共产党员”荣誉称号。当地老百姓亲切地称他为“海盐徐虎”。

Jiang Weirong was born in 1958 in Haiyan of Zhejiang Province. He is a representative of Provincial People's Congress, and a pipeline repairing worker of water supply company in Haiyan. On the award ceremony of “The Most Beautiful People—The Pride of Zhejiang” in 2012, Jiang Weirong was nominated. Moreover, he was awarded “The Professional Moral Model” in Jiaxing in 1998, and “The Top Ten People who Moved Haiyan City” as well as “Excellent Member of Communist Party” in 2006. Local people all kindly call him “Haiyan Xu Hu”. (Xu Hu: a man who is excellent in repairing and the character moved Chinese people)

【人物事迹】Character Story

地下管线被称为城市的“生命线”。姜伟荣所在的海盐自来水公司“保尔热线”抢修中心,就扮演着城市供水管道“120”的角色。30 多年来,不管是节假日还是深夜,不管是严冬还是酷暑,不管是狂风肆虐还是大雨滂沱,只要有抢修命令,有用户求助,他都能以最快的速度赶到现场。由于长期抢修管道,姜伟荣的手指不可避免要接触到氯化钙,导致所有手指都有不同程度灼伤,右手大拇指的指甲只剩下三分之一,灰黑开裂。对此,他只是淡淡地说:“不痛不痒,只是不好看。”姜伟荣还有一个身份——社区在职党员,他在社区成立了自己的党员服务工作室。社区里的离休干部、残疾人、孤寡老人,都有一张写有姜伟荣姓名和联系电话的卡片。家里自来水龙头坏了,马桶堵了,只要一个电话,姜伟荣随叫随到,免费上门服务。为提高服务效率,姜伟荣准备了两个工具包,一个放在单位,一个放在家里的车库,以便随时上门为用户解决难题。这一做,又是 20 年,共提供免费服务 1600 人次。在检修岗位上工作了 30 多年的姜伟荣,一双斑驳粗糙、几乎没有指甲的手见证了他多年来恪尽职守的职业操守。在社区志愿服务岗位上默默无闻地奉献,让他受到了社区群众的感谢和赞扬,也彰显了助人为乐的高尚品德。

Underground pipelines are called the “life line” of the city. The "pipeline hotline" of Haiyan water supply company where Jiang Weirong has worked plays an important role in the city. Over the thirty years, whenever on holidays or at midnights, in cold winter or hot summer, and no matter he come across great wind or storm, he could always come to repair pipelines right away if people called for help.

It is inevitable that Jiang Weirong will contact calcium chloride every day. Because of a long-term for broken pipeline repair, his fingers were burned to various degrees, with only one-third of right thumb nail left, to which he just said lightly, "the injured thumb nail doesn't cause pain or itch. It just doesn't look so good." Jiang Weirong has another role "incumbent party member in a community". He set up his own party member service workroom. Every retired cadres, the handicapped, orphans and widows have a card on which is printed Jiang Weirong's name and telephone number. On receiving a call from those people whose faucet and closestool is broken, Jiang Weirong will always appear in the first free time and provide service without payment. He prepared two toolkits which are placed in his company and garage respectively in order to enhance the efficiency of service. He has been doing this for twenty years and offering such free service to more than 1600 people. Serving as a pipeline worker for about 30 years, Jiang Weirong's rough hands almost without nails witness his professional spirit of duties fulfillment during so many years. In the meanwhile, Jiang Weirong volunteered in the community for many years. A lot of thanks and praises from the crowd all reflect his kindness and nobility.

【人物启迪】Character Enlightenment

正如姜伟荣所言,"美丽浙江"不仅仅是天更蓝、水更绿,更重要的是人人充满爱,人人愿奉献,有一个和谐的社会环境。只要每个人从自己做起,从身边的点滴小事做起,用一言一行去帮助那些需要我们帮助的人,这个社会一定会变得更加和谐,更加美丽。做一件好事不难,难的是一辈子做好事;为老百姓服务一次不难,难的是一辈子始终如一地为老百姓服务。

Just as Jiang Weirong has once said, "The beautiful Zhejiang is not only about bluer sky or greener water, but what is more important is that people are helpful and willing to give, thus a harmonious society will be built." Our society is sure to become more harmonious and beautiful if we do our part to help those who should be helped. Do a good deed is not difficult; what is difficult is to do good for a life time. Likewise, to serve people is not difficult; what is difficult is to serve people consistently during the whole life.

故事十二　彭彩荷——伟大的母亲 The Great Mother

【人物介绍】Character Introduction

彭彩荷,1956 年出生,浙江黄岩人。她担任台州市黄岩区头陀镇敬老院院长、头陀镇新界村党支部委员、妇女主任。

Peng Caihe was born in 1956 in Huangyan of Zhejiang Province. She is the director of a nursing house, the member of the Party Branch in Xinjie village as well as the women's director in Toutuo town of Taizhou.

【人物事迹】Character Story

30 多年来,彭彩荷用自己的双手收留、抚养了 11 个孩子,还用自己的肩膀挑起了有 72 位老人的敬老院的担子,人们都称她为"11 个孩子的妈妈和 72 位老人的女儿"。在彭彩荷第一次收养孩子的那一年, 她 25 岁,离异。此后,每当听说哪里有弃婴或孤儿,她就会把她们带到身边,好好照顾。没有生过孩子的她,学着给孩子换尿布、喂奶粉。为了养大这些孩子,她艰辛创业,卖过水果,办过货运站,开过小宾馆、小饭店,尝尽世间冷暖。她跑长途押运货物时,没工夫照顾儿女,就花钱雇了两个保姆,一个烧饭,一个照看孩子。她含辛茹苦,用母亲的坚韧撑起孩子的未来;她承欢膝下,用儿女的柔情担起老人的晚年。长年超负荷的工作,使她积劳成疾。2005 年,她患上了甲状腺瘤,每年都要跑杭州的医院治疗几次。尽管如此,她始终保持着乐观的心态。

30 多年光阴,青丝变白发,不变的是心底的善念,“老有所终,幼有所长”。她从一个人献爱心做好事开始,慢慢地在她周围形成了一个爱心团队,让爱不断接力、传递、涌动,终于汇成了爱的海洋。现在女儿们长大了,彭彩荷有了空闲时间,开始三天两头往敬老院跑,为孤寡老人洗衣、打扫房间、生火做饭。彭彩荷决定随着孩子们一个个地成家,她要开始专心照顾老人。她用自己的慈心和坚毅构建了生命最重要的维度,放飞着属于她的梦想,谱写了一曲人世间感天动地的爱的绝唱。

In the past over 30 years, Peng Caihe has taken in and raised eleven children personally and she has also shouldered the responsibility of taking charge of the gerocomium where 72 aged people has lived. People call her “the mother of 11 children and the daughter of 72 aged people”. In the year when she first adopted the child, she was only 25 years old and just divorced. After that, whenever she heard about an abandoned baby or an orphan, she would always bring them to her home and took good care of them. Though she has not experienced any pregnance and does not have her own baby, she learnt to change diapers for those babies and feed them. To raise these babies, she started many businesses, such as selling fruits, opening up freights station, hotel and restaurant, going through all kinds of difficulties in the process. During the period when she delivered goods over long distances, as she had no time to look after babies, she paid for two babysitters. One was in charge of cooking and the other was mainly responsible for looking after those children.

She works as a tender mother, shoring up kids' future with a mother's perseverance and strength. She cares like a dutiful daughter, brimming over the aged people's declining years with a daughter's inexhaustible tender affection. Taking the burden of constant work overload has resulted in her tiredness and broken health. In 2005, she got thyroid adenoma. From then on, every year she needs to go to Hangzhou to receive treatments several times a year. Even so, she still keeps optimistic.

The past years grayed her hair but did not wear away her ever-determined devotion and affection. The Chinese old saying that the old will be cherished and the young will be raised has motivated her to offer love and do good deed. Thus, around her a loving team has passed on the love so that streams of love can merge into the heart of every one. Now, Peng Caihe's children have grown up and she has some spare time. So she usually goes to the elderly nursing home to wash clothes, clean rooms and do some cooking for old people. She decides to spend more time to take care of the elderly after her adopted children get married one by one. Her kindness and determination has constructed the most important dimension in life which enables her dream to roar and her glory to spread. A piece of music composed with love is echoing in the world.

【人物启迪】Character Enlightenment

一个爱自己的人是渺小的,因为这是小爱;一个为别人活着的人是高大的,因为这是大爱。只有心中有大爱的人,才是“大写”的人,才是一个纯粹的人,才是一个最美的人。我们要为她鼓掌,为她喝彩,但更为重要的是,我们也要成为供养爱、传播善、创造美的一员。

A person who has a love only for himself is insignificant, for this love so called "small love". But a person who has a love for others is noble, for this kind of love is called "great love". Only people who are full of such "great love" can be noble and respectable. We all should applaud and appreciate her noble character, but what is more important, we should nurture love, transmit kindness and create beauty in our society.

故事十三　红日亭爱心老人 The Old Men Full of Love in Hongriting Pavilion

【人物介绍】Character Introduction

夏煮伏茶、冬熬热粥,温州红日亭的爱心老人们40多年风雨无阻,每天义务为过往的路人烧茶施粥,这个团队的平均年龄为70岁。他们荣获了2012年度“最美浙江人”和温州市鹿城区“十佳道德模范”荣誉称号。

Those warm-hearted elders in Hongriting Pavilion of Wenzhou have been serving the migrant workers voluntarily for 40 years, with herbal tea in summer and porridge in winter. Their average age almost reaches 70 years old. By doing so, they won "The Most Beautiful People of Zhejiang Province" in 2012 and "The Top Ten Moral Models" in Lucheng district of Wenzhou.

【人物事迹】Character Story

在温州市华盖山东麓,坐落着一个小小红日亭。有一支由家住附近的老人组成的团队,几十年如一日为过往的行人忙碌着。在红日亭服务的热心老人,从 20 世纪 70 年代初的五六人,增加到现在的二十多人,大多都已白发苍苍。他们中年纪最大的已经 86 岁,最小的也已经 61 岁。这些年里,有的老人因为身体的原因离开了,但又会有新的老人加入。热心的老人们从每年农历六月到中秋节烧伏茶,农历八月十五后开始煮粥,一直到腊月二十。这期间,他们还会根据一年的节气,变换花色品种,免费向路人供应芥菜饭、清明饼、端午粽、月饼、汤圆、糖糕等各种特色食物。据团队老人介绍,施粥摊现每天可供应 18 锅左右的粥,一般下午先烧 16 锅,第二天一早再烧两锅。一锅粥需要 2.5 千克大米,每次大约要用掉近 45 千克。一些热心的市民为他们送来锅子和大米。他们现日均施粥已到 600 碗,喝粥的大多是困难打工者。"红日亭"的老人们用伏茶和热粥给人温暖,同时他们的感染力和影响力,也在召唤着更多人行善。可是光施粥这块,团队每天都要在柴、米、油、水、电等方面支出 1000 多元钱。然而,红日亭的团队几乎每天都收到好心人捐助的不同的物资或爱心款,这些好心人的捐助是维持施粥点最重要的来源。这让这些并不富裕的老人们相信,红日亭团队的善举,一定能坚持下去。

There is a small pavilion named Hongriting located at the eastern foot of Huagai Mountain, Wenzhou city. A group of warm-hearted elders, who live near that pavilion, persist in helping migrant workers for decades of years. This group consisted of only five or six members in the early 1970s, but now the number has increased to over 20 and most of them are grey haired. The oldest one is already 86 years old and the youngest is already 61 years old. During these years, some aged people left because of their health condition, while some new members would join in the same time. Every year, those kind elders boil herbal tea from lunar June to Mid-Autumn Festival. And then they cook porridge until lunar December 20th. During that, they will also provide the homeless for free with various other special foods like fried rice with mustard, Qingming cake, Zongzi, mooncake, rice dumpling and Tanggao, according to the change of solar cycles. The elders said the porridge stall could provide 18 pots of porridge everyday. They usually cook 16 pots in the afternoon and finish the other two in the next day's morning. Since each pot of porridge holds 2. 5 kg of rice, the total volume per time amounts to nearly 45 kg of rice. And some warm-hearted citizens offer pots and rice to them. Now those elders provide over 600 bowls of porridge each day for free, mostly to those poor workers. However, everyday they need to spend more than one thousand yuan on rice, oil, water, electricity, and firewood, for providing enough porridge. They spread warmth to people with herbal tea and porridge, and also appeal to more people's kindness. Because of their influence, The team of Hongriting Pavilion receives donations almost every day. These donations from warm-heated people have become the main income to maintain their porridge line. People's enthusiasm lets the group believe that Hongriting's kindness can last for long time.

【人物启迪】Character Enlightenment

"红日亭"老人们用一杯茶、一碗粥向全社会传达了一种爱心善念。源自民间,发自老人的公益善举将会在广大人民群众中生根发芽。做一件好事易,做一辈子好事难。

The elders in Hongriting Pavilion convey a loving kindness to the whole society through a bottle of herbal tea and a bowl of porridge. The public charity originating from civil activity by the elders will take root and sprout among the people.

故事十四　孔胜东——好人有好报 One Good Turn Deserves Another

【人物介绍】Character Introduction

孔胜东，1964年生，浙江杭州人。他是浙江省杭州市公共交通集团有限公司第三汽车分公司三车队司机，曾获"全国劳动模范""中国青年志愿者银质奖""浙江省学雷锋标兵""杭州市十佳市民""浙江省最具影响力劳动模范"荣誉称号。

Kong Shengdong, born in 1964, is a bus driver from the third motorcade of the third car division of Hangzhou Public Transport Group Co., Ltd. in Zhejiang Province. He has been awarded the honorable titles of "National Model Worker" "Silver Medal of Chinese Youth Volunteer" "The Pacesetter of Learning Lei Feng of Zhejiang" "Top Ten Good Citizens in Hangzhou" "the Most Influential Model Worker of Zhejiang".

【人物事迹】Character Story

作为杭州市K28路公交车司机，孔胜东时刻把帮助他人，为乘客提供优质服务挂在心上。孔胜东的车上有不少"特色服务"。从1999年6月1日开始，他在车上摆出了茶水桶，每天在家烧好开水带到车上，供乘客免费饮用。为了方便乘客，孔胜东免费为公交车配备了常用药品、雨披、扇子等物品；同时，每个座椅背后都挂着便民袋，方便乘客放置垃圾或当呕吐袋。孔胜东甚至还为外地乘客考虑，在车厢里提供了自己设计制作的沿线导游图和车辆转乘示意图。2006年7月1日起，他又推出了免费阅报活动，每天购买杭城各大报纸放置在车厢醒目位置，方便乘客阅读，被乘客形象地称为"文化大餐"。他所驾驶的K28路公交车被乘客们亲切地称为"放心车""雷锋车"和"移动之家"。在他的示范带动下，他所在的车组年年被杭州公交集团评为"星级党员示范车"，所在线路也先后被授予"浙江省文明服务示范点""全国巾帼文明岗""全国三八红旗集体"等荣誉称号。

从 1986 年 3 月开始孔胜东参加了志愿者服务活动,每个周六晚上都在中山北路自己家门口设立义务修车点,为群众免费修理自行车。他还推出"特别承诺",免费上门为特殊群体修车。前几年,旧城改造,老房子都拆了,孔胜东一家也搬走了,可他仍然坚持每个周六的晚上准时出现在老地方。在这将近 30 年里,他不仅没有收过一分钱修理费,而且还从自己的收入中支出小配件和用电的费用。从 2004 年 5 月 1 日起,孔庆东还利用每个周六下午的业余时间,在汽车东站设立"便民服务台",为往来乘客提供免费咨询、指路、兑换零钱、打气和"反扒"宣传等多种服务。

As a bus driver of Line K28 in Hangzhou, Kong Shengdong is ready to help others and is happy to provide services of good quality to passengers from his bottom of heart. He offers many special services in his bus. For example, since June 1, 1999, he had put a tea bucket into the bus and brought boiled water from home everyday for passengers to drink freely. To bring convenience to passengers, he offers commonly used drugs, motion sickness bags, poncho, fans and other items for free. What's more, behind every seat, he hangs public baskets which passengers can use to litter or vomit. Besides, to facilitate the passengers, especially passengers from other cities, Kong Shengdong provides the route map involved K28 and the sketch map of transfer points that are all designed and made by himself. In addition, from July 1, 2006, he has launched an activity of free newspaper reading, purchasing many kinds of daily newspapers, which is visually regarded as a cultural feast by passengers. To facilitate passengers to read, these newspapers are all placed in prominent places. Therefore, his bus of K28 has also been called the "Assured Car", "Lei Feng Car", or "a Moving Home" by passengers. Driven and inspired by Kong Shengdong's spirit, colleagues in his team all learn from him and behave quite well and his group wins "Star Demonstration Vehicle" every year. K28 has also been awarded the titles of "Civilized Service Demonstration Sites in Zhejiang", the "National Women's Civilization Demonstration" and "March 8th Red-Banner Groups".

Kong Shengdong has participated in volunteer activities since March of 1986. Every Saturday night, he sets up a stall outside his home in North

Zhongshan Road to help people to repair bicycles with no charge. As for the special groups, he also likes to offer home service. Several years ago, because of the transformation plan of the old city, old houses were razed and Kong Shengdong's family also moved to another location. However, he still continues to provide bicycles repairing service in the original place on Saturdays. During these almost thirty years, he not only repairs bicycles for free, but also uses his own money to buy accessories and pay the electricity fee. Since May 1st, 2004, Kong Shengdong has set up a "Convenience Service Station" in East Bus Station every Saturday afternoon. He provides services such as consultation, direction, money changing, pumping air, and anti-griddle propaganda for free.

【人物启迪】Character Enlightenment

"帮助别人是件很快乐的事情,我会一直把它坚持下去。"孔胜东始终坚守着助人为乐的信念。做一件好事并不难,难的是一辈子做好事。

"It is a pleasure to help others and I will stick to it." Kong Shengdong never fails to believe that helping others is to help himself. It is not difficult for us to do one good thing, but it is difficult for us to keep doing good deeds through our life.

故事十五　"麻风村"的青年医疗团队 The Youth Medical Team in "Leprosy Village"

【人物介绍】Character Introduction

浙江省皮肤病防治研究所上柏住院部有十二位医护人员。他们荣获了

"全国麻风防治先进工作者"、国家级"青年文明号"、浙江省卫生系统"最美天使"、"最美浙江人"等荣誉称号。

Shangbo Inpatient Department affiliated to Zhejiang Institutes on Skin Disease Prevention and Control is staffed by 12 doctors. They are awarded such honorary titles as "Advanced Workers of the National Leprosy Prevention and Treatment", "National Youth Civilization Title", "The Most Beautiful Angel" in Health Systems of Zhejiang Province, "The Most Beautiful People of Zhejiang Province" and so on.

【人物事迹】Character Story

被外人称为"麻风村"的浙江省皮肤病防治研究所上柏住院部,位于湖州市德清县西南部的金车山中,现有 84 位老人,其中一、二级残疾 45 人,三、四级残疾 39 人。麻风病可引起皮肤、神经、四肢和眼鼻等的进行性和永久性损害,导致患者终身肢体畸残,有的断手残足,有的眼盲鼻塌,遭受精神上的歧视和肉体上的痛苦。几十年来,分配来的学生来了走,走了来,队伍始终不稳。现在,12 位 70 后、80 后医护人员采用 24 小时值班制,在有限的资源下长期为这些麻风病患者提供直接肌肤接触的细致服务。他们在这寂寞的山坳已坚守了 10 多年,远离家庭,做不了孝子、慈父、好配偶,但他们无愧于患者,无愧于人生。这支年轻的团队以其高超的医护水平相继吸引了来自英国、日本、印度的麻风病专家来此考察,得到了这些专家的认可和赞扬。

目前这里已经成为我国麻风病歧视及干预理论的发源地。原浙江省卫生厅厅长杨敬说:"婚姻法曾规定,麻风病病人不能结婚,他们无家、无亲人,是真正的弱势群体。为他们提供良好的医护服务和生活环境,对维护社会稳定、体现人类尊严具有非常重要的意义,也是我们政府、社会、公共卫生机构的职责所在。而政府的职责是由这些年轻人来完成的。我深深感谢这些年轻人。"

Shangbo Inpatient Department Affiliated to Zhejiang Institutes on Skin Disease Prevention and Control, called "leprosy village" by the outside, was located in Deqing county, southwest of Jinche mountain. In this village, there are 84 aged people, 45 of whom are with the first and secondary level of disabilities, 39 of whom are with the third and fourth level of disabilities. Leprosy can cause progressive and permanent damage to the skin, nerves, limbs and eyes. It will even lead to patients' lifelong physical deformities.

Disabled by blindness, the collapsing of noses or breaking of hands or limbs, the patients suffered mental discrimination and physical torment. For the decades, some graduates came and others went away, resulting in an unstable team. Now the 12 medical workers who were all born in the late 1970s and 1980s adopted a 24-hour on-duty system and provided a meticulous service involving skin contact for disabled leprosy patients. They have worked in this remote village for ten years, far away from their homes and not able to look after their family. Although they failed their families, they behave in a way valued by patients and this gives value to their whole life. Gradually, this young team's superb medical service has attracted leprosy experts from the UK, Japan, and India to visit this remoted hospital. These visitors were all amazed by their high-quality medical skills.

By now this leprosy village has become the source of theories of leprosy discrimination and intervention in China. The original director of Health Department in Zhejiang Province once stated, "the marriage law stipulates that leprosy patients cannot marry, therefore they do not have family support. Indeed they are truly the most vulnerable people in our society. To provide better medical service and living environment for them is of great significance in maintaining the social stability and reflecting people's dignity. It is also the point where the responsibility of our government, society and public medical institutions lies. I want to express my deep appreciation for those young doctors who fulfill government's responsibilities."

【人物启迪】Character Enlightenment

“麻风村”青年医疗团队以实际行动关爱麻风病患者和畸残者,使他们走出疾病的阴影,回归到温暖的社会中。这些充满幸福感的年轻人,默默地在这个远离县城、环境恶劣的“麻风村”奉献。他们不在乎偏低的待遇,只希望能书写自己精彩的人生,这是一种职业的幸福感。在今天这样的时代背景下,在祖国宽广的大地上,他们的无私付出和辛勤耕耘,十分值得境遇良好的人们深思。让我们一起对他们多一份关爱。

The youth team of "leprosy village" shows great concern and care for leprosy patients, the deformed and the disabled through practical action and leads them out of the shadows of disease to embrace the warm society. These young people with full happiness devote themselves to serve patients in such a remote "leprosy village" with poor working environment. They don't care about low salary, but want to create their own wonderful life. This is a kind of feeling of professional happiness. In such background of our times, their selfless devotion and hard work are really deserving deep reflection by people living in wealthy conditions. Let us show more caring to them.

故事十六　羊耀周——卖菜为助学 Selling Vegetables for Funding Students

【人物介绍】Character Introduction

羊耀周，磐安县普通卖菜老人，1935年出生，浙江金华磐安人。他被评为"最美浙江人——2014浙江骄傲年度人物"。

Yang Yaozhou, a farmer selling vegetables, was born in 1935 from Jinhua of Zhejiang Province. He was honored as "The Most Beautiful Zhejiang Citizen—the Pride of Zhejiang" in 2014.

【人物事迹】Character Story

羊耀周靠在县城里荒废的五亩山地上种菜为生。他住着简陋的泥墙屋，吃着粗茶淡饭，穿着几十年前的旧衣服，每天挑着担子往返约5千米的山路卖菜。

1999年，当他听说有一个品学兼优的大学生因为没有学费将被迫放弃学业时，就有了资助贫困学生完成学业的念头。21年来他坚持施善，将卖菜所得用来资助贫困学生，如今已帮助8人上了大学，共捐助8万余元。这些钱都是他早出晚归，省吃俭用，靠挑着菜担子一点点积攒起来的。

为了攒钱,老人省吃俭用,对自己几乎到了吝啬苛刻的地步。他住的黄泥平房里物品杂乱地摆放着。靠后窗墙边的那张床上,垫被是一张已变成黑色的棉胎,两床被子一床没有被罩,另一床的被罩已很破旧,白色的枕头也变黑了,连枕头后面的石灰墙也被汗水弄黑了。老人舍不得花钱买新被新衣,因为担心没钱资助贫困大学生了。自上山以来,他平时穿的,都是人家送的旧衣服。

老人每天卖菜的收入少则十多元,多则六七十元。一年到头买化肥需要花费四五百元钱。为了节省这笔不小的开支,每年夏季与秋季,老人常在凌晨四五点钟,到县城中街的一些市民家里挑大粪,挑到1.5千米外的山顶时天还没大亮,多时一年要挑上100多担大粪。为了让那些孩子能早点上大学,羊耀周老人卖菜精打细算,总是希望能多卖点。受他资助的大学生工作了把钱还给他之后,他又将这些钱捐赠了出去。

Yang Yaozhou makes his living by growing vegetables. He lives in a rough house, has simple diets, wears used clothes and shoulders a load to go to the county and back covering around 10 kilometers to sell vegetables.

In 1999, when Yang Yaozhou heard that an excellent student had to drop out of school because he was unable to afford the tuition fee, he decided to subsidize the student until he graduated. For 21 years, he has insisted on funding students by selling vegetables. Till now he has totally contributed over 80 000 RMB for 8 students and they have successfully attended the college.

In order to save money, the old man lives frugally and treats himself almost harshly. The cottage he lives in is cluttered with a lot of goods. On the bed are blackened mattress and two quilts, one without cover and the other with very shabby cover. The white pillow is becoming very dirty and the wall behind the bed is getting black because of his sweat. The old man is reluctant to spend money on clothes and quilts. Otherwise, he would have no money to subsidize students. His clothes are all from other people.

Yang Yaozhou's income is varying from 10 to 70 yuan a day. It costs him about 500 RMB to buy fertilizer every year. To save this large amount of money, in summer and autumn, he usually gets up at 4 or 5 a.m. to go to the cottage to shoulder a load of dung. Often it is still dark when he returns from the cottage and sometimes he can shoulder more than 100 loads a year. He is shrewd in money matters when selling vegetables so as to earn more and let those children attend school earlier. When these children return money to him, he will then subsidize others.

【人物启迪】Character Enlightenment

尽管已经80岁高龄,但老人依旧不忘用自己的力量撑起贫困大学生的明天,倾其所有,不求回报。生活异常清苦,但老人却显得如此充实而满足。他从帮助别人中得到了巨大的快乐,感觉心情和身体都特别好。他感恩老天给了他健康的身体,感激那些从不还价的人对他的信任和温暖。做好人,做对的事,善意就能够传递。而得到帮助的人,终有一天,也会转身助人。

Though Yang Yaozhou is already 80 years old, he still wants to help impoverished students and he doesn't ask for anything in return. His life is extremely impoverished, but he lives his life to the fullest and feels very satisfied. He feels very happy when helping others, while his emotion and body are very good. He really appreciates that he is healthy and gets trust and warm his customers give him. Being good and doing the good, he believes that he can pass kindness onto others. Those who get help from others will try to help others in the future.

故事十七 张文龙——善待每一个陌生人 Be Kind to Every Stranger

【人物介绍】Character Introduction

张文龙,1988年出生,浙江金华人,是浦江县堂头中学的一名教师。2015年他被评为"最美浙江人——2014年度浙江骄傲人物"。

Zhang Wenlong, born in 1988, is a teacher in Pujiang county, and from

Jinhua, Zhejiang Province. He was honored as "the Most Beautiful Zhejiang Citizen—the Pride of Zhejiang" in 2014.

【人物事迹】Character Story

2013年8月,张文龙年仅19岁的妹妹张文倩出车祸不幸去世。通过与父母沟通之后,张文龙决定捐献妹妹的器官。张文龙认为虽然挽救妹妹生命的奇迹未能出现,但可以用爱心创造奇迹。张文倩的器官成功拯救了3名陌生人。妹妹过世没多久,不幸接踵而来,2014年4月张文龙患有小儿麻痹症的父亲患上了尿毒症,同样需要做肾脏移植手术。在红十字会和浙江卫视的安排下,张文龙一家参加了"中国梦想秀"节目,"梦想助力团"成员表示愿意出资15万元帮助他们。然而令人扼腕的是,在节目播出前两小时,父亲在家门口被一辆越野车撞飞,当场死亡。张文龙拒绝了"中国梦想秀"栏目组的帮助,希望把钱捐给社会上更需要帮助的人。

父亲去世了,张文龙勇敢地承担起了照顾母亲的责任。作为一名教师,妹妹走的时候,因为教毕业班,在处理妹妹后事时,张文龙仅向学校请了三天假就赶回学校上课。父亲离世后,又因初三毕业班的学生马上面临中考,他还是只请了三天假,就毅然带着同样先天残疾的母亲回到学校。

经历了这么多,张文龙依然相信世界充满了爱。他认为一个人的力量也许很渺小,但如果每个人都愿意做一些力所能及的善事,那么最终将出现一股巨大的力量,推动我们的社会前进,真正实现和谐。

In August, 2013, Zhang Wenlong's little sister, Zhang Wenqian who was only nineteen years old, died of the car accident. After communicating with his parents, Zhang Wenlong decided to donate his sister's organ. Zhang Wenlong thought that the doctor couldn't save his sister, there still can be miracles. Doctors used Zhang Wenqian's organ successfully saving three strangers. However, before long, in April of 2014, Zhang Wenlong's father who was stricken with poliomyelitis was diagnosed with uremia. Therefore, he needed renal transplantation. With the help from Red Cross and Zhejiang TV, Zhang Wenlong's family attended the "China Dream" program. Dream Assistance Group decided to donate 150 000 RMB to help them. Unfortunately, two hours before the broadcast, Zhang Wenlong's father was also hit by car and was dead on spot. Zhang Wenlong rejected the help from the program and he hoped that money can be given to those who need help more.

After his father's death, Zhang Wenlong takes the responsibility to take care of his mother. As a teacher teaching graduating class, during the period of preparing affairs, he only asked for three days' leave and then went back to school. Similarly, when dealing with his father's funeral affairs, because his students are preparing for the senior high school entrance examination, after three days' break, he took his mother and went back to school.

After going through so many things, Zhang Wenlong still believes that the world is full of love. One person's power is small, but if everyone is willing to help others, it can promote the society's process and harmony.

【人物启迪】Character Enlightenment

除了"爱"之外,世界上最美丽的动词是"帮助",张文龙及其一家正是用实际行动书写了一次充满大义大爱的最美丽的"帮助"。面对亲人先后离世的噩耗,他始终坚信爱心可以"创造奇迹,延续生命",传递正能量。他们以道德的力量、人性的美好,延续了人间的温暖,成为社会发展的正能量。我们都是柔软的动物,会接受善良回报善良,会付出一点爱收回无限爱,希望大家都有坚强的意志力战胜邪恶,让世界充满爱。

Except for love, the other beautiful verb in the world is "help". Zhang Wenlong and his family impress us with practical action by helping others. Facing relatives' death, Zhang Wenlong still believes that love can create miracle, extend life and pass on positive energy. They show their energy by the power of morality and happiness. We are all emotional animals, and we will accept goodness and give goodness in return. We will show our love and enjoy others' love. Everyone can use the strong willingness to overcome evil and fill the world with love.

故事十八　潘克勤——跨国救助 International Aid

【人物介绍】Character Introduction

潘克勤,1987 年出生,浙江杭州人,是浙江省听力语言康复中心的听觉言语康复教师。她曾荣获“浙江省第五届红十字公益之星”“省残联优秀共产党员”“杭州市十大青年英才”“最美浙江人——红十字感动人物”等称号。

Pan Keqin, born in 1987, is a hearing and speech recovery teacher from Hangzhou, Zhejiang Province. She was honored as “the Star of Red Cross Public Welfare” “Excellent Member of Communist Party in Provincial Disabled Federation” “Top Ten Outstanding Youth in Hangzhou” “The Most Beautiful Zhejiang Citizen—Red-Cross Top Ten People” and so on.

【人物事迹】Character Story

2009 年,潘克勤踏入浙江省残联举办的听力语言康复中心,成为一名听障儿童康复教师,从此与公益事业结下了不解之缘。潘克勤不仅专注于康复教学的本职工作,在工作之余还积极投身到志愿服务中。在早年求学期间,她就有过多次献血的经历,并产生了登记捐献造血干细胞的想法。2010 年 9 月,她成功登记并加入了中华骨髓库。

2012 年 2 月 22 日,潘克勤接到红十字会的电话,得知一名韩国的白血病患者与她的造血干细胞样本配对成功,期望她能及时捐献造血干细胞,并说明了捐献造血干细胞的过程,给了她一个星期的时间考虑。她心想,孩子们的课,有时间可以补;即将到来的全国轮训班还有机会参加,但人的生命就只有一次,于是她决定捐献。

两次采集总共 6 小时,潘克勤在北京空军总医院成功捐献 272 毫升造血干细胞混悬液,为远隔千里的韩国白血病患者带去了生的希望。她也成为浙江省第 107 例造血干细胞捐献者,同时也是浙江省第二位跨国(韩国)的光荣捐献者。

出人意料的是,一年之后远在韩国的白血病患者病情出现反复,唯一的救治途径就是潘克勤再次捐献。当红十字会的工作人员再次联系潘克勤征求她的意见时,潘克勤非常爽快地答应了。而她唯一的要求,仅仅是“不想麻烦太多人”,希望能低调地完成这件事。潘克勤再次赶往北京为千里之外的患者送去生命火种。最终,韩国患者成功治愈康复。

In 2009, Pan Keqin entered Zhejiang Hearing and Speech Recovery Center, and became a recovery teacher. From then on, she has an affinity with public affairs. Pan Keqin not only concentrates on her teaching work, but also devotes herself into volunteer work. During the period of study, she has joined blood donation several times and had the idea of registering for donating hematopoietic stem cells. In September of 2010, she successfully registered at the Chinese Bone Marrow Bank.

On February 22, 2012, Pan Keqin answered a phone calling from the Red Cross and heard that her hematopoietic stem cells sample exactly matched those from a Korean patient with leukaemia. They hope that she can donate her hematopoietic stem cells in time. They clearly explained the whole process of donating and let her consider it for about one week. Though she needed to teach children and took part in a training class, she thought people only have one life. Therefore, she decided to donate for that patient.

After collecting for six hours, Pan Keqin successfully donated 272 milliliters suspension of hematopoietic stem cells in Beijing Air Force General Hospital. She brought hope for the Korean patient millions of kilometers away. She became the No. 107 hematopoietic stem cells donator in Zhejiang Province, and also became the second transnational donator in Zhejiang.

Beyond all expectations, one year later, that Korean patient relapsed and the only method was that Pan Keqin donated again. When the worker from the Red Cross asked for Keqin's opinion, she was quite willing to help the patient again, and she replied to the worker without any hesitation. Her only request was that she hoped they could complete it in a low-key manner. Pan Keqin hurried to Beijing again to send “the kindling of life”. Finally, they successfully cured the Korean patient.

【人物启迪】Character Enlightenment

她用自己的细心帮助听障儿童学会聆听,学会说话,融入社会;用自己的热心数年如一日的帮助他人,激扬青春,无悔奉献;用自己的爱心帮助残疾家庭重获希望,走出困境,走向光明;用自己的勇气,一次又一次地为白血病患者点亮生命的希望。这位普通而又不平凡的85后教师,用自己的实际行动,为杭州这座美丽的城市增添了一抹亮丽的色彩。

With carefulness, she helps the hearing impaired children to learn how to listen, speak and step into the world. For several years, she helps others, exerts her every youthful effort, and regretlessly contributes for the society. With love, she brings hope for families with the disabled and helps them get out of the trouble and turn from darkness to light. With courage, she has kindled the light of hope for the patient with leukaemia. This normal teacher impresses us with practical action in her twenties, and adds a bright color for this beautiful city.

参 考 文 献

第一章 务实 Pragmatism

故事一 王法金——新时代的马天民 Ma Tianmin in the New Age
http://qjwb.zjol.com.cn/html/2009-06/29/content_4915163.htm
故事二 郑小平——独臂鸿雁 Messager with One Arm
http://difang.gmw.cn/zj/2013-10/10/content_9132971.htm
故事三 孙炎明——警界保尔“Pavel Korchagin” in Public Security Organization
http://baike.baidu.com/link? url=TJRQoRk0jl16PJXiV0iKGDOAEZophrfsiUmpmIz4gsE5lkTUQz5-KujMs3TKaGDdMe8-uAXAKBKhq_OyBQOryK
故事四 钟杏菊——自家医生 Our Family Doctor
http://zjnews.zjol.com.cn/05zjnews/system/2011/06/29/017636131.shtml
故事五 俞佳友——为民记者 A Journalist of the People and for the People
http://cpc.people.com.cn/GB/67481/94157/217131/index.html
故事六 吴强忠——最美人民公仆 The Most Beautiful Public Servant
http://legal.china.com.cn/2013-07/24/content_29510811.htm
故事七 张思洋——大学生的好保姆 A Good Keeper of College Students
http://zj.sina.com.cn/edu/dzyx/2012-08-28/0743894.html

故事八　蒋定军——十字路口的艺术家 The Artist at the Crossroad

http://society.people.com.cn/GB/223276/203009/238532/17554827.html

故事九　周兆木——环保卫士 An Environmental Protection Activist

http://lgbj.fuyang.gov.cn/yffc/230847.jhtml

故事十　何剑兴——困难职工的贴心人 A Helpful Man of the Needy Workers

http://character.workercn.cn/c/2013/07/13/130713084249001638342.html

故事十一　高彩珍——杭州的姐 A Female Taxi Driver in Hangzhou

http://doc.qkzz.net/article/b3e4081a-3b3d-42c8-89cc-7b974e9ca1e6_2.htm

故事十二　史文斌——电力服务明星 A Service Star Electrician

http://zjnews.zjol.com.cn/05zjnews/system/2015/02/06/020502631.shtml

故事十三　高水华——残疾人企业家 A Disabled Entrepreneur

http://blog.sina.com.cn/s/blog_9024fa6701015qs5.html

故事十四　葛明霞——情感教学的创新者 An Innovator of Emotional Teaching Method

http://zjnews.zjol.com.cn/05zjnews/system/2011/09/09/017832547.shtml

故事十五　黄　斌——荒岛英雄 A Hero in a Desert Island

http://zjnews.zjol.com.cn/05zjnews/system/2010/10/12/016993361.shtml

故事十六　杭兰英——百姓喜爱的好支书 A Good Secretary Loved by People

http://www.zj.xinhuanet.com/2014news/zfhly/index.htm

故事十七　朱志根——浙江“水军”的功勋旗手 The Meritorious Coach of Zhejiang Swimming Team

http://sports.sohu.com/20140516/n399633568.shtml

第二章 守信 Trustworthiness

故事一 陶晓莺——家政女皇 The Queen of Homemaking Service

http://biz.zjol.com.cn/05biz/system/2011/10/15/017915796.shtml

故事二 吴乃宜——诚信老爹 The Trustworthy Dad

http://www.wenming.cn/sbhr_pd/xiaozhuan/cssx/201309/t20130912_1467106.shtml

故事三 杨冬林——开锁大王 The King of Locksmith

http://zjnews.zjol.com.cn/05zjnews/system/2011/09/15/017843823.shtml

故事四 陈金英——奶奶商人 Grandma in Business

http://www.zjol.com.cn/05zjol/system/2013/02/16/019149455.shtml

故事五 吴 斌——最美司机 The Most Virtuous Driver

http://news.ifeng.com/society/special/zuimeisijiwubin/

故事六 蒋引娣——一诺千金的农家女 Promise is Debt

http://zjnews.zjol.com.cn/05zjnews/system/2009/08/31/015784958.shtml? COLLCC=2120267524&

故事七 董忠岳——心中没有欠条 No Wages Strips in My Hands

http://www.zgshengsi.com/News_View.asp? NewsID=46985

故事八 陈 林——诚实立身 信誉立业 Being an Honest Man and Establishing a Trustworthy Enterprise

http://www.zjwmw.com/07zjwm/system/2015/04/23/020618326.shtml

故事九 吴岩兴——老吴热线 Lao Wu Service Hotline

http://www.zjwmw.com/07zjwm/system/2011/11/14/017994928.shtml

故事十 周言松——百姓的好干部 People's Good Cadre

http://news.qz828.com/system/2012/06/01/010487203.shtml

故事十一 田思嘉——烈火青春 Burning Youth

http://baike.baidu.com/link? url=SLy7h5PcSveOmR0k3OUqLN9V8D-XGQM7XiS47QZh4ZjCZ6Zyi51vPF4pLKdRYRuAgYtfmP9uB0YGMxfSKK0iW_

http://www.baike.com/wiki/田思嘉

故事十二 郑樟瑞——一个50年的承诺 A 50-Years' Promise

http://www.sxwmw.gov.cn/sxhr/201208/t20120827_330604.html

故事十三 邵宝林——诚信商家 A Trustworthy Businessman

http://baike.baidu.com/link? url=mBYuwmXVVpTydF5AVeDL0yroKFC5HO47Q6d-ZdP5FaClaBTnje_6QvKNAILb1m1-kxdmQ-nskm6wwmlrnyu3gK

http://zjrb.zjol.com.cn/html/2011-09/15/content_1087712.htm? div=-1

故事十四 汪南南——眼盲心不盲 A Blind Man with a Clear Hear

http://zjnews.zjol.com.cn/system/2013/11/22/019719724.shtml

http://www.zjwmw.com/07zjwm/system/2013/09/18/019602214.shtml

故事十五 胡惊雨——支教教师 A Volunteer Teacher

http://nbrb.cnnb.com.cn/html/home/yzrd/2012/0711/37555.html

故事十六 梅光汗——重情守信 An Affectionate Man Who Keeps His Promise

http://www.zjwmw.com/07zjwm/system/2014/06/11/020076653.shtml

http://zjnews.zjol.com.cn/system/2015/01/17/020467365.shtml

第三章 崇学 Studiousness

故事一 谷超豪——大师的求学路 A Master's Studying Life

http://baike.baidu.com/link? url=CMN6s4ed5A0QrbfgoXB_45Vy3Qmw8dttn3aXR9u0pA7xP9oTastJ2EaNGt9dGJSo2L_usDPg8PMeeG9KtqgXGq

http://zjrb.zjol.com.cn/html/2010-01/12/content_227272.htm? div=-1

故事二 杨晓丽——不言放弃 Never Give Up Studying

http://baike.baidu.com/link? url=6YwO3q42WE1Ug1b7rUjm7krxMgWD5-DjZv-sZQqo4W76kZ3bhfqExsFWOeq0a1-6CJ1ysuO6g281K3HAKoeEuK

故事三　许　欢——困境中寻出路 Seeking Way Out of the Difficult
http://baike.baidu.com/link? url = 9iWxKBSIXE-WpAvAni0R——aZ7G5X1jQOMOrJl_WcG2FrmaJ9xAg2XWnFjuyFCEY4zFhSrW27ywwLXwzTScmNZK
故事四　陈宇峰——科研达人 A Master of Scientific Research
http://econet.zjgsu.edu.cn/news/ShowArticle.asp? ArticleID = 348
故事五　曹秋芳——侍孝学习两不误 Neglecting Neither Filial Piety Nor Study
http://baike.baidu.com/link? url = lCVQM6CfiFAMgQ8BOJ6b5QZrCF7tPvBntBApoGv20IVsSz9gaafOxSc_qJtfoi_xZfwTkPrBb2jb4o0jKq5EPa
故事六　洪佳琳——钻研弱智教育 Studying on Education for Mentally Retarded Children
http://www.spe-edu.net/Html/tjnews/197001/332.html
故事七　束沛如——教与学相结合 Combining Teaching with Learning
http://www.zczyedu.net/newsInfo.aspx? pkId = 561
故事八　张献斌——农业技术推广者 Agricultural Technology Disseminator
http://baike.baidu.com/link? url = uRFpxdVCSSC87ANO9q7klHPfJkjhlnbfH5pCQXGFOUao44u61h_mw2WgpBzRMsu_c6fflmveEcY-e545Ti1mOa
故事九　徐　业——坚持自学的维和警察 A Peace-Keeping Police Persisting in Self-Studying
http://ohnews.zjol.com.cn/system/2011/08/04/010864296.shtml
故事十　朱佳龙——把优秀当成一种习惯 Taking Excellence as His Habit
http://www.zjol.com.cn/05zjol/system/2011/12/10/018066331.shtml
故事十一　慎祖佩——坚守与钻研 Sticking to Her Post and Doing Research
http://zjnews.zjol.com.cn/05zjnews/system/2004/08/30/003268393.shtml
故事十二　徐爱华——政策高参 A Senior Policy Adviser
http://zjnews.zjol.com.cn/system/2015/01/15/020464960.shtml

http://www.legaldaily.com.cn/zt/content/2012-12/27/content_4096735.htm?node=28929

故事十三 吴文武——技术能手 Technical Expert

http://www.chinahighway.com/news/2011/612411.php

故事十四 方 重——从中专生到副行长 From a Secondary Technical School Student to Be a Deputy President of a Bank

http://www.153w.com/html/78/n-111278.html

故事十五 阮林根——爱钻研的民警 An Assiduous Policeman

http://www.zj.xinhuanet.com/newscenter/focus/2014-09/16/c_1112496395.htm

http://baike.baidu.com/link?url=vmK5swLys6tJjhuO8cQXwbIjPRB9tkV1naMPzGAgjvO3LXZBkSfxyKyIgf3lidj51fHodVxeKFFfiAz24YmSZ_

故事十六 汪建华——眼神作家 A "Winking" Writer

http://news.ifeng.com/a/20141226/42801017_0.shtml

http://hzdaily.hangzhou.com.cn/hzrb/html/2013-01/29/content_1426038.htm

http://www.hzxh.gov.cn/art/2015/01/23/art_chnl798_108887.html

第四章 向善 Kindheartedness

故事一 吴菊萍——最美妈妈 The Most Beautiful Mother

http://news.sohu.com/s2011/wujuping/

故事二 王海文——南丁格尔奖得主 A Winner of Florence Nightingale Prize

http://www.wenming.cn/sbhr_pd/xiaozhuan/jlaq/201403/t20140310_1791628.shtml

故事三 方亚儿——不是亲人,胜过亲人 Not Close Relatives, but Closer than Families

http://zjnews.zjol.com.cn/05zjnews/system/2012/10/08/018856335.shtml

故事四 周晓丽——光明使者 The Lightbringer

http://news.sina.com.cn/s/2012-06-03/021924525632.shtml
http://www.aikan8.com/life/84post8415931.html
故事五　贾建平——法官妈妈 The Judge Mother
http://old.chinacourt.org/html/article/200607/11/211102.shtml
故事六　张　杰——瘦弱老人造福社会 A Thin Old Man Benefits the Community
http://qjwb.zjol.com.cn/html/2007-07/01/content_1632070.htm
故事七　2300 位宁波市民 2300 Ningbo Citizens
http://news.163.com/08/1103/08/4PQHNLIC0001124J.html
故事八　黄小荣——最美爸爸 The Most Virtuous Father
http://zj.sina.com.cn/zt/news/zmbb/
故事九　陈斌强——百善孝为先 Of All Virtues Filial Piety is the Most Important
http://zj.sina.com.cn/news/d/2012-10-17/073526868.html
http://www.jhnews.com.cn/zt/node_15121.htm
故事十　石进才——希望老人 An Old Man Full of Hope
http://www.tuanjiebao.com/2009/2-1/11948.shtml
故事十一　姜伟荣——海盐“保尔热线”“Paul Hotline” in Haiyan City
http://www.hcyjw.cn/content.aspx? id=739555929451
http://www.hydjw.gov.cn/NewsContent.aspx? id=10396
http://zj.qq.com/a/20130131/000039.htm
故事十二　彭彩荷——伟大的母亲 The Great Mother
http://hzdaily.hangzhou.com.cn/dskb/html/2011-02/25/content_1022974.htm
故事十三　红日亭爱心老人——The Old Men Full of Love in Hongriting Pavilion
http://zjrb.zjol.com.cn/html/2012-08/28/content_1718069.htm? div=-1
http://epaper.wzrb.com.cn/content.aspx? id=88845
故事十四　孔胜东——好人有好报 One Good Turn Deserves Another
http://zjnews.zjol.com.cn/05zjnews/system/2012/03/08/018249820.shtml
http://www.china.com.cn/17da/2007-10/14/content_9049152.htm

故事十五　“麻风村”的青年医疗团队 The Youth Medical Team in “Leprosy Village”

http://www.qnsb.com/news/html/2013/zhejian_1209/48978.html

故事十六　羊耀周——卖菜为助学 Selling Vegetables for Funding Students

http://panews.zjol.com.cn/panews/system/2015/01/18/018941877.shtml

http://panews.zjol.com.cn/panews/system/2012/10/11/015584585.shtml

故事十七　张文龙——善待每一个陌生人 Be Kind to Every Stranger

http://www.jhnews.com.cn/2014/0714/390793.shtml

故事十八　潘克勤——跨国救助 International Aid

http://zjnews.zjol.com.cn/system/2014/06/27/020109350.shtml

http://www.zjredcross.org.cn/web/comm/context.jsp?MenuIds=40&articleRelationId=3602